NEW ENGLAND AND THE SEA

THE AMERICAN MARITIME LIBRARY: VOLUME V

The schooner *Alice S. Wentworth,* leaving Nantucket Harbor. *Courtesy John W. Leavitt.*

New England

and The Sea

By Robert G. Albion

William A. Baker

Benjamin W. Labaree

Marion V. Brewington, *Picture Editor*

For Jeanne Cullen with best wishes,

Benjamin W. Labaree

Mystic, CT
8 July 1986

MYSTIC SEAPORT MUSEUM, INC.
Mystic, Connecticut

The excerpt from "The Dry Salvages" by T. S. Eliot (page 87) is reprinted by permission of Harcourt Brace Jovanovich, Inc.; copyright, 1943, by T. S. Eliot; copyright, 1971, by Esme Valerie Eliot.

Library of Congress Cataloging in Publication Data

Albion, Robert Greenhalgh, 1896–
    New England and the sea.

    (The American maritime library)
    Bibliography: p.
    1. New England—Commerce—History.   2. Shipping—
New England—History. I. Baker, William A., joint author.
II. Labaree, Benjamin W., joint author. III. Title. IV. Series.
HF3151.A65   387′.0974   72-3694
ISBN 0-8195-4052-8
ISBN 0-913372-23-4 pbk.
(Previously ISBN 0-8195-6046-4)

To the Memory of New Englanders Lost at Sea

Contents

List of Illustrations ix

Preface xiii

I. The Roots of a Maritime Heritage 3
    The New England Coast 3
    Exploration and Early Settlement 12
    Ships and Fish 21
    Colonial Commerce 32
    A Maritime Heritage 43

II. The Heroic Age, 1775–1815 45
    The Seaports 45
    King Commerce, 1775–1807 54
    Sea Lanes in Wartime 64
    The Twilight of Federalist New England, 1807–15 .. 76
    Perils of the Sea 86
    A Generation of Enterprise 96

III. The Golden Age, 1815–1865 97
    New England's Ports 98
    Distant Seas and Whaling 105
    The Atlantic Trade 118
    The Domestic Coasting Trade 124
    The Fisheries 135
    Shipbuilding 140
    The Civil War 150

IV.   The Dark Age, 1865–1914   161
        Foreign Commerce   161
        Coastal Commerce and Navigation   175
        Fisheries   191
        Danger at Sea   198
        The New England Playground   206
        Yachting   215
        Retreat from the High Seas   225

V.   The Twentieth Century   227
        Foreign Commerce and Shipbuilding   227
        Coastal Commerce and Navigation   240
        The Fisheries   251
        Safety at Sea and Harbor Improvement   258
        New England Playground   267
        A New Era   276

Epilogue   280

Index   284

Charts

Charts of the New England coast appear following page 299

List of Illustrations

The schooner *Alice S. Wentworth*   *frontispiece*

A map of the coast of New England   5

Typical rock-bound coast of northern New England   9

Sandy beaches of southern New England   11

A chart of the Atlantic Ocean   13

Conjectural picture of the pinnace *Virginia*   18

Mayflower II   20

Reproduction of the ketch *Adventure*   22

Wood-blocks of late eighteenth-century vessels   24

A late eighteenth-century fishing sloop   30

The American schooner *Baltick*   34

Boston Harbor, 1723   37

The sloop *Hannah*   41

Gull's-eye view of the sloop *Hannah*   41

Crowninshield's Wharf, Salem, Massachusetts, 1806   50

The ship *Franklin*   57

The ship *Columbia*   58

The ship *Boston*   59

The ship *Bethel*   65

Model of the Continental frigate *Raleigh*   66

John Paul Jones recruiting Yankee seamen   70

Broadside funeral elegy on Capt. James Mugford   72

The ship *Mount Vernon*   74

Broadside satirizing Jefferson's Embargo   77

The schooner *Lidia*   82

The Salem ship *Postillion*   86

Boston Light, 1723   88

Boston Light, 1789   88

The ship *Perseverance*   90
Model of a Massachusetts Humane Society lifeboat   91
The brig *Eunice*   93
Cross-staff; Davis quadrant; Hadley's quadrant; spyglasses   95
Portland, Maine, 1865   103
Boston Harbor, 1857   104
The Western Factories at Canton, China   106
The ships *Levant* and *Milo*   108
Getting off sandalwood at Dula, Timor   108
Dix Cove, Gold Coast, West Africa, with the brig *Herald*   111
The hermaphrodite brig *Zaine*   111
Drying sheds and boilers for curing *bêche-de-mer*   113
American vessels whaling in the South Pacific   115
Drying yard for baleen   117
The Cunnarder *Britannia*, 1844   120
The S. S. *Governor*   131
A stone sloop   134
The harbor of Rockport, Maine   134
Appleton's Wharf, Marblehead, Massachusetts   137
The heeltappers *Hannah* and *Joseph*   137
The last working pinky, the *Maine*   139
The Great Gale of 1846 on the Grand Banks   139
Fisherman handlining for cod   140
The clipper ship *Dashing Wave*   143
Gold Rush poster   144
Design for the figurehead of the ship *Morning Light*   147
The clipper *Flying Cloud*   147
The four-masted ship *Great Republic*   148
Donald McKay's shipyard in East Boston   148
Loading guano at the Chincha Islands   149
The "Stone Fleet" whalers   152
The U. S. S. *Kearsarge*   155
Confederate commerce-raider *Sumter*   157
The Boston waterfront, *c.* 1890   165
Immigrants landing in Portland, Maine   165
Deck view of the ship *Ice King*   167
The Down-Easter *A. J. Fuller*   169
The ship *Henry B. Hyde*   169
The Atlantic Works shipyard in East Boston   170
The steel ship *Dirigo*   171
The steel bark *Kiaulani*   172

The Bath Iron Works, Bath, Maine   174
The Boston-Bangor steamer *Camden*   174
The S. S. *Providence*   177
The shipyard of the New England Company at Bath, Maine   177
The steamer *Portland*   178
The S. S. *Kennebec*   178
The S. S. *State of Maine*   180
The Boston-New York steamer *Harvard*   180
Windbound schooners in Portland harbor   183
Ice schooners   183
The stone schooner *Annie & Reuben*   184
The five-masted schooner *Governor Ames*   184
The six-masted schooner *George W. Wells*   187
The schooner *Thomas W. Lawson*   187
The coal barges *Lonestar* and *Oakland* . . . the tug *Underwriter*   188
The knockabout fisherman *Helen B. Thomas*   194
Fishermen under construction at Essex, Massachusetts   194
Friendship sloop   195
Oystering in Long Island Sound   197
Boon Island Light House, Maine   199
Perkins Island Light and Fog Signal, Kennebec River, Maine   201
Launching the Plum Island Life-Saving boat   203
The S. S. *Gen'l Lincoln*   209
The New York Yacht Club squadron off Newport, Rhode Island   210
Poster advertising coastal service   213
Bar Harbor, Maine, *c.* 1900   214
Sandbaggers off New London   217
The sloop yacht *Shadow*   218
The sloop yacht *Gloriana*   221
The Cup-defender sloop *Reliance*   222
The steam yacht *Navarch*   224
Boston T-Wharf before World War I   229
Wooden steamship and yard of L. H. Shattuck   230
The U. S. S. *Lexington*   230
The steam yacht *Corsair*   233
The S. S. *Veragua*   233
The S. S. *Augustus P. Loring*   235
The New England Shipbuilding Company, South Portland, Maine   236
The U. S. S. *Nicholas*   236
The S. S. *Manhattan*   239
The S. S. *Boston*   239

The S. S. *Naushon* 243

The schooners *Hesper* and *Luther Little* 246

The rum-runner *Arethusa* 250

The trawler *Boston College* 253

The fishing schooner *L. A. Dunton* 254

The Block Island boat *Roaring Bessie* 257

Setting lobster traps off Monhegan 257

Cape Cod Canal 259

Buzzards Bay Entrance Light Station 261

Watch Hill, Rhode Island, before the 1938 hurricane 264

Watch Hill, Rhode Island, after the 1938 hurricane 264

The dude schooner *Mercantile* 271

The seventy-six rater *Ranger* 273

The twelve-meter *Intrepid* 275

The whaleship *Charles W. Morgan* 278

Preface

MORE than 350 years ago the first white settlers came by sea to the shores of New England. Although most of their descendants have since moved inland, some families have remained for generations along the seacoast, where they have been joined by other, more recent immigrants. Over the years New Englanders have used the sea as a source of livelihood, as a means of transportation, and as a playground. The need to work together along the waterfront and out at sea has given generations of mariners a keen sense of community. Yankee vessels have carried American produce to markets all over the world and have returned with luxuries as well as foreign commodities much needed at home. The tales of experiences brought back by New England's mariners have broadened the horizons of those who remained behind. And until well after the Civil War Yankee-built vessels formed the backbone of the nation's merchant marine. Toward the end of the nineteenth century increasing prosperity enabled people from all over the eastern United States to spend some of their leisure time enjoying the New England seacoast, and since then the expanding popularity of yachting and boating has brought new business to the region. Almost from the beginning New Englanders have had to learn new ways of making a living from the sea, but despite these changes, they have never lost their respect for the strength and beauty of the ocean around them.

This book has been a labor of love for its three authors. Each of us has lived within sight and sound of the New England coast for much of his life and has made a specialty of its maritime history. In the summer we have taught together at the Frank C. Munson Institute of American Maritime History at Mystic Seaport, Connecticut. Chapters I and II of this book, and the Epilogue, have been written by Benjamin W.

Labaree, Chapter III by Robert G. Albion, and Chapters IV and V by William A. Baker. We wish to acknowledge our gratitude to the members of the staff of the G. W. Blunt White Library at the Seaport, and to Marion V. Brewington, of the Kendall Whaling Museum, who served as picture editor.

Those desiring bibliographical suggestions for further reading should consult Robert G. Albion, ed., *Naval and Maritime History: An Annotated Bibliography* (4th edition, Mystic, Conn., 1972).

Robert G. Albion
William A. Baker
Benjamin W. Labaree

February 1972

NEW ENGLAND AND THE SEA

I

The Roots of a
Maritime Heritage

AMERICA'S maritime heritage began with the settlers who came to New England during the seventeenth and eighteenth centuries. Until the traumatic Atlantic crossing few of them had had any experience with the sea, and for most the passage to the New World was more than they wanted. But the New England soil proved difficult to cultivate, and the ocean offered new opportunities. A number of settlers therefore began to look to the sea for their livelihood, and America's rich maritime tradition was born.

The New England Coast

What was it about the coast of New England that so attracted European settlers in the early seventeenth century? To learn about the New World the founders of Plymouth Colony and Massachusetts Bay could only turn to the reports of explorers, each of whom had his favorite part of the coast. For the Englishman John Brereton, accompanying Bartholomew Gosnold in 1602, it was the view from a hilltop near the present harbor of Quisset, overlooking Buzzards Bay.

> We stood awhile like men ravished at the beauty and delicacy of this sweet soil; for besides diverse clear lakes of fresh water (whereof we saw no end) meadows very large and full of green grass; even the most woody places do grow so distinct and apart, one tree from another, upon green grassy ground, somewhat higher than the plains, as if Nature would show herself above her power, artificial.

3

In 1606 the French explorer Samuel de Champlain was nearly over-whelmed by the beauty of the coast of Maine, as generations of sailors have been ever since. One island was particularly attractive:

> It is very high and notched in places, so that there is the appearance to one at sea as of seven or eight mountains extending along near each other. The summit of the most of them is destitute of trees, as there are only rocks on them. The woods consist of pine, firs, and birches only. I named it Isle des Monts Deserts.

One of the most influential of all explorers to record his impressions of the New England coast was Captain John Smith, whose *Description of New England,* published in 1616, was widely read throughout the old country. For Smith the shore of Massachusetts Bay was

> the Paradise of all these parts; for here are many Isles planted with corn, groves, mulberries, savages' gardens, and good harbours, the coast is for the most part high clayie sandy clifts, the sea coast as you pass shows you all along large corn fields and great troops of well proportioned people. . . . Of all the four parts of the world I have yet seen not inhabited . . . , I would rather live here than anywhere.

The explorers of New England came gradually to know what the coast looked like and what its resources were, but they had no idea of how the region came to look as it did. Yet so important is New England's topography to its later development that we must begin with an understanding of the area's physical origins.

Although the geological foundations of the region were established about 500,000,000 years ago, the major force which determined the shape of the land as we know it today — "the scenery maker," as one scientist has called it — began its work only within the last 600,000 years. This force was a series of glaciers that moved down across the face of New England. The last, or Wisconsin, stage of glacial activity, whose final wave began about 30,000 years ago, buried the highest mountain-tops in its path, pushed along rocks and stones, which it ground into sand, and by its sheer weight depressed the level of the land in many places throughout the region. Only the ocean waters warmed by the Gulf Stream could check the steady flow of ice.

The terminal moraine — the line of farthest advance — of the final Wisconsin ice sheet runs the length of Long Island to Montauk Point,

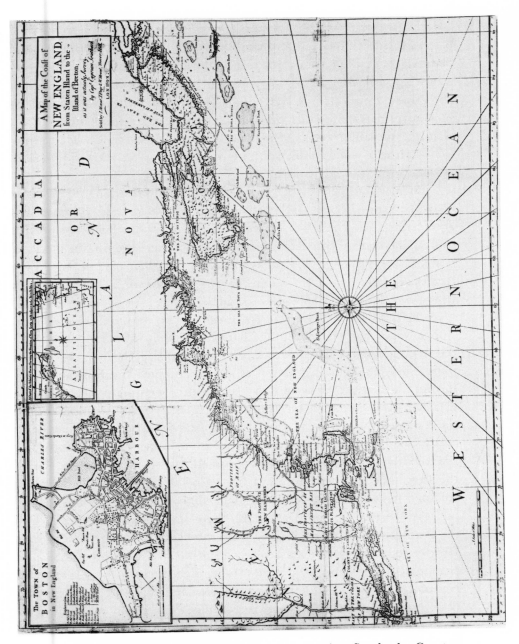

A map of the coast of New England, by Capt. Cyprian Southack. *Courtesy Kendall Whaling Museum.*

passes outside of Block Island, and bisects both Martha's Vineyard and Nantucket. It then continues east to form Georges Bank, some fifty miles beyond Cape Cod. It is no accident that the moraine coincides with these "outposts" of New England; they in fact were formed by successive glacial deposits piled high upon earlier foundations. This terminal moraine can be seen today by those who know what to look for — a line of smooth hills running roughly east-west with a plain sloping off southward to the ocean.

During these periods of glacial activity, such an immense quantity of ocean water became frozen that the sea level dropped as much as 450 feet and the coast line extended many miles out from the present shore. The continental shelf — the broad plateau reaching in places as much as 200 miles beyond today's coast — was then part of the North American land mass. Its outer margin is marked by deep canyons where rivers ran their course to the ancient sea.

When the last Wisconsin ice sheet began to recede, more than 15,000 years ago, several things happened. Meltwater ran off toward the sea, carrying sand and other debris to create the outwash plains found along the southern half of Martha's Vineyard and Nantucket and forming also the treacherous shoals offshore. Temporary halts in the glacier's retreat created recessional moraines. The most important of these shaped the northern edge of Long Island, including Orient Point and Plum Island, thus giving a boundary to Long Island Sound. The line of this recessional moraine continued east to form Fishers Island, the Elizabeth Islands chain, and Cape Cod itself. When the ice sheet resumed its withdrawal, meltwater etched river valleys like the Kennebec, the Merrimack, and particularly the Connecticut more deeply into the landscape, while at the same time the ocean's level gradually rose. Up the river valleys the sea advanced, filling in Penobscot, Casco, and Narragansett bays and flooding low-lying areas such as Long Island and Nantucket sounds. Smaller valleys and lowlands became protected harbors, while the ocean waters surrounded numerous mountaintops, isolating them as coastal islands or long peninsulas, especially along the coast of Maine. Some of the drowned hills were drumlins — hillocks formed by the glacier itself, such as the islands of Boston Harbor. By about 10,000 B.C. the "scenery maker" had retreated inland, leaving the coastal region much as we know it today.

But nature was not entirely finished with the face of New England when the last glacier retired, nor will it ever be finished. For 12,000 years the winds and the waters have worked a never-ending process of shaping and reshaping the land. The beaches of Cape Cod and Rhode Island, the southern margins of Martha's Vineyard and Nantucket, and the naked coast from Cape Ann to Cape Elizabeth have bent to the relentless pounding of the sea. Even the hard rock of Mount Desert Island has given ground at the Thunder Hole. Currents have so altered the bottom of Nantucket Sound and the shoals offshore that chartmakers nearly despair of providing accurate depths. From the mouth of every major New England river has come tons of silt to obstruct the channels of the estuaries. In recent centuries the sea has taken away more land than it has given back, yet tidal action has also joined former islands like Marblehead, Nahant, and Hull to the mainland by long bars and has added many square miles of new land at numerous points along the shore. The wind too is a builder. Around the edge of Ipswich Bay and on Cape Cod it has carved immense dunes out of the sandy residue left behind by the glaciers.

The New England coast from Provincetown south and west to Watch Hill is the most changeable shore in North America. Instead of the well-defined line found north of Cape Cod, the southern shore is simply the boundary where at any given moment in time sea meets land. When we realize that the ocean has been rising at an increasing rate (now estimated at two feet per century), we cannot doubt who the ultimate victor will be, unless a fundamental change checks the present trend.

Calm water would have little effect on the shore. It is the sea's constant movement that makes it so destructive. Swells caused by distant wind patterns over the open ocean, localized wind conditions nearer land and, most important, the flow of the tides combine to keep the seas in perpetual motion. Tidal rise varies along the New England coast from less than two feet in parts of Nantucket Sound to over thirty feet at Eastport, Maine. More generally a three-foot tide is found south and west of Cape Cod, a ten-foot tide north and east. In the narrow passages along the coast the navigator must know the set of the tide. At times it runs through Woods Hole at a four-knot clip and through the Race at the eastern end of Long Island Sound at nearly six. If a westbound mariner catches a favorable ebb in Buzzards Bay, he can add more than twelve miles to his progress by riding the next flood in through the Race. Beyond Cape Cod one must also reckon with the tide in passages like the Fox Island Thoroughfare, Eggemoggin Reach, and the Western Way. Crossing the mouth of the Kennebec River off Seguin, or Bass Harbor Bar, or Petit Manan Island Bar against the current can be sloppy going. Many a coaster has anchored outside in preference to bucking an ebbing tide to his destination. All along the coast New Englanders put the tide to work, turning water wheels to saw timber and grind grain, and some still dream of generating electric power by tidal dams in Passamaquoddy Bay. On a more modest scale the ten-foot tides beyond Cape Cod give the mariner opportunity to career his boat for minor repairs and a midseason paint job.

Men who live and work along the coast of New England spend much of their time studying the weather, for they know that at some time life itself may depend on their knowledge. It is not so much that New England weather is more violent than elsewhere as that it changes more often through a greater range of extremes. Pleasant weather is much the same along the whole New England coast. In summer the good day breaks clear, except for a spot or two of low-lying fog which the sun's warmth burns off quickly. A gentle northwest wind brings the land warmth to the edge of the sea but dies down in late morning. By noon or shortly after, the prevailing southwesterly begins to stir — "the main event of the coastal day," as one veteran has observed. Gaining strength rapidly, it may reach a velocity of fifteen or twenty knots by four o'clock, kicking up whitecaps in the shallow water of the bays and bringing a haze into the air that obscures the distant landmarks. By six o'clock the wind has subsided, and it generally dies altogether with the sun. Sometimes evening carries a night wind from the northwest that seems to blow high overhead rather than close to the earth's surface.

Bad weather tends to be somewhat worse north of Cape Cod. There much of the mainland lies exposed, while to the south barriers like Long Island, Martha's Vineyard, and Nantucket protect the mainland from the brunt of the ocean's fury. Two weather systems converge over New England, one that flows in from the west over the Great Lakes, the other pushing up the Atlantic seaboard from the south. To the wary the approach of a storm gives ample signs — a steady drop in the barometer, a shelf of high clouds closing in the sky, a shift of wind into the east. The coast is then in for a day or two of rain, sometimes heavy and wind-driven, with inshore waters whipped into a nasty chop and angry swells rolling in from the open ocean. On the average it rains

Typical rock-bound coast of northern New England, the shoreline, looking north from Great Head, Mount Desert, Maine. *Courtesy Peabody Museum of Salem.*

during one day out of three in New England, with three or four inches of accumulation month in, month out.

Occasionally a tropical hurricane rides up the Atlantic seaboard and slashes into the New England mainland before veering out to sea or dissipating its force in the Canadian woods. In 1635, 1815, 1938, and most recently in 1961, spectacular hurricanes have staggered the coastal communities and decimated fleets of vessels. Lesser tropical storms have appeared more frequently. The extremely low atmospheric pressure allows the storm tide to reach abnormal heights, flooding the lowlands and harbor fronts with churning waters. A wind shift coinciding with rising water can create tidal waves several feet high that rush into bays like Narragansett or into wide river mouths like the Thames at New London. Torrential rains flying before fierce winds add to the hurricane's destruction.

Winter comes to the coast of New England rather late in November with a cycle of freezing and thawing that makes sleet and slush commonplace. Ice forms on the rigging and decks of vessels offshore, crowds in against wharves and fish houses, and chokes the anchorages in all but the largest harbors. Gales are far more frequent in winter than at other seasons — and more dangerous too, not only because of the cold but also because wet snow, driven by the easterlies, cuts visibility to near zero at sea. When a sharp cooling of the winter air occurs, sometimes the ocean appears to be steaming. This "sea smoke" briefly reduces early morning visibility but quickly burns off with the sun and is rarely troublesome. Spring comes reluctantly along the edge of the sea because the ocean warms less rapidly than the land. Many of the most devastating storms have struck the coast in mid-March; but by the end of the month the ice has left the coves, and winter is over.

With the coming of summer the mariner has to reckon with one of the coast's most notorious characteristics: fog. Warm, moist air carried into the region by summer southerlies meets the cold air chilled by offshoots from the Labrador Current. Because cold air cannot hold as much water vapor as warm air, the cooling process condenses the moisture into countless droplets that remain suspended in the atmosphere. Only when the air is warmed by the sun or is replaced by drier air from the northwest will the fog dissipate. The ocean waters from Nantucket to Eastport are the real fog-breeders. During many summers the horns on the Pollock Rip lightship and at West Quoddy Head have oper-

Sandy beaches of southern New England, lobster shacks, dories, and fish barrels, near Gay Head, Martha's Vineyard, Massachusetts. *Courtesy Peabody Museum of Salem.*

ated on the average nearly one out of every two hours throughout July, though along the coast as a whole one would not ordinarily encounter summer fog more than about 20 percent of the time. West of Nantucket, where the water is warmer, fog is less frequent.

Until the fog burns off, the cautious mariner remains at anchor. If he must be under way, he sould be prepared to encounter one of nature's strangest phenomena. Fog seemingly suspends the laws of physics and plays havoc with man's judgment as well. Sound waves become so distorted that the horn or bell one is sailing toward might suddenly fall silent, only to have its signal come crashing down a moment later without warning. A period of intense searching into the mists for a bell buoy will convince the lookout that he sees the sought-for mark in a dozen different places. When the real buoy appears, his confidence is so shaken that he hesitates to make a positive identification. The fogbound sailor lives in a private world whose horizon is often less than fifty feet away. His only purpose in life is somehow to maneuver his domelike hemisphere safely past unseen rocks, shoals, and other vessels.

The varieties of shape and substance of terrain along the New England coast are too numerous to describe, but they have left a lasting impression on generations of seamen. The low, easy shore of Connecticut along Long Island Sound, with its broad harbors and river mouths; the deep indentation of Rhode Island's Narragansett Bay, where fertile islands are moored like large vessels in the stream; the offshore islands, Fishers, Block, the Elizabeths, Martha's Vineyard, Nantucket left behind by the retreating glacier; the grasping hook of Cape Cod reaching into the Atlantic, gathering around it dangerous shoals; the great harbors of Massachusetts, Plymouth, Boston, Salem, Gloucester; rockbound Cape Ann protecting the soft dunes of Ipswich beyond; the long, plain line of shore north to Cape Elizabeth; the Maine coast stretching eastward, with its bony peninsulas capped by bold headlands, its offshore islands, and its countless harbors carved from stubborn granite faces that look seaward — this is the coast of New England.

Exploration and Early Settlement

The first men to know northeastern America were of course not Europeans at all; they were a mixture of Caucasian and Mongoloid migrants whose ancestors had crossed the land bridge over the Bering Sea from the Asian mainland some 20,000 years ago. Artifacts recently found at Bull Brook in Ipswich, Massachusetts, suggest that man first came to the coastal region as early as 10,000 B.C., hard on the heels of the retreating glacier. Archeologists cannot prove that these settlements continued uninterrupted thereafter, but evidence of later inhabitants abounds throughout the northeastern corner of the continent. The "red-paint people," for instance, who decorated themselves with a derivative of iron oxide, have left numerous grave sites along the coast. The "oyster-shell people" were another early group. Enormous shell heaps along the banks of the Damariscotta and Kennebec rivers remain as mute testimony to their epicurean appetites. Significantly, these people, like the Indians and Europeans who followed, found the coastal regions of New England a land of promise.

At the time of the first European explorations, New England was the home of several Indian tribes belonging to the Algonquin family. While dependent for subsistence primarily on forest game and modest garden crops of corn, squash, and beans, these tribes spent the summer months along the seacoast, fishing for herring and alewives and enjoying

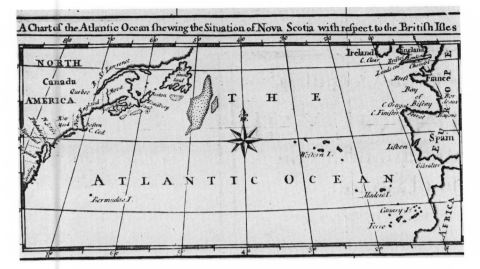

A chart of the Atlantic Ocean, showing the situation of the Grand Banks, New England, and Europe, drawn by Capt. Cyprian Southack, *c.* 1700. *Courtesy Kendall Whaling Museum.*

the succulent clams and oysters of the bays. Often they ventured forth in their birchbark canoes to establish fishing camps on the offshore islands. The Penobscots made particularly good use of the resources of their bay, fishing with spears, weirs, and woven traps. Much of their catch they dried and stored away for winter use. These Indians, along with Abnakis, Wampanoags, Pequots, and Narragansetts, were those best known to the Europeans who first came to the New England coast.

The early history of what we now call New England is inseparable from that of the Maritime Provinces of present-day Canada. In fact, the original grant to the Council for New England in 1620 included Nova Scotia, Cape Breton Island, and Newfoundland to the forty-eighth parallel. A glance at the map will show why the European voyagers usually made their first landfall along the coast of the Maritimes. Furthermore, the offshore fishing banks which attracted so many Europeans belong, geologically speaking, to the entire region, which was only later divided by the political border between today's Maine and Canada. The maritime history of New England, therefore, properly begins with the first recorded explorations along the northeastern coast of North America.

Bjarni Herjolfsson did not plan to discover the North American

continent in the summer of 986 A.D. He and his companions merely
sought to make passage from their home in Iceland to the Norse settlement in Greenland. But conditions familiar to all men who have sailed
New England's waters intervened. First a raging northeaster drove
Bjarni's sturdy knorr far to the south of his intended route. Then, as
the storm subsided, the mariners found themselves wrapped in a dense
bank of fog. Not having the advantage of the magnetic compass, they
could only sail aimlessly about until, after many days, the sun broke
through. Bjarni then shaped a course to the northwest, where he hoped
to find the coast of Greenland. Soon the first signs of nearby land
appeared — the abundance of birds, perhaps a steeper chop to the
shoaling water, the land warmth, and the pungent smell of distant vege-
tation. Bjarni had never seen Greenland, but he had been told to expect high, ice-capped mountains. Much to his amazement, the land he
soon sighted lay low against the sky and was heavily wooded. What he
and his followers discovered was, in all likelihood, the island we know
as Newfoundland.

Bjarni Herjolfsson finally did reach Greenland and, perhaps a bit
shaken by his experience, settled down at the colony there; he never
went to sea again. But the story of his discovery spread through the
Norse villages. About ten years later Lief, son of Erik the Red, reached
manhood and was eager to seek faraway lands as his father had done.
He went to Bjarni, learned all he could about the lands to the west, and
bought Bjarni's knorr for a voyage of discovery. Lief and his band of
thirty-five men set sail in the summer of 1001. Where they landed has
been the subject of one of the most heated arguments in all history.
Recent scholars using techniques of archeology unknown to earlier in-
vestigators have concluded that Lief rediscovered Newfoundland and
spent the winter of 1001–1002 probably at L'Anse aux Meadows. With
the coming of spring Lief and his followers returned to Greenland with
enthusiastic tales of their adventure and of the land Lief called Vinland
because of the wild grapes they discovered there. Other Norsemen followed, one band led by Thorfin Karlsefni establishing what it hoped
would become a permanent settlement on Newfoundland in 1009. But
a fierce battle with the Indians proved discouraging, and they returned
to Greenland within two years. Historians and archeologists have not
yet found conclusive evidence of any subsequent Norse settlements on
the North American continent, although further explorations may well

have continued until the Greenland settlements themselves disappeared around 1400.

Over the years many historians have belittled the significance of Norse accomplishments in North America. Some have been motivated by a partisanship favoring explorers of other nationalities — Italian, Portuguese, Irish, or Welsh. Others have pointed to the fact that no permanent settlement in America resulted from the Norse voyages and declared that their discoveries, while interesting, were of little importance because they were not followed up. Similarly consigned to the byways of history are the exploits of the German, Basque, and French fishermen who reportedly frequented the banks off Newfoundland throughout the fifteenth century.

Conservative historians credit the "discovery" of North America to the Genoese captain John Cabot and his son Sebastian, who sailed under English colors in 1497. Like Columbus five years before them, the Cabots sought a westerly passage to the Orient and unwittingly encountered the American continent instead — probably the coast of Newfoundland or Nova Scotia. Cabot went ashore to plant Henry VII's royal standard, establishing England's claim to the New World empire. Upon his return to England, he reported seeing dense forests of trees suitable for ships' masts and codfish so plentiful that his men hauled them out of the sea in buckets! Not surprisingly, fish and timber would soon become the staple products of New England.

It was the presence of large quantities of fish that brought increasing numbers of Europeans to North American waters during the sixteenth century. It was no accident that this region offered such abundance. The offshore banks were shoal enough (about two hundred feet deep) for light to reach the ocean floor and sustain the plants so necessary to the life cycle of bottom fish like haddock and cod. On these offshore banks, currents from the north bearing plankton animals met those from the south with plant life, giving sustenance to herring, mackerel, and other surface fish. The Grand Bank was the largest and best-known fishing ground, covering over forty thousand square miles off Newfoundland. Georges Bank off Cape Cod, with ten thousand square miles, was next in size and importance.

Fishing fleets from France, England, and Portugal sailed out in early spring, worked all summer, and returned in September laden with cod, mackerel, and salmon for markets all over Catholic Europe.

Some of the crews established land bases, putting out from coves in small boats to nearby grounds, drying their fish on shore, and living in huts during the season. Larger vessels stayed on the banks all summer while men salted down the daily catch in the holds. Whale oil and walrus skins were other North American resources that found a profitable market in Europe.

In 1524 Giovanni da Verrazano returned from a voyage to North America, bringing his French sponsors the first full account of the mainland south of Nova Scotia. Verrazano coasted north from Cape Hatteras to Cape Cod, discovering New York Harbor, Block Island, and Narragansett Bay in the process. In the year following a Portuguese sailor, Estevàn Gómez, mapped the remainder of the New England coast north of Cape Cod while sailing under the Spanish flag. Within a generation after Columbus, in short, European explorers had discovered the broad outlines of the North American coast. So crude were the early charts, however, that only after extensive exploration in the coming years would the details of the New England shoreline become clear. Much of this additional information was brought together toward the end of the sixteenth century by the English geographer, Richard Hakluyt, whose writings provided future generations with both the knowledge and the inspiration necessary for the founding of an overseas empire.

With the opening of the seventeenth century, English interest in America turned increasingly to exploitation. While some men still nourished the futile hope for quick wealth through the discovery of gold and silver mines, others looked to more gradual development of the region's resources. Such systematic ventures called for the investment of considerable amounts of capital, more than any one man was willing to risk. Consequently, groups of merchants and others combined to sponsor voyages to America in search of marketable resources. In the spring of 1602, for instance, a number of Bristol merchants sent Bartholomew Gosnold to plant a settlement in New England. After thoroughly exploring Cape Cod (which he named for the numerous fish found there) and the islands of Nantucket and Martha's Vineyard, he chose Cuttyhunk Island in Buzzards Bay for his site. A good start was made toward establishing the colony during the late spring, but the men chosen to stay behind changed their minds, and the whole group returned to England in midsummer. All was not lost, however, for in addition to the experience gained in New England, Gosnold's expedition brought home a cargo of sassafras, highly valued as a specific for syphilis.

In 1606 King James I granted lands in America to two joint-stock companies, the Virginia Company and the Northern Virginia Company, which was later reorganized as the Council for New England. The line between the grants was drawn at the thirty-eighth parallel, through Cape May. The following year each company established a trading post on its grant. The Virginia Company's colony at Jamestown became justly famous as the first permanent English settlement in America. The group sent out by the Northern Virginia Company was less successful. Headed by a Devonshire man, George Popham, brother of its principal backer, the expedition arrived off the Maine coast in July 1607 and headed for the mouth of the Kennebec River, where it landed. The colony survived the winter, but Popham did not. Without firm leadership and discouraged by a series of misfortunes, the remaining members of the company seized the first good opportunity to abandon the project and returned home in the summer of 1608. The Popham men did make one contribution of note: they constructed the first vessel built in America by Europeans, the thirty-ton pinnace *Virginia*. Some of the survivors of the colony may in fact have remained in America, perhaps at Pemaquid, or Monhegan Island, or Damariscove, but the evidence is only circumstantial.

During the first years of the seventeenth century, the New England coast was alive with European explorers. Among them were the French Sieur de Monts and his more famous companion Samuel de Champlain, who established a base at the mouth of the St. Croix River in 1604. For the next three years they explored the New England coast as far as Woods Hole. The Dutch showed a similar curiosity in North America, stemming from Henry Hudson's rediscovery of the river now named for him. In 1614 Adriaen Block explored Long Island Sound, sailed up the Connecticut River for fifty miles, and poked around Narragansett Bay. Fishermen of several nationalities set up summer quarters on Monhegan and other islands along the coast, and some of the men undoubtedly wintered over, by plan or otherwise. The English did not welcome the presence of "foreigners" in the territory they had staked out for themselves — in fact, an expedition from Virginia destroyed two French outposts in Maine — but it would take many

Conjectural picture of the pinnace *Virginia*, built at Fort Popham, Maine, 1607. Watercolor by John F. Leavitt.

years and several wars before England could call this corner of North America its own.

Onto the New England scene came one of the legendary men of history, Captain John Smith. He had been a member of the council in Virginia, and his friendship with the Indians had helped save the colony from extinction. Smith was an adventurer of heroic stature. Before his death in 1629 he had traveled to all four parts of the known world — Europe, Asia, Africa, and America — and had even served time as a slave in Turkey. In 1614 the Northern Virginia Company hired Captain Smith to explore the coast of New England. His book *A Description of New England* and its accompanying chart, published in 1616, proclaimed his infectious enthusiasm for the region. Like others before him, Smith was impressed not only with the beauty of the coast but also with the abundance of timber and fish.

Englishmen advocating colonization in the New World had several goals in mind. Among them were finding commodities, like fish and furs, salable in Europe; supplying the mother country with such strategic materials as mast trees and naval stores; and providing a market for English cloth goods, which were just now coming into surplus production. But to establish a successful colony, more than money was required. Not until men could be found who were determined to overcome hardships of climate, ill health, and skimpy provisions would New England see its first permanent settlement.

Such a group were the Pilgrims, a small sect of English Puritans who since 1606 had been living in exile in the Netherlands. Backed by London investors hoping for profit, the Pilgrims agreed to establish a trading post in the vicinity of present-day New York. After innumerable delays, landfall was made at Cape Cod in November 1620, but the *Mayflower* could not clear the shoals stretching south beyond Nantucket. Instead the group landed at Provincetown and, after exploring the area, finally settled at Plymouth harbor, which Captain Smith had named six years before. Although illness carried off half the population in the first winter, some fifty survivors stuck it out and within five years established Plymouth as a permanent colony.

Once the Pilgrims proved it could be done, other Puritans looked to New England as a place to escape religious persecution at home and to found a community according to their own principles. A small group settled at Salem in 1626 and were joined by others in 1628. By 1630 a dozen or more little settlements were scattered along the New England coast from Pemaquid Point to Plymouth. In that year the Massachusetts Bay Company sent an expedition of over a thousand to the lands granted it the previous year. This territory extended from a line three miles north of the Merrimack River to a line three miles south of the Charles, thus embracing Boston Harbor. Further immigration during the next seven years increased the population to over ten thousand people. By 1640 Massachusetts Bay included thriving new settlements at Newbury, Ipswich, Gloucester, Salem, and Marblehead, among others along the coast. Plymouth Colony established trading posts in Maine, at the head of Buzzards Bay, and on the Connecticut River at Hartford. A splinter group from Massachusetts Bay also settled near Hartford

Mayflower II, at sea under all sail. *Courtesy Plimoth Plantation.*

and another at Springfield, while still another company founded New Haven in 1638. With Roger Williams and his fellow exiles in Narragansett Bay and John Winthrop, Jr., at the mouth of the Connecticut River, the New England coast was well populated within two decades after the Plymouth colony struggled through its first hard winter. Although some pioneers did move into the interior by midcentury, the significant early migration was along the coast.

One need not look far to discover why almost all the first settlements in New England were coastal. The interior forests, difficult to penetrate and none too promising as farmland, harbored in addition Indian tribes who were becoming increasingly hostile as the white population continued to grow. In the early years the New Englanders did establish a profitable fur trade with the natives, but the Dutch at Albany and the French in Quebec soon cornered this trade for themselves. Less than a decade after the Puritan migration of 1630, the English settlers found themselves in deadly battle with the Pequots and other native tribes. This war and others to follow had all the ferocity of a European religious war, which to the Puritans it was, for they considered the Indian heathens to be agents of the Devil himself.

As the settlers came by the sea, so they would live by the sea. For without the promise of a staple crop like Virginia's tobacco or the sugar of the West Indies, New Englanders had to look to the ocean for survival.

Ships and Fish

For the most part the men who came to New England in the seventeenth century had little to do with the sea until their crossing. The beginnings of maritime New England were the result of acquired skills rather than of long tradition brought over from the Old World, although a handful of trained shipwrights could be found among the early settlers. Needless to say, not even the most ingenious Yankees could have established a maritime economy except under favorable circumstances. In addition to the topography of the coastline with its broad harbors, nature provided other advantages. Perhaps the most important of these was the abundance of timber, easily accessible along the banks of the many rivers that ran into the interior forests. Without

Reproduction of the ketch *Adventure*, a late seventeenth-century vessel, built in 1970 for the South Carolina Tricentennial Commission. *Courtesy William A. Baker.*

timber Yankees could not have built the vessels that became the foundation of New England's maritime enterprise.

The first vessel built by English settlers in America, the thirty-ton pinnace *Virginia,* slid into the Kennebec River in 1607; but except for small craft suitable for coastal fishing, shipbuilding did not become an important industry in New England until the middle of the seventeenth century. For one thing, the task of carving settlements out of the wilderness monopolized the energies of the first generation. Furthermore, the economy of coastal New England advanced but slowly beyond the stage of subsistence farming and fishing. Yankees were first encouraged by the possibilities of trade with other continental colonies and with the West Indies during the English Revolution of 1640–60 and the Dutch wars that lasted until 1678. Once these routes opened, others followed, for under the English navigation laws enacted at this time, vessels built and manned by American colonists could trade throughout the empire.

By the end of the seventeenth century, shipbuilding had become a major activity at a dozen different sites throughout coastal New England. The most active locations were, not surprisingly, found at the mouths of rivers like the Mystic at Charlestown, the Merrimack at Newbury, and the Piscataqua. But almost every settlement with access to tidewater launched one or two vessels each year. Finding skilled labor was the shipbuilder's most difficult task, for he could not always assure steady work for a full-time crew. Nor could he afford to tie up capital by laying aside timber for seasoning. Consequently, many a New England vessel was built by a novice crew from green timber, virtually assuring a short and perilous career.

The vast majority of New England-built vessels were sloops and ketches, two rigs most useful in the coastal and West Indian trades. On the average these vessels ran about thirty tons and were manned by crews of five or six; they were usually rigged with square topsails along with the gaff fore-and-aft sails characteristic of the rigs. Later in the century came brigantines and barques of fifty tons or more. For the fishermen local yards turned out small pinks and shallops, the latter evolving into the famous Chebacco boats of Massachusetts. The ketch began to give way around 1720 to the schooner, which thereafter became the far more common type of two-masted vessel along the coast, although variations on all these rigs continued throughout the eighteenth century. On the high seas, large brigs and, later, snows dominated the Atlantic routes between New England and Europe, these vessels ranging in size from about 100 to over 300 tons by the eve of the Revolution.

By that time New England yards were launching new vessels at the rate of one a day. The larger square-riggers averaged about 70 tons burden, while the smaller sloops and schooners were nearer 20 tons. New England accounted for about two-thirds of the new vessels constructed in the colonies by the Revolution.

In the earlier part of the colonial period a shipyard usually began construction only upon the order of the future owner. Builder and merchant could then agree upon specifications for the vessel and contract terms. At least a part of the building price was usually met in Eng-

Wood-blocks used by Ezekiel Russell of Salem, 1775–77, of the principal types of late eighteenth-century vessels: a ship; a sea sloop; a schooner; a brig. *Courtesy M. V. Brewington.*

lish goods, hardware, or other articles needed by the yard owner. One such contract, signed in 1750 by Tobias Langdon of Portsmouth, New Hampshire, and Samuel Pray of Kittery, called for Pray

> to build at his building yard at Kittery a Brigatine of the following dimentions r Scantlings, that is to say, Fifty one Feet by the Keel in Length Strait Rabbit; Breadth by the Beam Twenty one Feet, the Rake of the Stem to be three fifths of the Length of the Beam, Depth of the Hold to be Ten Feet, to have Two Decks and to be Four Feet between Decks and Two Feet to be allowed out of the Rake of the Stern & added to the length of the Keel, all the Timbers to be of a Proportionable thickness & Sound, the outside planks to be good sound White Oak two inches thick & three inches thick where arcording to the Rules of good Building they ought to be of that Thickness. The Quarter Deck to run so far forward as to take in the Main Mast and Pumps. . . .

Pray was to be paid at the rate of £25 per ton, half in bills of credit of New Hampshire, Rhode Island, or Connecticut, half in good English or West Indian goods.

Because of the abundance of timber, colonial shipyards turned out vessels at least 30 percent cheaper than English builders could match. A good many New England vessels were therefore sold abroad, both in the mother country and in continental ports, often after their thrifty owners had sailed them over with a profitable cargo. Such vessels, built on speculation and destined for distant owners, could not have been among the better examples of New England workmanship. But most vessels built along the New England coast remained in the hands of friends and neighbors; indeed, the builder himself often took a share in the vessel as partial payment for its construction. Serving in the fisheries or in the coastal and West Indies trade, such a vessel might have a useful life of ten or fifteen years. By then, if the shifting sands off Cape Cod or the sunken ledges of the Maine coast had not already claimed her as a victim, rot would probably have worked into her timbers. At some point the cost of repair came to exceed the economy of purchasing a new vessel, and if the owner could not palm his craft off upon an unsuspecting West Indiaman, she was consigned to the flats of a back cove, where the bones of countless vessels came to final rest.

It was fish that brought Europeans to American waters in the first place, and it was fish that would provide the foundation for the prosperity of those Europeans who came to settle in New England. Although the early colonists relied in part on fish for subsistence during their first years of hardship, it remained for a Salem minister to point out the potential wealth that lay beneath the waters off the coast. In 1653 the Reverend Hugh Peter visited several communities in Massachusetts urging the inhabitants to invest their meager resources in the fishing industry. Equally important, Peter also succeeded in rousing the interest of English investors in providing funds for the purchase of necessary equipment. In the same year the General Court of Massachusetts Bay established a commission to manage the infant industry; and four years later, along with other encouragements to the business, fishing vessels and equipment were exempted from taxation for a seven-year period. At the same time, several laws attempted to maintain standards of quality in the marketing of fish and to prevent the taking of cod and mackerel during their spawning season. This double policy of public encouragement and regulation of the fishing industry, established early in the seventeenth century, remained a fixture throughout the remainder of the colonial period.

Soon every village caught the fever. From Salem and Marblehead it spread eastward around Cape Ann and northward through Ipswich, Rowley, and Newbury. The Isles of Shoals, off the New Hampshire coast, and Richmond Island off Cape Elizabeth, like Monhegan and Pemaquid beyond, had first been settled as fishing outposts. Now they sprang to life — along with similar communities to the south of Boston, such as Nantasket, Scituate, and Barnstable — as fishing became maritime New England's major industry.

At first the New England fishermen confined themselves to working the waters close inshore. They erected weirs to seal off schools of herring in the coves and established stages along the riverbanks to fish for sturgeon, salmon, and alewives. Others chose to work areas a few miles off the coast, within an easy day's sail from their home ports. On Matinicus Sou'sou'west Ground, Jeffries Ledge, and Stellwagen Bank were found the cod, haddock, and pollock which became the backbone of the export trade. Still farther offshore in the Gulf of Maine lay Cashes Ledge, Marblehead Bank, and New Ledge, while some fifty miles east of Cape Cod the waters around Georges Bank invited the more adventuresome men to try their luck. Currents ran so swiftly across Georges that fishermen dared not anchor, fearing to be dragged under. At first offshore fishing was carried on in small shallops, manned by crews of three or four. Boats working the outer banks often required a fourth man, who remained on shore to oversee the salting and drying of each catch. Fishermen generally shared the profits of their trips rather than working for wages, and profit sharing has ever since been a characteristic aspect of the fishing industry.

Not until after the middle of the seventeenth century did New England fishermen venture as far as the banks off Sable Island or Newfoundland in any great numbers. But soon more than six hundred Yankee vessels manned by some four thousand men were swarming over the rich grounds each year. Generally three trips to the banks were made, with the first catch in the spring bringing in the best quality, known in the region as "dumb fish." Cod generally fell into three categories according to their quality. The best, or "merchantable," fish was reserved for export to Spain and Portugal, where it commanded the highest prices. The "middling" sort was bound for the Portuguese Atlantic islands and the prosperous English colony of Jamaica. The remainder of the catch, inelegantly referred to as "refuse fish," went to the other British islands in the Caribbean, primarily as food for the slaves working the sugar plantations. The southern continental colonies of America formed another important market for New England fish, and of course Yankees themselves ate far more of their catch than pride perhaps would allow them to admit. By the end of the seventeenth century, the lowly cod had indeed earned its subsequent place of honor in the State House of Massachusetts as the symbol of prosperity.

Before the end of the seventeenth century, pursuit of the cod involved New Englanders in something more than the world of commerce. Sending their vessels on increasingly ambitious voyages along the coasts of Nova Scotia and Newfoundland, they inevitably came into competition with other English and French fishing interests long since established along the edge of the Grand Banks. The Yankees got on quite well with their English cousins in Newfoundland, although the fishing activities of both groups caused much concern at home. In his aptly named essay, *The Nature of Plantations and their Consequences to Great Britain, Seriously Considered* (1669), Josiah Child had remarked on the decline in the numbers of English-based vessels fishing off the Grand Banks. Seventeenth-century theorists considered the fishing industry important not only as a source of national wealth but also as a training ground for future naval seamen and as an incentive to

shipbuilding. In a famous (or infamous) passage Child waspishly concluded that "New England is the most prejudicial Plantation to the
Kingdom of England," not only because it raised no commodities of
value to the mother country but also because its fishing was in direct
competition with the home industry. Although the mother country did
harass its settlements in Newfoundland, it did not seriously interfere
with the New Englanders who frequented the northern banks, for on
balance most authorities, including Child himself, recognized the importance of the fishing trade to the overall prosperity of New England.

Far more serious was the clash between Yankee fishermen and those
of French Canada, who by the middle of the seventeenth century had
become firmly established in numerous settlements along the North
Atlantic seaboard. French officials seized New Englanders and encouraged Indian bands to plunder their vessels and encampments whenever
possible. As a result of depredations during King Philip's War (1675–
76) and King William's War (beginning in 1689), hardly an English
settlement remained along the Maine coast east of Casco Bay. When warfare temporarily ended in 1697, the French controlled the entire northern coast from Penobscot Bay to Labrador, with the exception of the
eastern half of Newfoundland. New England's fishing industry was at
low ebb. Salem alone lost fifty-four our of sixty vessels through enemy
action and adverse weather. The French took every advantage of their
superior position to drive the English colonists clear off the banks. By
the turn of the eighteenth century they completely dominated the northern fisheries and monopolized the European market. The Yankees were
left to do the best they could on the grounds closer to their home ports.

Not until the victorious conclusion of Queen Anne's War in 1713
would New England's fortunes turn for the better. By the terms of the
Treaty of Utrecht the French abandoned Nova Scotia, renounced the
right to fish along its shores west of Sable Island, and gave up all claims
to Newfoundland as well. But they did retain Cape Breton Island and
were allowed to dry their catches along the western shore of Newfoundland. From these bases they continued to work the Grand Banks with
extraordinary success until after the middle of the eighteenth century,
one contemporary observer estimating that there were upwards of a
thousand French vessels on the banks each season, bringing in a catch
worth more than $4 million. The French were by no means out of the

picture until they were all but driven from the North American continent at the end of the Seven Years' War in 1763.

But after 1713 the way was clear for a return of New Englanders to the cod grounds off Nova Scotia and Newfoundland. The Yankees wasted little time taking advantage of the opportunity. Indicative of the change for the better was what happened in Marblehead. When the Reverend John Barnard arrived to take over his new parish in 1714, he found the inhabitants "dismally poor" and generally as "rude, swearing, drunken, and fighting a crew as they were poor." While some residents of neighboring Salem uncharitably insist that 'Headers have changed little since, more objective evidence suggests that the resurgence of Yankee codfishing brought a new vigor to all the towns along the North Shore and established Marblehead as the industry's recognized leader. Within twenty years after the Treaty of Utrecht the town boasted a fleet of 120 fishing schooners manned by more than a thousand men, figures that would grow slowly but steadily in the coming years.

By midcentury the industry had settled into a number of patterns. The shallop gave way to the sloop and schooner of fifty tons or more, manned by a crew of seven or eight. The men now fished "on their own hook," meaning that a daily count of each man's catch was kept and he was compensated proportionally at the end of the trip. A good vessel with an able crew made five trips, or "fares," each year, including runs to the banks around Sable Island and to Georges Bank off Cape Cod. In a good season a schooner might bring in catches worth about $1,800, but much of the profit went to the Boston and Salem merchants who dominated the export trade. These men often sent their outward-bound trading vessels to the fishing ports of the North Shore, where they could pick up a cargo of fish for the West Indies or Portugal more cheaply than at Boston itself. The fishing ports thus became loading stations not only for local exporters but for other shippers as well.

By the decade before the American Revolution, New England's cod fisheries employed an average of nearly 5000 men, who sailed to the grounds in more than 500 vessels. Each year they marketed a catch worth about $1 million. In addition there were the mackerel and herring fisheries worked by several hundred smaller vessels. About 10,000 New Englanders, including the mariners who carried the catch to mar-

A late eighteenth-century fishing sloop. Watercolor by M. F. Corne. *Courtesy Peabody Museum of Salem.*

ket and the men who cured the fish on shore, found employment in the fishing industry by the eve of the Revolution. Next to Marblehead as the leading fishing port stood Gloucester, with Plymouth and Salem far behind. The first two towns accounted for nearly 60 percent of the catch, but more than twenty different ports sent vessels to the cod grounds each year.

Allied with the cod fishery but rather different from it was the whaling industry. Europeans had valued the majestic whale for its oil long before the settlement of New England, and when residents along the coasts of Rhode Island, Cape Cod, and Nantucket discovered right whales close inshore, they recognized the worth of their good fortune. At first whales were spotted from shore stations, from which crews put out in longboats to capture their prey and tow its body onto the beach. There the blubber was "cut in" and "tried out" in large pots to extract the valuable oil. At one time or another, inhabitants of most New England coastal towns probably took a turn at shore whaling, but by the end of the seventeenth century the activity began to move offshore. From that time forward, whaling became the special preserve of two Massachusetts towns, Nantucket and Dartmouth (later New Bedford).

So completely did Nantucket and Dartmouth dominate the business that by the eve of the American Revolution, 230 of 304 whaling vessels hailed from those two ports and accounted for over 80 percent of the oil shipped to market. First the whalemen ventured to the shoals south and east of Nantucket; then larger vessels were fitted out for longer voyages to the Grand Banks, the straits of Belle Isle, and finally the Arctic waters of Davis Strait. Most of the vessels were sloops of eighty to one hundred tons, carrying two whaleboats and a crew of thirteen. In a procedure little altered for the next century, the boats set off in pursuit at the first sign of a whale in the offing. Approaching as close as possible, the boatsteerer hurled his harpoon deep into the whale and then made the line fast for what was called a Nantucket sleigh ride, as the victim towed its tormenters all over the ocean. When the whale slowed from exhaustion, the boat approached once more, and the quarry was dispatched by repeated thrusts of a sharp lance. Brought back to the sloop, the carcass was stripped of its blubber, which was boiled in large tryworks constructed on the foredeck. The oil was then stowed below in casks.

Early in the eighteenth century one Nantucket captain accidentally discovered a sperm whale far offshore. This species was prized for its oil of especially high quality and for spermaceti, a waxlike substance found in the whale's head. Sperm oil burned with unusual brightness, and candles made from spermaceti had no equal. Thereafter, Nantucketers specialized in the pursuit of the sperm whale — an adventure that took them on voyages far out beyond the Gulf Stream, to the Brazil Banks off South America, and finally, in the nineteenth century, into the Pacific Ocean. In 1771 Nantucket's catch alone was worth nearly $500,000 on the London market, much of it delivered in vessels from Dartmouth and Nantucket belonging to the Rotch family.

Whaling, then, took its rightful place alongside the cod fishery as a major source of valuable exports for Yankee merchants. Without these commodities New Englanders would have been hard pressed to pay for the goods they imported from the mother country.

Colonial Commerce

Many Americans have the idea that their colonial ancestors were left to fend for themselves once they arrived in the New World. For the vast majority of colonists who settled down as family farmers, it was essentially true that imperial authorities offered neither encouragement nor interference. But those settlers and their descendants who took to the sea for their livelihood had to reckon with an array of rules and regulations, some helpful, others restrictive in nature. Colonies existed to augment the wealth of the entire empire, so said the mercantilists of the day, and to assure prosperity certain principles had to be established and enforced.

These principles took shape through a series of navigation acts adopted by Parliament during the latter half of the seventeenth century. The first principle was that of the closed empire, within which only vessels of English construction and registry and manned by predominantly English crews were permitted to trade. The second was that certain products of the colonies were so valuable that they could be sent only to the mother country. Among the most important of these "enumerated commodities" by the mideighteenth century were tobacco, rice, indigo, sugar, and naval stores. Some of these crops, and others as well, were in such demand that bounties were offered for their production. The third principle was that, because the colonies were important as a market for goods manufactured at home, products of other European nations (with limited exceptions) could be shipped to America only through the mother country, where they were subjected to high duties. Since colonial vessels and their crews qualified as English under the law, the commerce of New England developed largely under the influence of these regulations. Not until political grievances arose in the decade preceding the Revolution did colonial merchants voice serious objections to the mercantile restrictions imposed by the mother country.

Within this system, New Englanders had developed several distinct patterns of commerce before the end of the seventeenth century. Colonial merchants were free to trade with all other English colonies in the New World and with most foreign colonies as well, except during wartime. Americans could carry all the natural produce of any English colony to the mother country and could sell nonenumerated articles to any European nation willing to buy. They could return to America with salt for the fisheries or with wine from Madeira or the Azores, and of course they could import manufactures from the mother country without limitation. The most important, though least spectacular routes went coastwise to the middle and southern colonies and to the Maritime Provinces, while the best-known run took the Yankee traders to the English and foreign West Indies. The third route, across the Atlantic to English and European ports, carried the most valuable cargoes.

Yankees became traders for the simple reason that they needed many articles of English manufacture. Since their region produced little that the mother country required, New Englanders had to exchange their wares with other colonies to obtain products which did command a favorable market in England. The life of a Yankee trader was thus one long search for what the English merchant called "returns" — commodities or bills of exchange with which overseas customers could purchase English manufactures to sell back home. The primary source of these returns was the West Indies, where planters who produced the staple crops in great demand in England were at the same time in great need themselves of the food and lumber products which New England had in abundance.

The West Indies route thus became the starting point for almost all successful New England merchants. From local farmers and other nearby points of supply they put together an assorted cargo for a sloop or schooner bound for the Caribbean. Often the vessel, or at least the goods on board, had several owners, who shared the risks and profits. These cargoes were made as varied as possible because a full load of any one article might well glut the market at some of the smaller islands. A typical cargo often included barrel staves and hoops, shingles and boards, dried or pickled fish, flour, bread, butter, peas, beef and pork, and occasionally horses, cattle, and poultry. Other popular items, especially in the eighteenth century, were manufactured goods like spermaceti candles, bricks, furniture, and even house frames, knocked apart for easy shipment but easily reassembled once ashore.

Because of the number of potential markets and the uncertainty of conditions, merchants generally gave shipmasters wide discretion in the sale of cargoes. The captains and sometimes other members of the crew were also given a "privilege" of shipping some goods on their own account. In addition, captains usually earned commissions on the

sale of the owners' cargo. Occasionally a captain became too familiar a figure at a particular island. "I am too well acquainted here," wrote Captain Wright to his owner in Newport. "They begin to demand credit much longer then I chuse to give them and if I refuse them they are much affronted and tell me, I may be damned and they will not deal with me any more." Under this and other discouraging circumstances the shipmaster simply sailed off to another island.

New Englanders often stopped first at Barbados. Not only was it among the largest of the British islands, but it was also farthest to windward; from there, each subsequent call at another port meant a simple run before the trades, rather than a painful beat upwind. As the economy of Barbados declined in the eighteenth century, Jamaica and other islands to the west became more popular. Of course the Americans were not limited to the British possessions for markets, and they often found better conditions at French, Dutch, and Spanish colonies. Dealing with foreign officials was not always a simple matter, but Yankee tradesmen soon mastered the art of greasing the right palm at the right time and generally had little difficulty making a satisfactory sale. Trade with the foreign possessions became increasingly necessary in the eighteenth century as the New England colonies exported far more produce than the English islands could possibly absorb. Martinique, Surinam, St. Eustatius, and during wartime the Spanish port of Montecristi all attracted their share of Yankee traders.

Finding a market for his outward goods was only part of the captain's job, for he also had to buy at the lowest possible price a suitable return cargo for his owner. It was an unwritten rule of the trade that one should make his purchases in the same place he sold his outward goods, and the captain had to take both aspects of the market into consideration before committing himself to a particular island. Return cargoes consisted almost exclusively of sugar, rum, and molasses, for the islands produced little else of value to New Englanders. Only when faced with the prospect of failing to fill up his hold would a captain search about for another commodity to bring home, usually a small quantity of cotton, or ginger perhaps, or a load of salt for the fisheries obtained at Turks Island or Tortuga.

Some excerpts from the instructions given in 1727 to Captain John Touzell of the Salem sloop *Endeavour* by its owner illustrate well the role of the master:

> You are to take the first good opportunity of wind and weather and come to Sail with said vessell, directing your course and making the best of your way for the West Indies; and you may Touch at Barbados, St. Christopher's or Antegoa, or Jamaica, and if any good marketts att any of those Places, then you may dispose of my Cargoe . . . to my best advantage, and Purchase a Loading of good Mollasses, Some Rum, good Cotton wool, good Coca Nutts and good Indigo, and any other thing you may bring here with Safety, that will turn to advantage, or, if the markets are Low at the English Islands, then you may goe and Trade at Guardelupe, Cape Francois, or any of the french Islands, where you Can gett Permition to Trade, and with Safety, and bring my Effects as afforesaid. . . . Imploy your Coopers Diligently in making Cask for your Molasses which you purchase for me, make what Dispatch you Can back to New England to me. Leave no debts on my account, If possible to avoid itt, Butt Bring the whole Proceeds of my Cargoe in Such goods as I have mentioned. be Careful to pay your Port

Charges, and not to bring anything Home to endanger a Seizure of my Vessell. . . . So wishing you a Prosperous voyage, Comitt you to the Protection of Almighty God, I am

Yr Freind and Imployer,
Sam'll Browne

Bring Some Oranges and Limes

In the older islands of Barbados and Antigua, and at Jamaica as well, the planters much preferred to distill their own rum and gain the extra profit from its manufacture. Indeed, Jamaica rum remained a favorite among the wealthy colonists, particularly at New York and in the southern provinces. By 1700 rum began to challenge beer as the most popular alcoholic beverage among the common folk, and the distilleries of New England required more and more molasses. Although regarded as inferior to the West Indies variety and often inelegantly referred to as "stinking rum," the New England product undersold other varieties and found a ready market throughout the colonies. The high cost of sugar also made molasses the common sweetener in most households, and before long the demand became so great that it could no longer be met by the British islands alone. Yankee merchants therefore turned to the foreign West Indies for their supplies, where indeed molasses was the only staple they could legally purchase under the regulations imposed at most French and Dutch islands. This trade in turn provoked passage by Parliament of the Molasses Act of 1733, placing a prohibitive duty on foreign molasses in an effort to destroy New England distilleries and favor those operated by the West Indian planters. Only because of lax enforcement did the attempt fail.

The West Indies trade brought profits to New England merchants in several ways. The most obvious, of course, was the sale of sugar, molasses, and rum to shopkeepers or directly to consumers. Profits from sales made in New England were often taken in the form of lumber, fish, and provisions to make up future cargoes bound for the Caribbean, thus keeping the cycle going. The molasses and rum sold in the southern continental colonies often purchased plantation produce such as rice and tobacco, which in turn found a ready market in England. New Englanders generally preferred to buy bills of exchange with their sales to the southerners, however, so that they could reduce their own considerable debts in London. Not all rum went for domestic consumption, of course. A considerable quantity was purchased in New York for

Boston Harbor, 1723. A contemporary engraving attributed to William Burgis. Note the various types of small watercraft, including the forerunner of the Block Island boat and the Whitehall boat.

the Indian trade, and perhaps an even larger quantity found its way to the African coast in the slave trade.

Historians of early New England have been slow to recognize how much of the region's prosperity depended upon the institution of slavery. Black servants were employed as carpenters in shipyards, as longshoremen and truckmen along the waterfront, and as mariners aboard vessels. Even more significant was that the tobacco, rice, and sugar plantations of the southern and West Indian colonies constituted the major market for New England produce such as fish and timber. Those Yankee merchants who prospered in the plantation trade were as much dependent on the institution of slavery for their riches as were the planters themselves. Some New England merchants, the slave traders, relied even more directly on human bondage for their business profits. Perhaps as much as 30 percent of the Africans imported into the continental American colonies made the notorious middle passage 'tween-decks on a Yankee-owned slaver. Still other New Englanders counted on selling much of their rum to British and American merchants directly engaged in the slaving business. The coffers of some of New England's proudest families were filled with profits from this trade.

Whatever the ultimate destination of the commodities brought back from the West Indies, profits depended on further commercial transactions, particularly involving coastal trade with other colonies. In an era when roads were too crude for the portage of bulky cargoes, coastal and

TABLE 1
New England Colonial Commerce

A. TONNAGE IN SHIPPING 1770

	New Hampshire	Massachusetts	Rhode Island	Connecticut	Total New England
OUTWARD TONNAGE					
to Gt. Britain	1,910	13,778	955	426	17,069
So. Europe	185	5,419	755	180	6,539
W. Indies	12,419	20,957	6,779	9,923	50,078
Coastwise	5,678	30,128	12,172	9,734	57,712
Total outward	20,192	70,282	20,661	20,263	131,398
INWARD TONNAGE					
from Gt. Britain	1,200	13,916	400	210	15,526
So. Europe	—	6,213	101	—	6,314
W. Indies	10,300	19,917	7,121	8,656	45,994
Coastwise	3,862	25,225	11,045	10,357	50,489
Total Inward	15,362	65,271	18,667	19,223	118,523

B. WEST INDIES TRADE 1772

		New Hampshire	Massachusetts	Rhode Island	Connecticut	Total New England
IMPORTS						
cocoa (lbs)	Br.	4,650	82,594	—	—	87,244
	For.	63,300	166,393	37,652	192,952	460,297
coffee (lbs)	Br.	19,734	13,740	—	23,086	56,550
	For.	—	166	593	—	759
cotton (lbs)	Br.	16,330	19,900	2,767	1,050	40,047
	For.	33,260	127,171	15,892	26,944	203,267
molasses (gals)	Br.	9,783	32,660	30,539	1,700	74,672
	For.	521,538	2,047,529	586,329	269,805	3,425,201
rum (gals)	Br.	165,875	178,756	155,750	313,690	814,071
	For.	—	—	—		
Sugar (lbs)	Br.	168,372	709,004	149,544	108,614	1,135,555
	For.	106,085	2,356,590	148,922	103,558	2,715,124

EXPORTS	
Wheat (bu.)	16
Corn (bu.)	5,995
Bread/flour (ton)	970
beef/pork (bbls)	6,555
fish, dried (quin.)	251,720
fish, pkld (bbls)	22,644
rum (gals)	1,090
boards (ft.)	28,297,527
shingles (no.)	19,035,742
hoops/staves (no.)	8,292,938
naval stores (bbls)	347

inland waterways served as the country's highways. Nearly half of Connecticut's tonnage in 1769, for instance, plied the coastal routes. Local traffic was so great that records fail to tell us, for instance, how often Gloucester vessels brought a cargo of fish into Salem, say, in exchange for English cloth goods and ironware or a few hogsheads of rum. Nor can we measure for certain how dependent the towns of Narragansett Bay were on Newport as their entrepôt. But the newspapers in the major ports tell of the comings and goings of little sloops and schooners by the score each month, while the movements of smaller watercraft such as shallops and "gundalows" went largely unreported.

A somewhat clearer picture is given of coastwise voyages between the continental colonies. With only occasional fluctuations throughout the eighteenth century, nearly half the vessels entering Boston and an even greater proportion of clearances made passages from or to one of the other twelve continental colonies. When all of British North America is included, the coastal trade appears even more dominant. For the year 1768, for instance, 430 vessels entered Boston from the other continental colonies, while 164 more came in from the Maritime Provinces — 594 out of a total of 879 entrances. Measured by tonnage, the figures are of course less impressive, because coastal vessels were invariably sloops and schooners measuring on the average thirty or forty tons in contrast to the larger vessels engaged in the West Indies and Atlantic trades.

We have already seen that the molasses imported from the West Indies and the rum into which much of it was distilled were important articles of trade to almost every New England merchant. New England fish and timber products, like shingles and staves, also found a market in other colonies. In addition to acquiring commodities necessary to keep the West Indies trade going, such as fish, timber, and provisions, the New England merchants imported from the middle colonies quantities of wheat and flour and other produce for consumption at home, along with considerable amounts of pig and bar iron. Thus, while the plantation colonies of the continent shipped most of their staples to Great Britain and southern Europe, New England was also a significant market.

Records kept at Annapolis, Maryland, in the years before the Revolution give an excellent picture of coastal trade between New England and the Chesapeake region. In December 1759 the schooner *Elizabeth,* twenty-five tons, entered from Salem with a cargo of fish, sugar, molasses, and cheese. One month later she cleared for home with several hundred bushels of wheat and Indian corn and one barrel of pork. Within two months she made another voyage with much the same cargo. The sloop *Hannah* entered Annapolis in May 1766 in ballast, having already discharged her cargo in Philadelphia. The master then took on board a large quantity of flour, with which he cleared for Newfoundland. There he probably exchanged his cargo for a load of fish or perhaps for bills of exchange. One of the most varied cargoes coming into Annapolis was on board the schooner *Darby* in 1771, when she entered with candles, shoe leather, 3 dozen axes, 1 desk, 2 tables, and 380 pairs of shoes. She cleared for Marblehead a few days later with the usual assortment of corn, pork, flour, and beans. Sometimes New Englanders stopped in the middle colonies on their way to or from the West Indies; and occasionally a vessel, such as the schooner *Betsey* in 1767–68, would make a voyage or two between the Chesapeake and the Caribbean before returning home at all. In any case, coastal commerce played an essential part in the overall activity of the Yankee trader. Without the produce and markets provided by the other colonies, New England's commerce could not have been sustained at prosperity levels for long.

The fact that the West Indies and coastwise trade routes accounted for the vast majority of clearances from a busy harbor like Boston suggests that commerce with the Old World was relatively unimportant to New Englanders. It is true that New England was less dependent upon the mother country as a market than were the plantation colonies to the south, but the northern colonies purchased the products of Great Britain in equally large quantities. Furthermore, the countries of southern Europe were important markets for New England produce and an equally good source of salt (needed in the fisheries) and bills of exchange. Numerous Yankee traders had well-established connections with mercantile houses in the Azores, in the Canary Islands, and on the Iberian peninsula. To these correspondents they consigned cargoes of lumber products, rum, and the best New England fish. Like any voyage the run to southern Europe had its ups and downs. When William Pepperrell sent his brig *Kittery* from Portsmouth to Cadiz in 1751 with a cargo of fish and lumber, the fish was so bad it sold well below the regular market. Still worse, before the cargo could be delivered, a hurricane drove the brig ashore, a total loss. Another New England mer-

The Sloop *Hannah,* in a gale during a voyage from Cadiz to Boston in 1753. From watercolors in Capt. Robert Treat Paine's log. *Courtesy Massachusetts Historical Society.*

Gull's-eye view of the sloop *Hannah,* hove to, with the tiller lashed down, in the same gale. *Courtesy Massachusetts Historical Society.*

chant active in the Iberian trade was Jeremiah Lee of Marblehead. In 1770, Lee's ship *Vulture,* 110 tons, called at Annapolis, where her molasses, fish oil, and shoes were sold for a cargo of wheat and flour, which the *Vulture* then carried to Lisbon.

No figures more graphically tell the story of the New Englanders' search for returns than those involving direct trade with Great Britain. In 1772, for instance, New Englanders purchased British products valued at over £800,000, yet the region exported to the mother country only £126,000 worth of its own commodities in return. In contrast, over £500,000 worth of produce left the Chesapeake colonies in payment for a like value of imports. New Englanders could send no wheat, corn, flour, or bread of their own. Worse still, England accepted no New England rum, at least in that year, and only seven quintals of dried fish! Were it not for the export of whale oil from Nantucket and Dartmouth, worth over £100,000 in 1772, the New Englanders would have made a poor showing indeed.

Another staple product of New England that found a market in the mother country was the mast trees of New Hampshire and Maine. Samuel Pepys described the arrival of five mast ships from New England during a war with Holland in 1666 as "a blessing mighty unexpected, and without which, if nothing else, we must have fallen last year." In 1692 the mast ship *Diligence,* having brought into Portsmouth a mixed cargo of English cloth goods and hardware, departed in the fall with twenty-one masts and numerous spars and frame pieces for the naval dockyards of England. Other products of the northern woods, including hoops, staves, and boards, found a market in the mother country, although more often timber was sent across unsawn. Occasionally merchants simply lashed some logs together, stepped a mast, and found some brave souls to sail the raft over to England. Unfortunately for their prosperity, New Englanders never took full advantage of the opportunity to export naval stores — pitch, tar, and turpentine — to the mother country, where these articles were in great demand. Rural Yankees avoided working for other people as much as possible.

Most New England merchants could not obtain sufficient returns to offset their continuing imports from home, and on paper remained indebted to their British correspondents right up to the outbreak of the Revolution. Aaron Lopez, one of Newport's most affluent merchants, owed the London house of Hayley and Hopkins over £12,000 by 1774.

But American importers continued to make a good profit on the goods they sold at retail. British merchants in turn kept right on filling American orders, helpless to do otherwise since their livelihood also depended on the continuation of the Anglo-American trade. In the five years just before Lexington and Concord, the American colonies altogether annually imported over £2,700,000 in British goods, of which New England accounted for more than one-quarter. To the English merchant of the day these shipments represented his best opportunity for profit. "The [British] merchant makes an allowance for the loss on the imports or returns," one observer commented in 1775, "and therefore his chief attention is given to exports, from which he expects such an advantage as will compensate for the loss on the returns."

A Maritime Heritage

At no time during the colonial period was more than one out of ten New Englanders in any way associated with maritime life. Yet the activities of this small fraction gave to the region a special flavor that has remained to this day. In an era when most Americans were farmers, supporting their families on holdings of a few hundred acres, how could one group of colonists set a tone far out of proportion to its size? For one thing, the daily life of the seafaring Yankees, so different from the ordinary settler, has drawn the attention of contemporary observers and modern historians alike, who have singled them out as a special breed. But, in the long run, their importance lies in the nature of their contributions to the lives of their fellow Yankees.

What the mariners of New England did was to transform their native land from a random collection of farming communities and give it a place of significance in the world at large. By shipping surplus agricultural products to distant markets, the mariners helped many farmers to rise above the subsistence level. By sending out to every country store a variety of English manufactures, from clothing to hardware, merchants made possible a steady increase in the standard of living and the level of productivity throughout the region. And by the variety of their own activities — distilleries, shipyards, and retail shops, as well as shipping itself — maritime entrepreneurs created the urban seaports that offered an alternative way of life for New Englanders eager to move off the farm. Equally significant was the civilizing effect, for the life of the Yankee mariner became a part of the wider world around him — the world of the Carolinas and Cadiz, of the Chesapeake, the Caribbean, and London itself.

II

The Heroic Age, 1775–1815

THE PERIOD from 1775 to 1815 has been aptly called the Heroic Age in American maritime history. War raged over the seas for twenty-nine of these forty years. During twelve years America was itself at war with Great Britain, and New Englanders along the coast lived under the constant threat of bombardment and invasion. Through much of the period Yankee shipmasters faced attack from belligerent warships and privateers. Owners tried to adjust to wildly fluctuating business conditions, seeking new markets to offset their losses along traditional routes. For all New Englanders who lived by the sea, it was indeed an Heroic Age.

The Seaports

One important by-product of New England's maritime activity was the growth of the seaport. Unlike other sections of colonial America, where ports such as New York, Philadelphia, and Charleston came to dominate the commerce of a large area by the middle of the eighteenth century, New England was a land of many seaports. To be sure, the influence of New York and Boston was widespread, and by the early nineteenth century these ports would come to overshadow the entire region. Yet many of the smaller ports throughout New England developed special commercial activities of their own, and they maintained their distinct character long after their economic importance had waned.

Boston and Newport were already urban centers at the end of the colonial era; but in the next half-century many another New England port grew from a large village to a cosmopolitan city, the home of complex enterprise and sophisticated culture. Wharves and warehouses lined its waterfront, where longshoremen unloaded a bewildering assortment of cargoes from near and far. Shipyards, sail lofts, and mastyards crowded along the shore, and ropewalks stretched out nearby. In almost every quarter of the town were the two-story, often gambrel-roofed houses of the artisans, with their ground-floor shops and upstairs living quarters. Watchmakers, sellers of charts and nautical books, and tailors who featured seafaring garb had special status here. In most of the seaport shops the customer could find a large quantity of recently imported foreign goods, whose quality usually surpassed that of American wares until well after 1815.

Along two or three streets, including the inevitable High Street and Pleasant Street, stood the square-built homes of the merchants and their affluent associates. Generally of brick construction after 1790, these buildings towered above neat courtyards and outbuildings, and from their upper chambers or roofs one could usually catch a glimpse of the harbor. Inside were silver and furniture from the shops of America's finest craftsmen, along with china and hangings from the Far East. A remarkable number of these houses served for generations as the family homes and still stand, with furnishings virtually intact, as monuments to New England's age of affluence.

Into Market Square in the center of town farmers from outlying communities brought their produce and mingled with the cosmopolitan population of the seaport. Ships' crews often included some foreigners and a good many lads from the interior of New England and from other states as well. Among the artisans were men who had learned their trades in distant lands and had come to America to escape military service in this age of war and to better their station in a more mobile society. A few shopkeepers were women, single or widowed, who proved fully capable of making their way in the "man's world" of business. Among the artisans and laboring people worked a number of blacks freed by their New England owners during the era of the Revolution or descended from slaves who had earlier gained their liberty. A few of these men owned property and could vote, but social attitudes were hardening at the turn of the century, and the black man's rights never did gain full recognition in the northern towns. Down the streets of New England's seaports walked men from all over the world, some to stay, others to move aboard the next vessel clearing outward.

As early as 1760 Connecticut was compared to "a cask of good liquor, tapped at both ends, at one of which Boston draws, and New York at the other." But at least the development of an active commerce along the coast and to the West Indies had tied the region's many prosperous farms to the outside world since the late seventeenth century. New Haven, New London, and Stonington harbors enjoyed relatively deep water, while river ports like Middletown and Norwich had the advantage of reaching far into the interior as marketplaces for the surrounding countryside. Farmers bringing in their surplus crops could purchase in exchange English goods imported via New York or Boston. This role as entrepôt to a thriving agricultural community brought growth and prosperity to the ports of Connecticut.

The emergence of New Haven as an urban center gained symbolic recognition in 1784 when the central part of the old town was set off and incorporated as a city. Although the population in this part of town numbered only a little over 3000, the community had long since outgrown the original eight residential blocks which surrounded a ninth central square, the Green. To the west were the three brick buildings of Yale College, while along Chapel Street to the south stretched the shops of local artisans and storekeepers. The newer area of town spread out to the southeast, flanking the road to the waterfront. There Long Wharf reached into the deeper water of the harbor, while around it were clustered the warehouses and other wharves that formed the center of the city's maritime activities. Some thirty vessels hailed from New Haven in 1784, mostly engaged in the coastal and West Indies trades, and weekly packets ran to New York and New London.

In the first generation after the Revolution, New Haven began to develop local industries on a significant scale. A sugar factory and a woolen mill soon appeared, joined by numerous shops that produced items like clocks, carriages, and buttons. In 1789 Eli Whitney established just over the city border in Hamden his famous gun factory, based on the pioneering principle of interchangeable parts. At the same time, the city continued to grow as a seaport. By the efforts of a hard-working black artisan working mostly alone, Long Wharf was extended an additional 1500 feet in 1810 to enable the larger vessels of the period to use its facilities. The local fleet had increased in number to nearly eighty, still predominantly in coastal and West Indies commerce, with an occasional voyage to Europe and the East.

Life in New Haven was not all business. Around the college centered a vigorous intellectual and cultural community led by President Timothy Dwight and the poet John Trumbull. Along with the ministers of the Congregational churches, most other professional men, and virtually all the merchants, they formed an establishment whose grip on the city's political and social power was for a time unshakable. As in other New England seaports, New Haven's Federalists seemed to thrive on their hatred of Thomas Jefferson and of the principles for which they thought he stood. But the times were changing in the first years of the nineteenth century, and men who constantly looked back to a simpler era had difficulty leading the community into the future.

To the eastward, along the shore of Long Island Sound, other important maritime communities had long thrived. Saybrook, at the mouth of the Connecticut River, never did realize its full potential because oceangoing vessels sailed right by its wharves bound upstream to Middletown and Hartford. In 1807 the Middletown customs district, in fact, had the largest registered and enrolled tonnage of all ports between New York and Cape Cod. New London and Norwich, on the other hand, did succeed in sharing the commerce of the Thames River valley; while Stonington, Connecticut, and Westerly, Rhode Island, vied for domination of the region bordering on Fishers Island Sound. Except for New London's whaling interests, all of these ports played a similar role, serving as outlets for the produce of inland farming communities and bringing to them the manufactured goods of other towns and other lands.

In Narragansett Bay a remarkable change took place in the years after the close of the Revolution. Until the 1760s the town of Newport held sway as the dominant commercial center of Rhode Island. It was, in fact, one of the leading ports of eighteenth-century America. Its distilleries turned out thousands of gallons of dark New England rum, which the merchants used as currency to purchase country produce and goods marketable in Europe. A number of its most prominent merchants imported slaves into the West Indies and engaged in trade with the French and Dutch islands in time of war — activities which merchants in other ports also pursued, though not so successfully.

If the Wantons, Champlins, and other leaders of Newport thought they could continue to dominate the trade of Rhode Island, they did not reckon with the energy and ingenuity of the Browns of Providence.

By the 1760s the family's mercantile house was led by the founder's four sons, popularly known as Nicky, Josey, John, and Mosey. As the activities of this family expanded through the last half of the eighteenth century, so too did the fortunes of its native town. Providence had other advantages over Newport as well, among which was its location at the head of the bay on a commodious cove where the Seekonk meets the tidal flows of the Providence River. Newport, by contrast, was on an island, cut off from any land routes to the rest of the colony. Increasingly, farmers found Providence a more convenient market-place for their produce, and they began making purchases there as well. Soon the Newporters came to depend on their rival merchants up the bay for the commodities they exported. When in 1769 Moses Brown succeeded in his fight to locate in Providence the fledgling Rhode Island College (later to bear the family name), the intellectual and cultural future of his native town was assured. By 1790 the population of Providence had grown to within a few hundred of Newport, and expansion along the waterfront could hardly keep pace with the town's increased business activity. By 1802 its fleet numbered 120 vessels with a total tonnage of over 13,000, surpassing Newport's for the first time.

The Browns' operations had been diversified almost from the beginning, with a blast furnace and shares in a candle factory among their business interests. Now they branched out still further, teaming up with other merchants to form a bank and fostering a variety of other enterprises, including two bridges over the Seekonk River to link the town with Warren and Bristol. Moses Brown, who did not enjoy the countinghouse, left this end of the business to his brothers while he dabbled in other ventures. By far the most significant was the water-powered textile mill he established on the banks of the nearby Pawtucket River. When the Englishman Samuel Slater arrived at New York in 1790 with the plans of Arkwright's perpetual spinning machine in his head, he quickly learned of Brown's operation and offered his services. Brown had sense enough to subsidize the young man in the construction of the new machinery, and the year 1791 brought the birth of the American cotton textile industry, next door to the port of Providence. This juxtaposition of wharf and waterfall would have profound significance for New England in the century ahead.

To the east of Narragansett Bay came the ports of New Bedford, Nantucket, Barnstable, and Plymouth, whose continuing prosperity

Crowinshield's Wharf, Salem, Massachusetts, 1806. Oil painting by Georgy Ropes. Around the wharf are moored the *Fame, America, Prudent,* and *Belisarius. Courtesy Peabody Museum of Salem.*

followed the long-established businesses of whaling and codfishing. The heart of maritime New England in the years after the Revolution was of course Boston, which steadily increased its domination of the region's commerce. In 1807, the peak year of prosperity before the War of 1812, Boston's total tonnage surpassed that of the next three New England ports combined. Yet these other towns — Portland, Salem, and Newburyport (in order of tonnage) — along with Portsmouth, New Hampshire, had distinctive roles to play, not only as outports to Boston, but as centers of independent commercial enterprise in their own right. And the Maine coast east of Portland could no longer be brushed aside, for Bath, Waldoboro, and the Penobscot Bay area each had a greater tonnage than such better-known ports as Newport, New London, and Gloucester.

A study of the town of Newburyport during the early years of the new nation reveals a lot about New England seaports at a critical time in their history. Like most significant maritime centers, Newburyport served as an entrepôt for an extensive interior region. Situated at the mouth of the Merrimack River about forty miles north of Boston, it had since colonial days dominated the life of the lower Merrimack valley. With other seaports of New England the town enjoyed its most prosperous era in the first years of the nineteenth century. Let us take a closer look at Federalist Newburyport as a representative New England seaport.

Not all of the residents of Newburyport earned their livelihood by the sea, but an analysis of occupations made for the year 1773 and valid for later years as well suggests that a remarkably large number did have some association with maritime activities. Of the town's 700 adult males in a population of about 3,500, the occupations of almost 600 have been determined. Among the business and professional men were 140 who described themselves as merchants, shipbuilders, distillers, or shipmasters, all connected with the sea. In addition, the town's 21 shopkeepers depended on goods imported by water to stock their shelves. Artisans with maritime skills — 136 in all — included shipwrights, boatbuilders, sailmakers, coopers, mastmakers, and caulkers. Over 50 men described themselves as mariners, truckmen, or laborers, all of whom worked along the waterfront, and at least half of those whose occupations could not be found surely held similar jobs. All told, it would be fair to say that about 400 men, or nearly 60 percent of the adult male population, earned their living in some occupation connected with the sea.

The other side of the coin shows that around 300 Newburyporters had no first-hand connection with maritime activities, although of course every resident benefited indirectly from the prosperity of the waterfront. Those not working in maritime pursuits included the ministers, physicians, and other professional men; nearly 200 artisans, like cordwainers, blacksmiths, joiners, and cabinetmakers; some 27 yeomen still farming within the boundaries of the town; and doubtless a fair share of those men whose occupations cannot be identified. Even the seaports had something in common with the inland towns.

In the generation from 1773 to 1807 the population of Newburyport doubled, but there is no reason to believe that the distribution of occupations significantly altered. One important change did profoundly affect the people of the town, however. Most of the colonial merchant families could not weather the postwar depression that swept through the seaports of New England. In their places rose new men, many from the humblest of origins, to become leaders of Federalist Newburyport. Only five of the twenty-five wealthiest residents in 1790 bore any relation whatever to the top twenty-five of 1767. At the turn of the century, among the most prominent men were a former cordwainer, a former chaisemaker, and a man whose previous occupation had been that of leather dresser.

In politics Newburyport at the turn of the nineteenth century, like other New England seaports, was staunchly Federalist. Most merchants had no reason to oppose the party that had been in power during their own rise in wealth and influence. Indeed, all who were respectable and proper in New England in 1800 seemed to support the candidacy of President John Adams for reelection. Not only was Thomas Jefferson a Virginian, but he was also widely believed to be an atheist, an admirer of revolutionary France, and an enemy to American commerce.

Seldom in American life has the political arena been marked with more bitterness than during the first fifteen years of the nineteenth century. In Newburyport the Federalists outnumbered their Republican counterparts by a margin of two or three to one in most of the significant elections. Almost all Federalist leaders were among the older, established merchants and professional men in town, while the Republicans attracted younger men still working their way up. Jeffersonians tended to avoid basing their political campaigns on ideological issues, except to claim they were the defenders of democracy. No such reticence inhibited the Federalists, however, one of whom was proud to write in 1804: "We hate democracy — we have opposed it and we will oppose it with all our heart, with all our soul, and with all our strength. . . . We will never submit to be governed by a *scape-gallows* rabble."

The line between the two camps appeared in almost every aspect of life. The Congregationalist ministers were Federalist to a man, while the Presbyterians tended to be Republican. Each party had its own fire company, bank, insurance company, and Masonic lodge. While the Republicans invested in the Newburyport Turnpike running south toward Boston, the Federalists controlled the toll bridge leading north over the Merrimack. Even the militia companies had political overtones, the Federalists dominating the respectable Washington Light Infantry, while the Jeffersonians were left with the less prestigious artillery company.

The divisiveness of partisan politics in Newburyport typified the situation everywhere. In Boston, for instance, the Federalists made the funeral of one of their leaders, Fisher Ames, into a political event, and the deceased's own brother Nathaniel, a Republican, refused to attend. As one result of the political fighting, both Republicans and Federalists made a greater effort to attract popular support. More than once, however, a strained note appeared, as in the pitch for John Quincy Adams that ran: "Vote for Jack Adams; he is the seamen's and mechanics' friend: can do his duty aloft or below, and was brought up by his father, our old Federal Commodore."

Like many other Americans of their generation, New England's merchants took an ambivalent stance toward the institution of slavery. Some of them had owned household servants before the Revolution, and others relied on black bondsmen to work along their wharves and sail aboard their vessels. In the first half-dozen years after the war, all the New England states moved to abolish slavery, although it apparently died a slow death in some parts of Rhode Island and Connecticut. At the same time, however, New England merchants continued to depend heavily on commerce with the southern plantation colonies, and after 1793 a number of new Yankee fortunes were made in the West Indian carrying trade. Undoubtedly some New England shipowners resumed their active role in the slave trade itself, while others still supplied the rum and other commodities used in the business.

The positions of two former Newburyporters is revealing. Jonathan Jackson, like many prominent merchants, fell on hard times after the Revolution. One of several schemes he considered as a means of recouping his losses was to enter the African slave trade. Circumstances, apparently, rather than moral scruples prevented him from doing so. At about the same time, his intimate friend and former next-door neighbor on High Street, the lawyer John Lowell, successfully argued for the freedom of several slaves under the new Massachusetts Constitution.

To write off the merchants of the period as selfish and narrow-minded, with no feeling for the world beyond the countinghouse, would be unfair. One need only walk down Chestnut Street in Salem or along Newburyport's High Street to realize that the Federalists had style. Without their mercantile patrons, Charles Bulfinch and Samuel McIntire could hardly have made careers as architects. Merchants supported a full range of important civic and educational activities, such as parks, schools, and libraries. They patronized the traveling companies that gave frequent musical and theatrical performances. Under their encouragement the seaports of New England emerged from an earlier status as provincial country towns to become cosmopolitan centers of culture and learning.

King Commerce, 1775–1807

No business is more directly influenced by international affairs than a nation's maritime commerce, a fact particularly true in America during the period from 1775 to 1815. In these years American merchants were forced to make major adjustments to new situations on at least a half-dozen occasions, with at least as many minor adjustments in between. At times — during the Revolution and the War of 1812, for example — normal commerce came to a virtual standstill, replaced only by munitions voyages and the cruises of privateers and letters of marque. Between these cataclysmic wars, however, the merchants of New England enjoyed a period of prosperity not again equaled until the 1840s.

With hostilities between the new nation and Great Britain at an end by 1782, American merchants looked ahead to a new era. But the decade of the 1780s brought only disappointment and ruin to numerous merchants of the older generation. Because of their heavy investments in now-worthless state and congressional bonds and currency, many of them had no free capital with which to replace lost or worn-out vessels. Those who had built fast privateers for wartime service quickly learned how poorly suited such vessels were for peacetime trade, where cargo capacity and low operating costs outweighed speed in importance. The cornerstone of New England commerce, the fishing fleet, lay in shambles. Marblehead, for instance, had its prewar fleet of 12,000 tons reduced to 1,500 by war's end. As late as 1790 the value of fish exported from Massachusetts remained 30 percent below prewar figures.

Coupled with these problems was instability at home, generated both by the departure of many Loyalist merchants from the seaports and by the painfully slow process of establishing new governments and commercial policies. Worse still, the burden of wartime debt bore directly upon the property owners through heavy land and personal taxation, which further reduced the merchants' capital and drastically curtailed the farmers' purchasing power. Shipowners could not afford to order new vessels, nor could builders sell to English customers as before, because the use of American craft by British shippers in imperial trade was now prohibited. Construction along the Merrimack thus dropped from the ninety vessels launched in 1772 to only three as late as 1788, and shipyards elsewhere along the coast suffered comparably. Connecticut's fleet dropped by one-third between 1786 and 1790, confirming the decline. Idle shipyards meant unemployment for hundreds of artisans, further depressing public purchasing power.

The worst blow came in 1783, when Great Britain announced its commercial policy toward the new nation. Influenced by recent writings of Adam Smith, friends of America like Edmund Burke, young William Pitt, and the Earl of Shelburne had hoped to reopen the ports of the empire, particularly in the West Indies, to American vessels under a treaty of reciprocity. But conservatives in Parliament, perhaps with reason, feared an American takeover of imperial trade, and the way was clear for embittered British officials to inaugurate a policy of vengeance. American fish and meat products were excluded altogether from the British West Indies, and other produce, such as lumber, livestock, and grain, could be shipped in British vessels only. While Americans could trade directly with Great Britain, they were effectively deprived of the West Indian returns with which to buy British goods. American produce such as fish, whale oil, tobacco, and rice was either banned outright or subjected to prohibitive duties. By the middle of the decade the downward economic spiral seemed to have no end.

The fate of two merchants in Newburyport illustrates the crisis. On paper John and Nathaniel Tracy were the town's richest citizens toward the end of the Revolution in 1780, and even before the signing of peace they hopefully dispatched several vessels to France. But the tobacco and indigo on board was variously described by their Nantes factor as "the worst I ever saw," "of wretched quality," and of an appearance "more like blue Earth than Indigo." One of the vessels was a small privateer with limited cargo capacity; another leaked badly. By the end of 1783 the Newburyporters had lost heavily in the Nantes trade. Meanwhile, they imported quantities of English goods and soon owed Lane Son and Fraser of London over £6000 for articles that remained unsold in Newburyport. The firm declared bankruptcy, and Nathaniel Tracy went into retirement, the town having to abate his taxes in 1790 shortly before his premature death.

Nathaniel's younger brother John put up a stiffer battle, first operating a ropewalk, then heading west to Marietta on the Ohio River to attempt a fresh start; but when he returned for his family, he could not raise enough money to move them. In the end he swallowed his pride and sought a vacancy in the new federal government's customhouse. "I must look to my country — a Country that I neither spared property, labour, nor Attention to support, when in my power," he explained, "but on the contrary, the confidence I placed was my ruin. I do not reflect on myself or my Country — I was happy in sinking or swimming with them." John Tracy spoke for hundreds of New England merchants who, their vessels sunk by the enemy and their capital lost in unredeemed continental notes, could not adjust to the new world their patriotism had helped create.

To take the place of the older merchants who had left during the war, or who went into bankruptcy in the decade that followed, came a new generation. Rising largely from among the artisans, shipmasters, and privateers, these men had several advantages over their predecessors. For one thing, the profits they had accrued during the war were not tied up in defaulted bonds or in worn-out vessels and wharves. For another, they had relatively little land and other property on which to pay heavy taxes. Most important, perhaps, they were unencumbered by the older ways of conducting trade for, as Talleyrand once observed, "commercial habits are more difficult to break through than we imagine." The nouveaux riches of the post-Revolutionary generation in New England bore the names Cabot, Derby, and Crowninshield. It was an era that witnessed a former chaisemaker buy the mansion of a merchant for whom he had once built a carriage, an era that saw the holdings of a shoemaker turned importer rise from £400 in 1786 to £800 in 1790 and double again by 1793.

One major change that came with independence was the freedom to trade any place in the world where American merchants could gain admission. Farewell to enumerated articles, restrictions on direct imports from Europe, and the ban on voyages east of the Cape of Good Hope. Membership in the closed empire of Great Britain had served the colonies well on the whole, but now the Americans had to make their way in the world, without monopoly markets, English bounties, and the protection of the ever-watchful British fleet. To succeed in this new world challenged the ingenuity and energy of every New England mariner in the decades that followed the Revolution. In their search for new markets and for returns with which to buy the ever-desirable products of Great Britain, New England vessels would sail "to the farthest port of the rich East," in the words of Salem's municipal seal.

While not always the first Americans into such distant lands as China, India, and Sumatra, New Englanders came to dominate the

Ichp. Francklin

The second American trading vessel in Japan, the ship *Franklin* of Salem, under Capt. James Devereux, 1798. *Courtesy Peabody Museum of Salem.*

glamorous Eastern trade by the end of the century. As in commerce with Great Britain, the major problem was to find returns with which to purchase homeward cargoes of pepper, silks, tea, and chinaware. Among established American produce, only ginseng, a medicinal herb, commanded a market in Asia. The search for returns in the China trade took American merchants all over the Pacific. When John Ledyard, a Connecticut Yankee who had circled the globe with Captain James Cook, published a report of the Russian sea otter business, some New Englanders looked to the northwest coast of America. In 1788–89 Captain Robert Gray, in his ship *Columbia* out of Boston, found a supply of furs there and carried them to China, thereby establishing a pattern of trade that served New Englanders well for years to come. New Haven vessels specialized in sealing off Chile and Peru, drying the skins on a deserted stretch of the coast quickly dubbed the New Haven Green.

The ship *Columbia,* surrounded by Indians of the Northwest Coast, 1792. Painting on glass by George Davidson, a member of the crew. *Courtesy Massachusetts Historical Society.*

Other vessels stopped at the Sandwich Islands for sandalwood, another highly prized commodity on the Canton market, and for *bêche-de-mer,* but usually Americans had to part with scarce specie in order to obtain cargoes in Asiatic ports. Vessels from Providence, however, developed a new wrinkle in 1792 by carrying foodstuffs and other provisions to the new settlements in Australia, selling them there for bullion or sound British notes.

Another significant branch of the eastern trade centered on the French island of Mauritius (then called Ile de France) in the Indian Ocean. Declared a free port by its owners, Mauritius became a refuge for French emigrés after the Revolution broke out in 1789 and was a major entrepôt for the exchange of a variety of commodities. When

The ship *Boston*, captured by Indians at Nootka Sound, 1803.

Elias Hasket Derby of Salem decided to enter the eastern trade on a large scale, he sent his son out as master of the ship *Grand Turk* in 1787 to establish a base at Mauritius for the family's Asiatic business. There young Derby sold his cargo of fish, provisions, tobacco, rum, and flour — and, in fact, the vessel itself. He plowed the profits back into the homeward cargoes for some of the half-dozen other Derby vessels that sailed to Asia in the next two years, and in 1791 he hitched a passage home with a cousin. Throughout the 1790s American shipmasters calling at Mauritius either sold their cargoes there for coffee and sugar or, more often, fanned out to other ports around the Indian Ocean, including Mocha for coffee, Muscat for gum arabic, Bombay for cotton and textiles, and Java for sugar and coffee. Others continued to Canton for tea and other standard China trade items. The Browns of Providence sent their ship *General Washington* to Madras in 1787–88. There the supercargo reported that "the whole life and study of the Indians is to cheat you," but he did not hesitate to recommend that future shipments of

New England rum be labeled West India rum because the Indians could not tell the difference!

One of the most reliable and long-lasting American enterprises in the Far East was the importation of pepper from Sumatra. Opened in 1789–90 by the brig *Cadet* under Captain Jonathan Carnes of Salem, the pepper trade was soon dominated by that port so completely that Sumatra and its adjoining islands became commonly known as the Salem East Indies. In 1797 Carnes brought the first bulk importation of pepper into New York on the Salem schooner *Rajah,* a voyage that netted its owners a profit of 700 percent on their initial investment of $18,000. Yankees had already begun to export pepper to Europe, including the Netherlands itself, and by the beginning of the nineteenth century had established firm control of the world market.

Far more important than the Pacific trade to the prosperity of Federalist New England was the establishment of new lines of commerce with Europe. In 1791 American merchants were exporting more than $1 million worth of goods to each of five markets: Great Britain, France, Spain, Portugal, and the Netherlands. In addition, Yankee shipmasters found their way back into continental Europe's West Indian possessions ever more frequently, because the islanders needed New England's timber and fish. But the scarcity of adequate returns for the continental trade remained a great handicap, as American merchants continued to have difficulty finding means to pay for the quantities of goods imported from Europe. The opening of trade in the Pacific helped, but it was not yet enough. What Americans needed was to lay their hands on commodities that Europeans demanded in great bulk. When Nicholas Brown of Providence sent his ship *Hope* to Copenhagen in 1788 with tobacco, indigo, and New England rum, the voyage was not profitable. In subsequent years the firm more successfully purchased Russian goods at St. Petersburg with bills of exchange, although obtaining good bills remained a problem.

The outbreak of war between England and France in 1793 gave the Americans their chance, especially after hostilities reached worldwide dimensions before the end of the decade. Because Britannia ruled the waves, neither the French nor their continental allies could bring in the produce of their overseas possessions. As the French conquests spread, the British extended their blockade to cover all European ports from the Mediterranean to the Baltic Sea. From this situation Yankee merchants saw an opportunity to obtain their desperately needed returns. As neutrals they might carry West Indian produce, especially sugar and coffee, to the beleaguered Continent. Ordinarily, of course, the French reserved this trade for themselves; and by the so-called Rule of 1756, international custom decreed that trade closed to other countries in peacetime could not be opened to them as neutrals in time of war. The French were willing to admit the Americans, however, if the latter could find a way around the rule. In no time the Yankees adopted the practice of the "broken voyage," whereby they brought West Indian cargoes into American ports, unloaded and paid duties, and then reexported the goods as American. By granting a rebate, or "drawback," on the duties, the customs officials gave tacit approval to the practice.

American commercial profits now soared, and the merchants of New England were in the thick of the traffic, sharing the bounty with colleagues at New York, Philadelphia, and the Chesapeake ports. A few figures tell the story. In 1791 New England exported about $3.8 million worth of goods, almost exclusively of domestic growth and manufacture. By 1795 the region's exports had risen to $9.4 million, and by 1807 the total reached $24.1 million — a sixfold increase in sixteen years. Reexportation of foreign produce accounted for over 75 percent of this growth, but the sale of domestic produce abroad also rose as Yankee vessels carried fish, lumber, and provisions to the West Indies and to Europe.

Because of the rapidly changing world conditions during this period, shipmasters had to stay alert to obtain their cargoes under the most favorable circumstances. In 1799, for instance, the Dutch West Indies supplied more coffee than any other source, but by 1807 the Spanish, Danish, and French islands had taken the lead, with the Dutch East Indies next in importance. In the sugar trade the Spanish islands led the field in 1799, but by 1807 the French West Indies nearly matched them. As for markets, changes came even more swiftly. In the 1790s, Hamburg, Bremen, and the other Hanseatic ports received two-thirds of all American exports going into the Continent. By 1807, however, the Netherlands became the leading entry, with France, Italy, and Spain all exceeding the old Hanseatic towns. Alert shipmasters could enhance an owner's profits considerably by staying abreast of developments.

More important, only by such knowledge could the captain hope to avoid capture by the British or confiscation by the French, as the rules of the game constantly changed.

To see how the trade actually worked, let us look at an operation carried out by Newburyport's wealthiest merchant, William Bartlet. In January 1807, Bartlet sent Captain Andrew Wilson to the French island of Martinique in his eighty-ton schooner *Farmer*. On board was a typical New England cargo: fish, staves and boards, beef, butter, beans, and cheese. A few hats, shoes, and boots rounded out the list of exports, along with a little soap and household furniture. The cargo was valued at about $5000. In early May, Captain Wilson returned with 12,000 gallons of molasses, 35,000 pounds of brown sugar, and 3,500 pounds of coffee. The molasses undoubtedly went to one of the town's eight distilleries, but the other commodities were stored alongside cargoes which had been brought in since the beginning of the year from Guadeloupe, Santo Domingo, and Martinique by twelve other Bartlet vessels.

Now the merchant had enough coffee and sugar on hand to put aboard the pride of his fleet, the ship *Pomona,* recently returned from Calcutta. Captain Isaac Adams supervised the loading of over 400,000 pounds of sugar and 45,000 pounds each of coffee and pepper. In mid-May the *Pomona* cleared for Amsterdam. There Captain Adams disposed of his cargo and purchased 25,000 gallons of good Dutch gin and nearly 100,000 pounds of nails, along with assorted paints, steel, and cloth goods. When Captain Adams returned to Newburyport in October, he had a cargo whose paper value was about $80,000, all of which had been purchased with produce brought in from other parts of the world by Bartlet's far-ranging fleet.

Several voyages by vessels belonging to Nicholas Brown of Providence show what extraordinary profits were possible. In 1800 his ship *Charlotte* loaded a cargo of coffee, obtained earlier in Java at eight cents a pound, and sold it in Amsterdam at thirty cents per pound. The *Charlotte*'s master then purchased $23,000 worth of European goods, cleared for South America, and sold his cargo for $63,000. Eight years later Brown's ship *Asia* realized a fourfold profit in coffee sold at Tönningen, and in 1811 the same vessel sold tea purchased at $68,000 for $267,000 on the Copenhagen market.

For a while at least, neutral trade solved the problem of returns that traditionally plagued New England merchants. But benefits reached others as well. The expansion of trade demanded new and larger vessels, and now merchants were accumulating the capital necessary for construction. Hundreds of shipwrights found employment in yards throughout the region, while hundreds more cut the timber, forged the ironwork, and manufactured all the other accessories required in the new vessels launched each year. Farmers prospered as their produce reached expanded markets, not only abroad but in the burgeoning seaports themselves. All of these men brought their new earnings to the marketplace for the purchase of domestic manufactures and imported goods alike. Furthermore, wealthy men who earned their money ashore, like the Boston lawyer Fisher Ames, could now invest their savings in maritime ventures, for merchants always needed specie for their Asian voyages.

A glance at Newburyport reveals the extent of this prosperity. The town's total valuation increased fourfold between 1793 and 1807. The average resident was now worth $5000, three times more than in 1793; and more significant, the median property holding more than tripled, proving that the new prosperity affected most of the residents. The mastmaker Zebedee Cook saw holdings of $1665 in 1793 soar to $30,000 by 1807, while John Akerman, ropemaker, was now worth $4000 instead of the mere $165 of fourteen years before. More representative was the case of the laborer John Libbey, whose modest holdings increased from $165 in 1793 to $500 in 1807. One must search hard to find a resident whose fortunes actually waned during the period.

By 1807 the merchants who stood at the center of all this activity could no longer be disparaged as nouveaux riches. By the rapid social mobility that characterized nineteenth-century America, the Cabots, Crowninshields, and Derbys had already become "the Establishment." And the wise ones among them, sensing the importance of diversification, invested their gains in ventures with different risks from those of overseas commerce. When time began to run out on the booming neutral trade, these men and especially their sons were ready to follow the precedent established in 1791 by Moses Brown and shift their capital "from wharf to waterfall." Without the profits of the Federalist generation, however, the manufacturers of the next generation could not so easily have established New England's next important economic undertaking — cotton and woolen textiles.

Sea Lanes in Wartime

Lest we succumb to human weakness by looking only on the brighter side of history, we should recognize that the profits of neutral trade came amid the hazards of war. From the earliest colonial years onward, American merchants lost many vessels through sinking or capture on the high seas or by confiscation in port, for war was a commonplace condition, especially during the eighteenth century. Even during peacetime, lawless bands of pirates sometimes lurked in the passages between the Caribbean islands or pounced on vessels of all nations entering the Mediterranean Sea. During the Revolution and the War of 1812, not even New England seaports were safe from enemy attack.

The ways in which maritime New England waged war between 1775 and 1815 remained largely unchanged from colonial days. The smaller merchant vessels plying the open sea usually carried a gun or two with which to offer resistance if molested, but these weapons gave little hope of warding off a determined enemy. Larger vessels clearing for foreign voyages frequently mounted more numerous and heavier cannon. Their commanding officers often carried a letter of marque and reprisal, by which the government authorized them to capture enemy merchantmen. Such vessels, known simply as letters of marque, were primarily engaged in trading voyages, not commerce raiding. The vessels called privateers, on the other hand, had carte blanche to cruise on the high seas in search of prizes without the pretext of engaging in trade. In effect privately owned warships, these vessels carried heavier armament and larger crews than did the letters of marque. Although many privateers were former merchantmen converted by their owners, the most successful ones were built for speed and for improved performance to windward. The best of the privateers made a significant contribution to the design of sailing vessels.

Neither of these types contributed very much to the defense of their nation's merchantmen, except when one occasionally bested an enemy privateer or retook a captured prize. In fact, defense of its maritime interests was not young America's strong suit. The ease with which British naval units captured merchantmen and raided seaports proved an embarrassment to officials in both the Revolution and the War of 1812. New England made some contribution to the defensive effort by building several men-of-war, for their state forces as well as for the

The ship *Bethel* of Boston, a privateer during King George's War. This is the earliest known identified American ship portrait, 1748. Artist unidentified. *Courtesy Peabody Museum of Salem.*

Model of the Continental frigate *Raleigh,* built at Portsmouth, New Hampshire, 1776. Model by August Delin.

continental navy, and by constructing fortresses at the entrances to their harbors. New Englanders also relied upon the "spider catchers," eight- to ten-ton boats with twenty or thirty men, which put out from the seaports of Massachusetts to harass the British forces during the Revolution. But young Yankee patriots much preferred to ship out in privateers with the hope of rich prizes than to serve aboard a frigate doing convoy duty or to maintain shore watch for a possible assault from the sea. Besides, frigates and fortresses proved equally ineffective in the face of British attacks, and all told, New England took a heavy beating in both wars.

Long before hostilities broke out at Lexington in April 1775, commercial war between the mother country and the colonies had begun. In June 1774 the port of Boston was closed in retaliation for its famous Tea Party, and British naval units barred entrance to all but small coasters laden with firewood and provisions for the desperate population. Some Boston merchants moved to Newburyport, Salem, and Marblehead, and those ports helped pick up the slack. In the autumn the Continental Congress banned all importations from Great Britain and her colonies after 1 December and all exportations to those places after 20 September 1775. As each town established a committee to enforce these provisions of the Continental Association, a truly revolutionary government sprang up on the local level throughout maritime New England. Thereafter merchants who wished to remain in the good graces of their neighbors conformed to the new "law of the land."

The British ministry did not hesitate to retaliate in kind. If the Yankees refused to trade with the mother country, she would prohibit them from trading with anyone else. This she did as of 1 July 1775 by the New England Restraining Act, and for good measure she excluded the region's fishermen from the offshore grounds as well. Only Nantucket's whalers and the mackerel fishermen of Marshfield and Scituate escaped the ban, as a reward for the strong neutralist spirit within these towns. When the British ministry discovered later in the spring that New England did not stand alone in adopting the Continental Association, it levied similar restrictions on the trade of all the other colonies, save New York, Delaware, North Carolina, and Georgia. There it hoped in vain that leniency would encourage loyalty.

In its policy of commercial warfare against the mother country, Congress hoped to bring pressure on Parliament for repeal of the Boston Port Act and other obnoxious legislation through the petitions of British merchants and West Indian planters. These tactics had seemingly worked before in bringing repeal of the Stamp Act in 1766 and most of the Townshend duties in 1770. But by 1775 the British merchants had tired of playing pawn to the Americans, and besides, the Parliament had determined upon a policy of coercion.

Meanwhile, the Americans began to realize that as long as they continued under the restrictions of the Navigation Acts, their self-imposed ban on commerce with Great Britain hurt themselves more than the mother country. After the battle of Bunker Hill they realized how desperately they needed all sorts of military supplies, especially powder. Congress therefore encouraged a breach of British legislation by inviting foreign vessels to bring in war materiel and carry off continental produce like tobacco in payment. In the fall of 1775 the program to procure ammunition was placed under a secret committee of Congress and its activities greatly widened. Silas Deane of Connecticut sailed for France, where he helped set up a fictitious company through which the government poured vital war supplies for the American forces. Many of these cargoes came into Portsmouth, New Hampshire, because that part of the coast seemed relatively clear of British patrols.

Inspired by a combination of patriotism and profits, New England merchants sent their vessels off to procure powder and muskets wherever they could be found. One bountiful source was the French and Dutch West Indies. In July 1775, for instance, New London's Nathaniel Shaw dispatched Captain John MacKibbin in the sloop *Black Joke* with molasses, sugar, and coffee to Philadelphia. There he was to exchange his cargo for flour and staves and clear for Cap François, where Shaw had just learned that large quantities of powder had arrived. Other vessels sailed to Spain, France, and even British possessions in the West Indies, the demand there for American provisions proving stronger than the will to deny munitions to the continentals. By the following spring, direct voyages to France were common. In April the brigantine *Happy Return* cleared Providence with a cargo of sperm oil to be exchanged at Nantes for blankets, lead, gunpowder, and arms. Hopefully the Americans could accumulate needed munitions before the British fleet could close in.

In an effort to end this trade, the British Parliament had declared in the Prohibitory Act of December 1775 that the colonies were in open rebellion. Effective 1 March 1776 the act authorized the navy to seize any American vessel on the high seas; in addition, all foreign ships trading with the colonies were made legal prizes of war. Having been, in effect, kicked out of the empire and declared an enemy, the Americans retaliated in April 1776 by opening the ports of the thirteen colonies to the shipping of all the world's nations except Great Britain. This declaration of commercial independence denied in final language the authority of Parliament to regulate the trade of the colonies, a practice which the Americans had accepted with little question since the middle of the seventeenth century. To no one's surprise, the colonies declared their political independence within three months.

The effectiveness of Britain's declaration of war on American shipping depended, of course, on its execution by the fleet. The potential threat of the mother country's naval might had in fact persuaded a number of New Englanders who were ideologically uncommitted that loyalty to the Crown had much to be said for it. The fact that these loyalists ultimately ended up on the losing side resulted in large measure from the British navy's failure to press its advantage in the early months of the war. By the time the fleet had shaken out its peacetime cobwebs in 1778, the French had joined the Americans in a decisive alliance.

But the French men-of-war gave little protection to the New England coast either before or after the alliance of 1778. Meanwhile, British warships worked their will on any seaport their commanders wished to intimidate. Because of a refusal to ship masts for use of the fleet, the British burned most of Falmouth (later Portland), Maine, in October 1775. They subsequently bombarded several more ports, including Gloucester, New Bedford, Bristol, and Stonington. Later in the war came a devastating British raid on New London, led by Thames-born Benedict Arnold. Loyalists from Long Island joined expeditions against other Connecticut towns as well. The British held Boston until March 1776, and then in December they occupied Newport, maintaining a base of operations there until October 1779. Ports like Salem that escaped attack gained the advantage over the others at the war's end. In addition to bombardment and occupation, the Royal Navy sent out small tenders filled with marines to confiscate livestock and other provisions belonging to the colonists living along the shore or on coastal islands. Local minutemen did what they could to drive off the marauders, and many a small-town hero emerged as the defender of sheep and cows, but considerable damage was done. Several island communities along the coast of Maine had to be abandoned altogether, so exposed were they to assault from both navy and loyalist privateers based in Nova Scotia.

In the summer of 1775 Congress authorized the individual colonies to acquire armed vessels and to take whatever other measures they considered necessary to protect their harbors and commerce. John Adams had hoped for a more aggressive policy, one that would provide for an American navy, but moderates blocked the proposal until late in the year. Not until March 1776 did Congress finally authorize continental vessels, as well as the warships and privateers of individual colonies, to wage offensive war against British merchantmen. To be sure, most of the New England colonies had already outfitted a number of armed vessels and sent them out to scour the waters off their coasts. Washington had even taken the initiative to acquire a small fleet of his own to intercept vessels supplying the British forces besieged at Boston, but none of these forces could engage in battle with British frigates.

GREAT
ENCOURAGEMENT
FOR
SEAMEN.

ALL GENTLEMEN SEAMEN and able-bodied LANDSMEN who have a Mind to diftinguifh themfelves in the GLORIOUS CAUSE of their COUNTRY, and make their Fortunes, an. Opportunity now offers on board the Ship RANGER, of Twenty Guns, (for FRANCE) now laying in PORTSMOUTH, in the State of NEW-HAMPSHIRE, commanded by JOHN PAUL JONES Efq; let them repair to the Ship's Rendezvous in PORTSMOUTH, or at the Sign of Commodore MANLEY, in SALEM, where they will be kindly entertained, and receive the greateft Encouragement.---The Ship RANGER, in the Opinion of every Perfon who has feen her is looked upon to be one of the beft Cruizers in AMERICA.---She will be always able to Fight her Guns under a moft excellent Cover ; and no Veffel yet built was ever calculated for failing fafter, and making good Weather.

Any GENTLEMEN VOLUNTEERS who have a Mind to take an agreable Voyage in this pleafant Seafon of the Year, may, by entering on board the above Ship RANGER, meet with every Civility they can poffibly expect, and for a further Encouragement depend on the firft Opportunity being embraced to reward each one agreable to his Merit.

All reafonable Travelling Expences will be allowed, and the Advance-Money be paid on their Appearance on Board.

IN CONGRESS, MARCH 29, 1777.

RESOLVED,

THAT the MARINE COMMITTEE be authorifed to advance to every able Seaman, that enters into the CONTINENTAL SERVICE, any Sum not exceeding FORTY DOLLARS, and to every ordinary Seaman or Landfman, any Sum not exceeding TWENTY DOLLARS, to be deducted from their future Prize-Money.

By Order of CONGRESS,

JOHN-HANCOCK, PRESIDENT.

DANVERS: Printed by E. RUSSELL, at the Houfe late the Bell-Tavern.

John Paul Jones recruiting Yankee seamen for the U. S. S. *Ranger*, 1777. *Courtesy Naval Historical Foundation.*

Despite these efforts in the early years of the war to establish a regular navy, maritime New England's most significant contribution to the fighting was through the hundreds of privateers sent out from its ports. One must recognize that privateering, like smuggling, whaling, and clipper ships, is one of the glamour topics of American maritime history. As such, the story of privateering has sounded far better in the telling than in the original fact. With rare exceptions neither the individual engagements nor the profits earned by the owners and crews justify the ballyhoo surrounding the activities of these private warships, although for a while there was glory enough for all.

Yet privateering did have some effect on the course of the war and the well-being of New England. For one thing, the capture of heavily laden British merchantmen brought badly needed commodities into American ports. Furthermore, many seamen found profitable berths on board the privateers at a time when regular commerce had little to offer. Finally, to some extent, the loss of their ships and cargoes did hurt the British war effort in America, though no one would claim that the effect was in any way decisive. On the negative side, men badly needed in the continental army and navy avoided regular service by shipping out in privateers, and competition for armaments and powder drove up prices.

Toward the end of the war, privateering became extremely risky, with far fewer prizes than before and with greater American losses as well. One New England auctioneer specializing in the disposal of captured vessels and cargoes saw his business decline from twenty-three prizes in 1780 to only seven in 1782, the last year of the war. Despite all this, the glamour lingered on, both for the young bucks of the period and for war buffs of later generations.

As serious as were the British attacks on American seaports and their seizure of merchantmen at sea during the Revolution, at no time did the New England maritime activity come to a standstill. Merchants of the next generation, however, faced a British navy that during the War of 1812 was relentlessly efficient in shutting up the ports of New England altogether. And the interior was far from troublefree. No sooner had neutral trade begun in 1793, in fact, than Great Britain, France, and the Republican administration all threw in the way of Yankee prosperity an unprecedented series of obstacles.

The British could hardly be expected to tolerate American trade

A FUNERAL ELEGY,

Composed on the DEATH of the truly Brave and Heroic CAPTAIN
JAMES MUGFORD,

Late COMMANDER of the FRANKLIN PRIVATEER Schooner, lately fitted out from MARBLEHEAD, with a few 2 Pounders and Swivels, and 21 Men, who on the 17th of May, 1776, valiantly attacked and took a King's Store-Ship, 300 Tons, bound from Cork to Boston, mounting 6 Carriage Guns, besides Swivels, and 18 M___ ___ch is esteemed the richest Prize that has been brought into any Port in the AMERICAN COLONIES since the commencement of the War, having on board 1500 Barrels POWDER, designed for the Use of our cruel and implacable Enemies, the British Fleet and Army, employed to enslave the CONTINENT.——This brave and gallant HERO, most unfortunately for his COUNTRY, fell a sacrifice in Defence of its RIGHTS and LIBERTIES, on the 19th of the same Month, in a desperate Engagement with 13 Boats, manned with 200 Marines and Sailors from the British Fleet. This ELEGY is recommended to be preserved by all the FRIENDS to AMERICAN LIBERTY.

AH! who but mourns at the decrees of fate,
To snatch a YOUTH whose deeds fame will relate,
To weary mansions of the dead to rove,
And mix with the brave sons of war above.

The winged messenger of death, with his fierce dart
Was swiftly sent, and pierc'd our HERO the heart.
The Muse but weeps, whose breast is fill'd with woe,
We've lost a mortal scourge t'our Country's foe.

O! could his life been spar'd for a few years!
But ah! the brave is fled, and left a world in tears.
Wilt thou be prais'd? poetic pow'rs are faint,
Thy courage and thy valor half to paint:

To thee let Heroes grateful voices raise.
The brave and great may justly join their praise.
This Youth who was but in his prime,
Shall in COLUMBA's latest Annals shine,

Whose brightest deeds of glory and renown
Were late with wreaths of laurels crown'd.
Ye great and good! O mourn now with the Muse,
And weep on hearing of this awful news;

MUGFORD's no more, O let our tears now flow!
No more he lives the terror of our faithless foe.
Through thickest glooms, look back, immortal SHADE!
On that confusion which thy death hath made;

Or from Olympus' height look down and see
A Continent in grief bereft of thee.
Who taught thee, MUGFORD, in the pow'rs of night,
To vanquish numbers who oppos'd with might?

Who strung thy feeble arms with might unknown?
How great thy conquest, and how bright thy crown!
His morning sun, which rose resplendent bright
Was quickly mantled with the gloom of night.

But hark! in Heav'n's blest bow'rs your HERO hear,
And learn to imitate his courage here:
" Come WARREN, WOLFE, MONTGOMERY, join with me,
" We're glad we fought to set our Country free;

" Free from our Tyrant's mercenary sway:"
Thus spake those HEROES, whom the gods obey.
Grim Monarch! see, depriv'd of vital breath,
A youthful HERO in the dust of death:

Dost thou go on incessant to destroy,
Our griefs to double, and lay waste our joy?
Enough thou never yet wast known to stay,
Though millions die the vassals of thy sway:

Nor youth, nor science, nor the ties of love,
Nor ought on earth thy flinty heart can move.
The conq'ring brave, from his dire dart to save
In vain we ask the Sov'reign of the Grave.

Thy PARTNER sees thee mingle with the dead,
And rend the graceful tresses from her head,
Wild in woe, with grief unknown oppress'd,
Sigh follow sigh deep heaving on her breast.

Fair MOURNER there see thy lov'd MUGFORD laid,
And o'er him spread the deep impervious shade;
Clos'd are his eyes, and heavy fetters keep
His senses bound in never-waking sleep;

'Till time shall cease, 'till many a starry world
Shall fall from Heav'n, in dire confusion hurl'd,
'Till nature in her final wreck shall lie,
And her last groan shall rend the azure sky:

Not, not 'till then his active soul shall claim
His body a divine immortal frame.
But see the softly-stealing tears apace
Pursue each other down the MOURNER's face;

But cease thy tears, bid ev'ry sigh depart,
And cast the load of anguish from thine heart:
From the cold shell of his great soul arise,
And look beyond, thou native of the skies;

There fix thy view, where fleeter than the wind
Thy MUGFORD mounts, and leaves the earth behind.
Thyself prepare to pass the vale of night,
To join forever on the hills of light:

To thine embrace his joyful spirit moves
To Thee, the PARTNER of his earthly loves;
He welcomes thee to pleasures more refin'd,
And better suited to th' immortal mind.

Say, PARENT, why this unavailing moan?
Why heave your pensive bosom with the groan?
To JAMES, the subject of my mournful song,
A brighter world, and nobler strains belong.

Say, would you tear him from the realms above
By thoughtless wishes and prepost'rous love?
Doth his felicity increase your pain?
Or could you welcome to this world again.

Indulgent PARENT, weep not for thy SON,
Prepare yourself the heav'nly race to run;
When death shall snap the thread of life's twisted cord,
May you enjoy the blessed mansions of your GOD.

Broadside funeral elegy on Capt. James Mugford of Washington's Navy, 1776.
Courtesy Peabody Museum of Salem.

with their enemy, and in November 1793 they authorized naval units and privateers to seize all neutral shipping trading with the French West Indies. Throughout the winter, as one wag put it, "Britannia waived the rules." Although the policy eased the following spring, hundreds of American vessels were seized, and more than one hundred and fifty were condemned in prize court. When Captain Samuel Lawton of Newport fell victim to the British sloop of war *Hound* off Cap François in March 1794, he was taken into Jamaica. "There seems to be neither Law nor Justice here and they have got all my Cash from me therefore it is impossible to find friends here," he reported to his owners. "There is now in port forty od sail here and the chief of them libel'd and their tryals wont come on this four months. By that time their Vessels will not be fit to proceede home." Late in 1794 America and Great Britain settled some of their more serious differences by Jay's Treaty. One of the terms provided adjudication of claims from American merchants that ultimately resulted in awards of some $12 million.

Angered by this rapprochement between the United States and Great Britain, France took vengeance by turning its own privateers loose on American shipping. After 1796 insurance rates for West Indian voyages soared from about 6 percent to over 30 percent by 1798. Far worse, American crews gaining freedom after capture by French privateers brought back tales of barbarous treatment. As opinion began to swing against the French, New Englanders backed the Adams administration's decision to fight back. Local groups in Newburyport, Salem, and other New England ports raised subscriptions to construct several warships, which helped to bring the undeclared naval war with France to a successful close by 1800. Meanwhile, the government issued letters of marque to American merchantmen eager to defend themselves. In 1799 the twenty-gun Salem ship *Mount Vernon* did just that and more, warding off several French naval vessels and then capturing a privateer in full view of British vessels off Gibraltar. The *Mount Vernon*'s captain, Elias Hasket Derby, Jr., ultimately delivered his cargo in Naples for three times its original value.

No sooner had the United States settled, at least temporarily, its differences with France than the long-festering problem of the Barbary pirates demanded attention. Corsairs from Morocco, Algiers, and Tripoli had menaced European traders in the Mediterranean for years; but

The ship *Mount Vernon,* beating off French privateers in the straits of Gibraltar, 1799. Gouache by M. F. Corne, a passenger on the vessel. *Courtesy Peabody Museum of Salem.*

by the mid-eighteenth century the British, through a combination of blackmail and naval might, had been able to guarantee the safety of all members of their empire. One of the high costs of American independence was the loss of this protection, and in 1794 Congress authorized a permanent navy to cope with the situation.

In 1794 the master of a brig out of Berwick reported her capture just fifteen miles off Lisbon and gloomily predicted that "soon the whole western ocean will be infested with cruizers." By the beginning of the nineteenth century, seizures of vessels and enslavement of their crews had reached intolerable proportions. In addition, the young nation suffered embarrassing indignities, such as the Algerian dey's demand for warships. The thirty-six-gun frigate *Crescent* was one of four "tribute vessels" built at Portsmouth and handed over in 1798, fully laden with masts, sailcloth, and other strategic materials. Some New England mariners took out individual insurance policies at 2.5 percent to provide a ransom of $3000 in case of their capture. But after the

Quasi-War with France, naval units moved into the Mediterranean to convoy American merchantmen safely past the hostile coast. In 1803, for instance, the frigate *Philadelphia* recaptured the Boston brig *Celia* and freed her crew from the pirate vessel. Within a few years American vessels could once more ply the waters between Gibraltar and Italy with relative safety.

New England shipowners held their breaths when, in 1802, England and France made peace. Was the era of neutral trade to end after all? Fortunately for the profit-seekers, hostilities reopened with greater vigor than ever late in 1803; and as we have seen, prosperity soared to still greater heights along the New England seaboard. But with renewed warfare came further depredations against American commerce. One of the most persistent abuses was the British practice of impressing seamen off American merchant vessels. More often than not, these men were deserters from the stinking fo'c'sles of the British men-of-war, but not infrequently native Yankees stood condemned to years of service in the British fleet. Later, however, in an effort to discredit the Republicans' War of 1812, Salem Federalists like John Pickering and William Gray claimed that they knew of only thirty-five impressment cases out of 18,000 sailors employed in their vessels.

Nor was impressment the only problem facing the New England merchant, for in 1805 a British court handed down a sobering decision. The ship *Essex* had been seized en route from Barcelona to her home port of Salem, where she had intended to lay her cargo on shore to "Americanize" it before reloading and clearing for Havana. The court ruled what the Americans had known all along, that such a voyage was merely a dodge to cover what in actuality was a continuous voyage from one enemy port to another. For a time thereafter, British naval units swarmed all over American vessels — in the West Indies, off the coast of Europe, and even in the Indian Ocean. Most maddening of all, British frigates skulked just outside the three-mile limit off major American ports, requiring each merchantman coming their way to heave to and await inspection, often delaying the passage for a full day. A Portsmouth master reported in 1806 that the "infamous Henry Whitby" of the fifty-gun ship *Leander* had stopped him off Sandy Hook. "Frequently after our vessels had hove to, would he order shot after shot to be fired into them, with directions to the gunner to sink the damm'd Yankee rascals." One case of insolence followed another, behavior that even New England Anglophiles found difficult to defend. But as long as the profits of neutral trade continued to pour in, merchants refrained from criticizing the British too harshly.

In June 1807 England overstepped itself when its man-of-war *Leopard* brought the U.S.S. *Chesapeake* under fire and impressed four deserters from her crew. Promise of more humiliation came in November with Britain's latest Orders in Council, which required all vessels trading with any European port under Napoleonic control to stop first in England, unload its cargo, and pay duties before proceeding. The Jefferson administration found itself in a difficult quandary. Lacking the naval force to defend neutral rights, the president chose instead to avoid further losses by retreating from the seas altogether. With passage of the Embargo Act in December 1807, President Jefferson accomplished what the English, the French, and the Barbary pirates together could not — an end to neutral trade.

The Twilight of Federalist New England, 1807–15

The new Embargo prohibited all American vessels from engaging in foreign trade. Thus began one of the most distressing periods in the history of maritime New England. For the next five years commerce suffered through a series of disruptions that culminated in a devastating war with the world's foremost naval power. The close of hostilities in 1815 found New England stripped of its former prosperity and isolated from the rest of the union by its embitterment toward the national government.

It was certainly not the novelty of an embargo that angered New England merchants. Their patriotic fathers had used the tactic in the quarrel with Great Britain more than thirty years before, particularly in the Continental Association of 1774–75. Washington's administration levied an embargo in 1794 to protest British harrassment of American trade. The principle appeared sound enough. But to hardened Federalists Jefferson could do no right, even if he did adopt a policy used twice before in an effort to protect American commerce and to wring concessions from our boycotted foes. Furthermore, Jefferson's timing was bad, for in 1807 New England merchants had enjoyed their most prosperous

THE EMBARGO:

DEAR Sirs, it is wrong
To demand a new Song;
  I have let all the breath I can spare, go;
With the Muse I've confer'd,
And she won't say a word,
  But keeps laughing about the Embargo.

I wish that I could,
Sing in Allegro mood;
  But the times are as stupid as Largo;
Could I have my choice,
I would strain up my voice:
  'Till it snapt all the strings of Embargo.

Our great politicians,
Those dealers in visions,
  On paper, to all lengths they dare go;
But when call'd to decide,
Like a turtle they hide,
  In their own pretty shell the Embargo.

In the time that we try,
To put out Britain's eye;
  I fear we shall let our own pair go;
Yet still we're so wise
We can see with French Eyes,
  And then we shall like the Embargo.

A French privateer,
Can have nothing to fear;
  She may load and may here or may there go;
Their friendship is such,
And we love them so much,
  We let them slip thro' the Embargo.

Our ships all in motion,
Once whiten'd the ocean,
  They sail'd and return'd with their cargo;
Now doom'd to decay,
They have fallen a prey
  To Jefferson, Worms, and Embargo.

Lest Britain should take
A few men by mistake,
  Who under false colours may dare go;
We're manning their fleet
With our Tars, who retreat
  From poverty, sloth and Embargo.

What a fuss we have made,
About rights and free Trade,
  And swore we'd not let our own share go,
Now we can't for our souls
Bring a Hake from the shoals,
  'Tis a breach of the twentieth Embargo.

Our Farmers so gay.
How they gallop'd away.
  'Twas money that made the Old Mare go;
But now She won't stir,
For the whip or the spur,
  'Till they take off her clog, the Embargo.

If you ask for a debt,
The man turns in a pet,
  "I pay, sir? I'll not let a hare go;
If your officer comes,
I shall put up my thumbs,
  And clap on his breath an Embargo."

Thus Tommy destroys,
A part of our joys;
  Yet we'll not let the beautiful Fair go;
They all will contrive
To keep commerce alive,
  There's nothing they hate like Embargo.

Since rulers design,
To deprive us of wine,
  'Tis best that we now have a rare go;
Then each to his post,
And see who will do most,
  To knock out the blocks of Embargo.

Broadside satirizing Jefferson's Embargo. The portrait is presumed to be of Washington. *Courtesy American Antiquarian Society.*

year ever. With a favorable balance sheet, one can apparently tolerate a remarkable amount of insolence and even the loss of a few sailors to impressment and cargoes to confiscation. But Jefferson saw an embargo as the only honorable alternative to war in 1807, for the *Chesapeake-Leopard* affair had inspired belligerent cries from "hawks" all over the country, including New England. Knowing that the nation was too weak to fight, he turned to "measures short of war" in an effort to make American weight count for something in the European balance.

As news of an impending embargo spread along the seacoast, merchants frantically readied whatever vessels they had in port to clear outward before official notification of the act reached the local customhouse. Even for those that made it, freedom would be short-lived, for once they returned to an American port, they could not again clear foreign. By the spring of 1808 most of the absent pigeons had come home to roost, although a few vessels remained out to enter the freighting business between the West Indies and European ports until captured by British cruisers.

Only the fisheries and the coastal trade remained open to American shipping, but both offered numerous opportunities for evasion of the law. When Samuel Hadlock of Little Cranberry Island, Maine, finished hauling for cod on the banks off Newfoundland, he found his vessel heading for Portugal, possibly because of adverse conditions at sea (an acceptable excuse) but more likely because the price of merchantable fish had soared at Oporto. Once there, of course, he might as well bring home a worthwhile cargo. He netted enough from his salt and lemons to order a new schooner built for himself. Similarly, a Bostonian cleared on a rather unusual whaling voyage with 500 casks of bacon in the hold. In due course he returned from Halifax with, indeed, a cask of whale oil on board — along with several hundred bales of English woolens.

The coastal trade accounted for a far greater number of violations. Coasters were required to post heavy bonds to land their cargoes at another American port, but sometimes vessels made for the open sea instead. If caught, forfeiture of the bond wiped out any gain from the illicit trade, although occasionally the shipmaster might successfully plead that distresses of the sea had caused his erratic voyage. Never before had American vessels suffered such a rash of sprung timbers, split tops'ls, and broken spars. The coaster *Ploughboy* of Bangor left

Newport for Castine with provisions, only to put into Antigua under stress of weather. There the master undoubtedly had to sell his cargo to pay for "repairs" before heading for home. If he followed the example of others, his hold was empty, but the proceeds of his voyage had been cautiously sewn into the lining of his overcoat or perhaps stashed away under the cabin floor.

Smugglers reaped a handsome profit at both ends of the Atlantic coastline, at Passamaquoddy Bay opposite New Brunswick and along the St. Marys River between Georgia and Spanish-owned Florida. Coastal clearances from Boston to Maine ports other than Portland increased almost ninefold, from fifty-seven in 1807 to over five hundred in 1808. An astounding amount of flour came into Eastport as legitimate cargo, some 160,000 barrels during 1808 alone. Worth about four dollars each as they piled up along the American side of the bay, the casks brought three times that figure at Campobello or Grand Manan. No wonder the bay fairly crawled with small craft, for a man could make upwards of fifty dollars for one night's hard rowing. By the end of the year, however, government officials had had enough. The frigate *Chesapeake* ironically took station in the bay and put an end to the traffic that her encounter with the *Leopard* the year before had done so much to bring about.

But not all New England mariners could or would take advantage of loopholes in the system, and for them the Embargo spelled disaster. Newspapers published accounts of vessels laid up, yards acockbill, and of grass growing along the wharves of ports from Penobscot Bay west.

> Our ships all in motion once whitened the ocean;
> They sailed and returned with a cargo;
> Now doomed to decay, they have fallen a prey
> To Jefferson — worms — and embargo.

So wrote one contributor to a seaport newspaper. All the downward effects of the business cycle through which New England suffered in the 1780s closed in once more. Shipyards laid off workers in anticipation of a falloff in orders. Farm prices plummeted as the West Indian market shut down. The district of Middletown, specializing in the marketing of Connecticut Valley produce, exported no goods at all in 1808. The fisheries languished for similar reasons; and all the shopkeepers and artisans dependent on shipwrights, farmers, and fishermen for customers faced the future with despair.

The most spectacular losses struck the merchants engaged in the re-exportation of foreign goods. From a high of over $15 million worth of such trade in 1807, New Englanders managed to export less than $5 million in foreign produce during 1808. Overall, the value of New England's exports dropped from $24 million to under $6 million as the result of the Embargo. That any goods got out at all is testimony to the various ways in which New Englanders took advantage of the law's loopholes without actually smuggling. More than one merchant could trace his ultimate downfall to the Embargo, even though he might gamely hang on for a number of years.

One result of the Embargo which Jeffersonians particularly regretted was the wave of bitterness that swept political circles throughout New England. Never charitable in their opinion of the Republicans to begin with, Federalist merchants and their allies among the professions stormed and raged in town meetings, in letters to the editor, and in petitions to Congress. As the Embargo dragged on through 1808, some concluded that Jefferson's real objective was "the utter destruction of northern commerce"; others attributed authorship of the measure to Napoleon himself. Timothy Pickering of Salem suggested nullification as a proper means of protest for the New England states, and Newbury-port Federalists implored the General Court to "interpose" the state's authority in their behalf. The Boston *Gazette* even published a dark hint at secession. "It is better to suffer the amputation of a limb than to lose the whole body. We must prepare for the operation." And the Salem *Gazette* asked, "What charms can a *union* have for New England if all her commerce by land and water . . . must be sacrificed?" Other ominous signs appeared in some of the seaports, including the formation of armed guards "to defend their rights and privileges," the appointment of committees of correspondence reminiscent of an earlier revolution, and the castigation of all who helped enforce the Embargo as "enemies to their country."

By the end of Jefferson's second term, Republicans everywhere had reached the obvious conclusion that the Embargo had failed to earn any recognition of American rights from either belligerent. In its place Congress substituted the Nonintercourse Act of March 1809, which allowed Americans to trade with any port in the world except those under

British and French control. The following year Congress tried a different tack with the Macon Act. Effective May 1810, President Madison lifted nonintercourse with both belligerents, with the option to reinstate it against one power if the other agreed to rescind its restrictions against neutral trade. Napoleon saw no reason not to play the game, and by pretending to suspend his decrees, he succeeded in having nonintercourse renewed against Great Britain in May 1811. Thereafter, Madison steadfastly denied the overwhelming evidence that Napoleon had duped him; and so matters stood until a final embargo in April 1812, two months before the declaration of war against England.

One would expect the patterns of American commerce to be erratic during the years 1809–12, and indeed they were. The Spanish islands in the Caribbean continued to be the leading source of sugar for reexport and took over as the chief supplier of coffee as well, while imports from the Danish, Dutch, and French West Indies tailed off sharply because Napoleon kept them under tight control. The Swedish island of St. Bartholomew ranked second behind the Spanish possessions, and by 1811 the coast of Brazil began to supply significant quantities of coffee. In Europe American traders had to find new routes into the continent, since the ports of Holland and France were no longer accessible. Many took their chances against Danish privateers and extortionist officials in the Baltic Sea by calling at Danish, Swedish, and Russian ports, with trade to the latter nation a specialty of vessels from Massachusetts. American exports to this area increased nearly sevenfold from pre-Embargo days to a value of over $15 million in 1810. When the risks became too great, a number of shipmasters rounded North Cape to enter Archangel. Another major outlet for American produce was the Iberian peninsula, especially in the years after 1810, when Wellington's army of occupation demanded quantities of wheat and flour.

But at no time between the Embargo and the War of 1812 did American exports come close to reaching previous levels. New England's share of the export trade, which had reached a high of $24 million in 1807 and had dipped to less than $6 million in 1808, struggled back to only $14 million by 1811. The one consoling fact was that most of the loss was in the reexportation of foreign goods, while domestic produce nearly regained its pre-Embargo level.

The activities of the Newburyport schooner *Lydia,* owned by John and Philip Coombs, illustrate well the flexibility necessary for success-

Schooner Lidia of Newburi Port Entering the Port of Marseilles 10. November 1807.

The schooner *Lidia* of Newburyport, entering Marseilles, France, 1807. *Courtesy Peabody Museum of Salem.*

ful commerce during the period. Before the Embargo the *Lydia* had made a number of runs to the Mediterranean, carrying sugar, coffee, and fish to Spain, Marseilles, or Sardinia and returning with wine, glassware, and salt. In 1810 Captain David Haskell cleared for Alicante, Spain, with a cargo of fish, but instead of bringing the *Lydia* directly home, he headed north for Archangel, from which he returned to Newburyport in December with a load of iron, hemp, and cordage. The voyage to Russia was apparently so successful that the Coombs brothers decided to have the *Lydia* rebuilt along heavier lines. The refit converted the vessel into a brig, with her burden increased to 160 tons and a second deck added. Thus enlarged, she departed in May 1811 with sugar and cotton for Archangel and returned in October with another cargo of iron, sailcloth, and flax.

New England merchants sensed that they were at best enjoying only a brief Indian summer in the years after the Embargo. In their letters some gloomily predicted further restrictions, and others foresaw ultimate war with Great Britain. They were particularly annoyed that the nation seemed to be drifting, with no one issue or episode serious enough to justify hostilities but with no leaders committed to the preservation of peace. Southern and western Republicans uttered rash statements about seizing Canada or Florida or both, while others spoke darkly about ending the Indian menace on the frontiers. But in the long run, war came as the result of accumulated frustrations over British offenses — impressment, restrictions on commerce, and insolence on the high seas. Many Americans felt strongly that the young nation's honor must be defended at all costs, and Republicans from all sections, including New England, supported the war, though not always with the enthusiasm with which Federalists opposed it.

New England merchants were by ordinary standards probably no less patriotic than Americans from other parts of the country. But in 1812 they stood to lose more than most citizens from a war with the world's strongest naval power. It was no longer so much a matter of profits, although that was a factor; more distressing was the fact that their vessels, wharves, and homes stood naked before the British fleet. Their fathers' generation had suffered a similar fate during the Revolution, but that was in a worthy cause. To Federalists it seemed that the national government was telling them that they must sacrifice their all to salve the pride of partisan Republicans, and most of them would have none of it.

"What are we to do, my friend," wrote one New Englander, "now that this overwhelming calamity is at our very door?" What they did is a matter of record, honorable or not, depending on the standards by which one wishes to judge them. They refused to turn over control of their militia to the federal government; they withheld all possible support to the warfare on land and ridiculed the feeble showing of their fellow Americans in the field; they continued to trade with the enemy by land as well as by sea; and in the end some of them seriously proposed making a separate peace with Great Britain, while others symbolically raised the five-star flag of New England over coastal fortifications. No responsible officials seriously proposed secession, but more than one private citizen would have welcomed such a proposal. "What would your fathers have done? What *did* they do?" asked an Essex County minister of his flock in reference to the generation that had declared its independence of Great Britain. "Were your boat fastened to a fireship just ready to explode, would you not cut the painter . . . ?"

How badly the war hurt New England also depends on how one measures it. In its effect on foreign commerce, of course, nothing could have been more devastating. By 1814 the export trade had all but disappeared, with only $2.6 million in cargoes leaving New England ports, mostly domestic produce heading to Florida and the Spanish and Swedish West Indies. The fishing fleets lay idle alongside their big sisters in harbor, whose lower mastheads were protected by inverted tar barrels dubbed "Madison's nightcaps." Farmers again watched the disappearance of overseas markets depress the value of their produce, and even the coastal trade suffered severely, first from governmental restrictions and then from the hovering British fleet.

The small American navy — only seven frigates and nine other warships — succeeded in herding many New England vessels back to port at the outbreak of war, but by late 1812 Canadian privateers from New Brunswick and Nova Scotia began to take a heavy toll. The infamous *Liverpool Packet,* mounting only five guns, sent in over thirty prizes before being taken herself by the schooner *Thomas* out of Portsmouth. The American frigates were by this time bottled up in harbors from Chesapeake Bay northward, and all effective opposition to British naval might was at an end. Thereafter enemy frigates closed in on virtually anything that floated, from proud Indiamen to humble coasters. The British squadron had standing orders to halt fishing smacks and demand ransom of their skippers, almost too much for one British officer, who confided in his journal:

> Made the unfortunate master of a fishing boat . . . pay $200 for a ransom. The poor creature has a wife and seven children, no money, and was in debt for his salt and fishing lines even. He with great difficulty scraped up by sixpences and shillings the amount of the money at Provincetown and came on board with tears in his eyes. This is an ungenerous war against the poor, and unworthy of Englishmen. I am ashamed of Captain Epworth's conduct.

Enemy tenders raided seaboard towns throughout New England, though Cape Cod and Maine bore the brunt. In the summer of 1814 British forces landed at Castine in Penobscot Bay, raided Bangor up the river, and then took possession of the entire coast eastward to Passamaquoddy Bay, where they stayed until April 1815.

Despite these woes, New Englanders fared better than the residents along Chesapeake and Delaware bays, which the British blockade had closed earlier in the war and where thousands of redcoats landed to pillage and burn scores of towns, including of course the nation's capital. While Massachusetts managed, even in 1814, to export in one way or another goods worth over $1,000,000, all the ports of Chesapeake Bay together sent out less than $300,000 worth, and Philadelphia shipped no goods at all. Connecticut, oddly enough, *increased* its exports during the war, from about $700,000 in 1812 to over $1,000,000 in 1814, although the Middletown district was shut out almost totally from this wartime trade.

No amount of looking on the bright side can disguise the fact that the War of 1812 wreaked irreparable damage to foreign commerce throughout New England, especially in the smaller ports. Unable to weather the storm, merchants in the outports from Portland to New Haven went under, one after another, or else moved to Boston or New York. As a secondary consequence of the war, those two places increased their domination of New England's commerce until only ports like Salem, with its specialized trade with the East Indies, and the fishing towns of Gloucester, Marblehead, and New Bedford could claim to carry on the proud traditions of their forefathers. Maritime New England outside of these ports would enjoy a renaissance in the middle decades of the nineteenth century, but meanwhile it had only the memories of a glorious past to sustain it.

The Salem ship *Postillion,* lost at Wells Beach, Maine, 1781. Three views, showing the vessel under way, dismasted, and overset with the crew in the boat. Watercolor attributed to Ashley Bowen of Marblehead. *Courtesy Peabody Museum of Salem.*

Perils of the Sea

A man had no respect for the sea who, glancing back at the familiar shore as his vessel cleared the land, did not wonder for at least an instant whether this voyage would bring him safely back to his home port. A mariner's life was the most dangerous calling a man could choose during the age of sail. Many of Salem's more than four hundred widows in 1783 would have testified to that. Sunken ledges and sandy shoals reached out from the scenic New England coast to impale hundreds of hapless vessels driven before a winter gale or lost in a thick summer fog. T. S. Eliot was much later to write of the Dry Salvages, a ledge off the tip of Cape Ann:

> And the ragged rock in the restless waters,
>   Waves wash over it, fogs conceal it;
> On a halcyon day it is merely a monument,
> In navigable weather it is always a seamark
> To lay a course by; but in the sombre season
>   Or the sudden fury, is what it always was.

In his never-ending battle against the hazards of the sea, however, the mariner did not stand alone. Men who had gone to sea before him, and others who had not, dedicated themselves to making the seaman's life as safe as possible.

The earliest effort to reduce the danger of seafaring along the New England coast came with the establishment of lighthouses at the entrances of several ports. High up in rickety wooden structures, clusters of whale-oil lamps burned through the night, tended by keepers who often doubled as harbor pilots or worked as fishermen. Day or night, in clear weather at least, the approaching master could get his bearings from the tower and hopefully find the harbor channel.

The first light station in North America was built by the colony of Massachusetts Bay on Little Brewster Island in Boston Harbor in 1716. Vessels using the harbor contributed to its maintenance and to the salary of its keeper. Three years later a cannon was placed at the station to answer vessels in fog, the first such signal on the continent. Like most early structures, Boston Light fell victim to fire on several occasions, and during the Revolution it was destroyed twice, once by each side. The stone tower built in 1784 has stood ever since to mark the entrance to Boston Harbor. Other ports quickly followed Boston's example and established their own harbor lights. Nantucket built the first of seven successive structures on Brant Point in 1746, and Newport's Beavertail Light, the Gurnet off Plymouth, and New London's light were among other stations founded before the Revolution. All lighthouses built by local or state authority were turned over to the new federal government in 1789, eventually to become the responsibility of the U.S. Lighthouse Service, until absorbed by the Coast Guard in 1939.

In addition to the harbor lights, colonists marked channels into numerous harbors with buoys and day beacons. A public lottery pro-

To the Merchants of Boston this View of the LIGHTHOUSE
is most humbly presented. By their Humble Serv.ᵗ Wᵐ Burgis

The first known view of Boston Light, 1723, with a portrait believed to be of the "Province Sloop." *Courtesy Naval Historical Foundation.*

A South West View of the LIGHTHOUSE, situate at the Entrance of BOSTON Harbour

Boston Light, 1789, from an engraving in *The Massachusetts Magazine, 1789. Courtesy M. V. Brewington.*

vided markers at the entrance to the Connecticut River; Massachusetts placed buoys at the mouth of the Merrimack. Private groups often put buoys out in their own home ports, such as those placed by the Salem Marine Society. In 1797 the federal government assumed responsibility for establishing and maintaining buoys along the coast.

Shortly after the Revolution, mariners recognized the need for lighthouses that would guide vessels around offshore dangers as well. In 1784 Nantucketers succeeded in persuading the General Court to erect a lighthouse at the end of Great Point, a sandy spit jutting seven miles out into the shoals at the eastern entrance to Nantucket Sound. For years the keeper trekked out to the lonely post each night to light the lamps. Another station was established on Thatcher Island, a sea-swept ledge off Cape Ann, where in 1789 Massachusetts erected twin lights to distinguish the station from other beacons. At the entrance to the Kennebec River the federal government built a lighthouse in 1795 on Seguin, an island deriving its name from the Indian word for vomit, graphically describing the churning waters there. The most isolated station in the years before 1815 was undoubtedly on Boon Island, seven miles off the southern coast of Maine. In the first five years after its construction in 1811, three keepers in succession resigned because of loneliness. Hundreds of mariners owed their lives to the men who built the towers and kept the lights burning along the New England coast. .

The aid of lighthouses notwithstanding, vessels by the score pounded onto the rocks and shoals of New England each year. If wrecked in summer close to land, crew members had a chance of getting off with their lives, but if shipwrecked in the dead of winter, particularly on one of the numerous offshore ledges, they were doomed to perish in the ice-cold waters or to freeze to death high in the rigging. Not until after the Revolution did any organization in New England make rescue at sea its particular concern. Then in 1791 the Humane Society of Massachusetts, founded some years before to further "the preservation of human life," awarded a premium of £3 to a Frenchman who had saved four shipwrecked sailors near Nantucket. Throughout the nineteenth century the society made numerous awards for the rescue of survivors from the smallest harbor craft to the largest oceangoing vessels. Meanwhile the society, joined by a similar group in Newburyport, constructed huts along the outer reaches of the coast — at Plum Island, on the back side of Cape Cod, and on Nantucket — in addition to others

Salem-bound from Batavia, Java, the ship *Perseverance,* cast ashore near Tarpaulin Cove, Massachusetts, 1805. *Courtesy Peabody Museum of Salem.*

closer to Boston and Plymouth harbors. Inside these buildings the society endeavored to keep a supply of firewood and other articles for the use of shipwrecked mariners, although vandals not infrequently got there first. In 1807 the society built America's first lifeboat, a thirty-four-footer lined with cork, modeled after a whaleboat, and constructed at Nantucket. It was stationed at Cohasset and manned by a volunteer crew. From these beginnings would come the U.S. Life-Saving Service, an independent organization under the Treasury Department until it was merged in 1915 with the old Revenue Cutter Service to form the present Coast Guard.

Two other kinds of voluntary association performed important functions at the turn of the nineteenth century. One was the marine society, whose membership generally consisted of master mariners. Every considerable New England port from Providence to Portland had one such

Model of a Massachusetts Humane Society lifeboat in its horse-drawn or man-drawn cart, early nineteenth century. *Courtesy Peabody Museum of Salem.*

organization, while Salem could boast of two. The primary purpose of these groups was to provide for the support of widows and other dependents of its own members, but other activities soon emerged. The Salem East India Marine Society, restricted to masters and supercargoes who had sailed the Pacific or Indian Oceans, expected its members to keep journals of their voyages, reporting the discovery of islands and shoals and making charts of distant seas. From its founding in 1797 the society maintained a museum to preserve not only the artifacts brought back by its members but their logbooks as well. The societies recommended sites for lighthouses and lobbied in behalf of legislation to aid the advancement of navigation and commerce.

By the end of the eighteenth century, merchants and other men of means had banded together in many of the major seaports to establish insurance companies. These companies formalized the sharing of marine risks which merchants had practiced informally among themselves for many years. In time of peace the rates for routine voyages to Europe or the West Indies ran around 2 percent. During the War of 1812 they reached the nearly prohibitive level of 50 percent.

Of more direct help in preventing marine disasters was the appearance of printed sailing directions to guide shipmasters into strange harbors. The Bostonian chartmaker Cyprian Southack first published his popular *New England Coasting Pilot* around 1720, and throughout the eighteenth century local printers issued sailing directions for their own ports in broadside form. Many Yankee mariners relied on *The English Pilot,* whose fourth book covered North America, but despite occasional reprintings its information was often out of date. Worse still were the error-ridden tables available for celestial navigation. In 1796 the Newburyport printer Edmund March Blunt brought out the first edition of Captain Lawrence Furlong's famous *American Coast Pilot,* which contained harbor charts and sailing directions for the Atlantic and Gulf coasts. The master of a vessel standing in for New London, for instance, could learn that

> in beating in there is no danger, keeping the lighthouse bearing N. b E. ½ E. and N. b W. ½ W. When you come within 1 mile of the lighthouse keep about mid-channel of the harbour, leaving the lighthouse on the west side of you; you may stand within 5 rods of either shore, until you get up with a small Island of rocks upon the west side of the harbour. Give it a birth of twenty rods, there being a small ledge called *Melton's Ledge* which bears about N. E. from the Island of Rocks; you may anchor abreast of the town.

Much of his information Furlong pirated from various English books, but as subsequent editions appeared, he relied increasingly on recent surveys by reliable shipmasters. In addition to charts and directions, *The American Coast Pilot* included tide tables, courses from one major harbor to another, and many pages of miscellaneous information useful to the shipmaster.

To improve the quality of offshore navigation, Blunt published an edition of a standard work on the subject in 1799 as revised by Nathaniel Bowditch. Born in Salem of humble circumstances, Bowditch left school at an early age to work in a ship chandlery until going to sea. He combined his practical experience as a supercargo and shipmaster with his self-taught knowledge of mathematics to become an important navigator and astronomer. In 1802 the first edition of his *New American Practical Navigator* was simultaneously published in England and America. Thereafter, until the federal government took over the business of publishing charts and navigational tables in 1866, every New England shipmaster could rely on successive editions of Furlong's *Coast Pilot* and Bowditch's *Practical Navigator* to guide him through the dangerous waters of the Atlantic coast and to aid him in the difficult science of finding his way at sea. By 1800, in almost every seaport, retired shipmasters or landbound mathematicians opened schools where ambitious young men could learn the mysteries of navigation and better their chances for a master's berth.

As for the vessels in which New England mariners ventured forth

The brig *Eunice* of Salem, 145 tons, built at Barnstable, Massachusetts, 1803. After repairs on her hull, she could not be refloated through the soft sand, and the skipper built a huge cask around her and rolled her into the water. Watercolor by Anton Roux, 1806. *Courtesy Peabody Museum of Salem.*

at the turn of the century, only gradual changes were taking place. Most significant was an increase in size. Before the Revolution only a rare vessel measured 300 tons or more. After the war, brigs and full-rigged ships of that tonnage were far more common, especially in the Asian trade. They rarely exceeded 600 tons, however, and generally Americans preferred the convenience of moderate size, especially when entering port with a full hold. Yankee shipbuilders learned from the design of the Baltimore clipper how to sharpen the lines of their hulls to obtain greater speed and improved sailing qualities. Unlike privateers and pilot boats, however, cargo capacity and economy of handling remained more important than speed in the design of merchant vessels. In the fleet trading with the southern states and the West Indies a similar increase in burden followed the Revolution, with the schooner gradually replacing the sloop, which was thereafter largely confined to river and sound traffic and the shorter coastal runs.

Perhaps the most noticeable changes in design could be seen in the postwar fishing fleet, which replaced those vessels lost during the Revolution. The Chebacco boat, a two-masted vessel with the foremast

stepped well forward in the eyes, was first developed in the town of
Essex, north of Cape Ann. Some Chebacco boats were pink-sterned,
others were square-sterned, and all were bald-headed. These little vessels averaged about forty feet in length with a measurement of under
thirty tons and generally had a small cuddy forward where the crew
could take refuge in foul weather around a fireplace with a generous
supply of rum to fight off the chill. But these boats proved too small
for offshore fishing and were soon supplanted by the larger pinky
schooner that became so popular after the War of 1812.

Only one significant change had occurred in the procedure of designing vessels since the colonial era. In the mid-1790s two New England shipbuilders, Enos Briggs of Salem and Orlando Merrill of
Newburyport, each developed for his own use the so-called lift model
— a wooden half-model of a vessel's hull, composed of several layers,
or lifts, loosely pinned together, which could be separated after the
block of wood had been carved into its desired shape. In this way the
proportions could be taken off more easily and the lines laid down in
the builder's loft. Although in some ways a step backward, the making
of a model enabled some clever mechanics who could not draw plans
to achieve good results.

In other respects shipbuilding had changed little. A large number
of small, competitive yards remained characteristic of the industry, each
with a master carpenter and twenty-odd workers turning out two or
three vessels a year. Supplies of oak for frames and planking became
more scarce along the seaboard during the building boom of the period
1793–1812, but the yards located north of Cape Cod could still build
vessels at about thirty-five dollars per ton. While the War of 1812, like
the Revolution before it, put a temporary stop to construction, the industry recovered rather more quickly after 1815.

In design, construction, and rigging the shipbuilder did his best to
provide a seaworthy vessel for the owner and master. Men like Blunt
and Bowditch published the best surveys and astronomical tables available to improve the arts of pilotage and navigation. The government
constructed lighthouses and other aids to mark the most dangerous hazards along the coast, and the marine societies and insurance companies
did what they could to protect owner and master alike in the event of
losses. But seafaring remained a dangerous profession despite the best
efforts of the men who stood behind the mariners.

(upper left) Cross-staff, also called a Jacob's staff or a fore-staff, for taking altitudes of the sun or of the North Star to determine latitude, the most commonly used nautical instrument of the seventeenth and early eighteenth centuries. All crosses illustrated are reconstructions. *Courtesy Peabody Museum of Salem.* (upper right) Davis quadrant or back-staff, American, dated 1751, commonly used for sighting latitudes throughout the seventeenth and eighteenth centuries. *Courtesy Kendall Whaling Museum.* (lower left) Hadley's quadrant, probably English, dated 1767, commonly used for observations in the nineteenth century, though less commonly during the last two-thirds of the eighteenth century. Note the back sight and the diagonal scale for minute readings. *Courtesy Kendall Whaling Museum.* (lower right) Typical spyglasses used by mariners during the eighteenth and nineteenth centuries. The one with the octagonal barrel dates about 1770. One has a lithograph in the cover showing the Marryat flag signals. *Courtesy Kendall Whaling Museum.*

A Generation of Enterprise

In the thirty years between the end of the American Revolution and the beginning of the War of 1812, maritime New England underwent major changes. Its colonial commerce destroyed by the ravages of war and by political independence, the region's next generation of merchants developed new patterns in place of the old. They solved, at least temporarily, the problem of finding returns with which to pay for European manufactures, and at the same time they opened up other lines of trade that would serve American commerce well in the years to come. In the process the young nation's Stars and Stripes by 1815 had flown from Yankee vessels in virtually every port in the world, from Canton to Copenhagen, from Africa to Archangel.

One result of this expanded trade was the growth of the seaport from a provincial town to a cosmopolitan city. Prosperity brought new and more complex enterprises. Wealth also raised the cultural standards to a new level, for the affluent merchants of the Federalist period had no thought of wasting their money on cheap luxuries. But most significantly, mercantile capital gave rise to New England's first factories.

In short, the generation of merchants who prospered during this Heroic Age established the United States as a leading nation of commerce in its own right, while at the same time they helped to provide the basis for future industry. Few groups of men before or since have brought such major changes so swiftly to their native land by peaceful means.

III

The Golden Age, 1815–1865

VAN WYCK BROOKS, in *The Flowering of New England, 1815–1865,* describes the amazingly rich output of literature during the half-century embracing Emerson, Hawthorne, Thoreau, Longfellow, Bancroft, Prescott, Holmes, and Lowell. During those same years Yankee mariners, merchants, and shipbuilders combined to earn New England a similar superlative in the maritime field. After three decades of moderate progress, American seagoing activity reached a climax toward the end of the Golden Age, between the mid-1840s and mid-1850s. It was a period impressive not only statistically but also emotionally. Its exhilarating emphasis on speed was reflected in the names of the magnificent clippers — *Flying Cloud, Winged Arrow, Wild Rover, Whirlwind,* and many others.

Several outside happenings, from Ireland to California and China, combined to stimulate the booming conditions of that memorable decade. In 1844 Caleb Cushing's treaty, following close upon British success in the Opium War, opened Shanghai and other "treaty ports" to American commerce. In 1845–46 rains combined with a fungus blight to wipe out the potato crop upon which the Irish had depended for sustenance. The result was bitter starvation in Ireland; large numbers of those who did survive were brought across the Atlantic to New York, Boston, and other American cities. The Irish influx was followed shortly by substantial numbers from Germany, partly fleeing from the revolutions there. Those same rains led Britain in 1846 to repeal the protective Corn Laws, which had hitherto sharply curtailed the importa-

97

tion of American grain. Three years later, continuing their efforts to reduce governmental regulations, the British repealed their time-honored Navigation Acts.

Meanwhile, in 1845 and 1847 Congress followed the recent British precedent of subsidizing steamship lines and thus made it possible to establish services both across the Atlantic and to the West Coast by way of Panama. The most spectacular impulse came with the discovery of gold in California in 1848, followed shortly by discovery of gold in Australia. The rush of forty-niners to San Francisco not only meant unexpected business for the subsidized steamers on the Panama route but also brought merchant sail to its climax with the California clippers, built by the score for the stormy Cape Horn run. The Australian gold rush gave a brief extension to their usefulness.

American shipping reflected these various influences both in quality and in quantity. The most striking result was the creation of the graceful clippers, originally for trade with China and then with California. The first of these fast clippers were built in the mid-1840s to bring tea from the newly opened port of Shanghai. The word *clipper* meant "streamlined." In the pursuit of speed, however, the ship's cargo capacity was cut down by nearly a third.

The increasing transatlantic trade called for less spectacular types of vessels. The Black Ball and other sailing packets — those "square-riggers on schedule" — could carry only a part of the rush of immigrants to America. Consequently, many large ships were built to fill that new demand. Most numerous of these were the substantial but less elaborate ships needed to carry cotton and other cargoes. Many of these vessels became the specialities of Maine yards. There were also the new crack sidewheelers. These subsidy steamships, like the earlier sailing packets, were usually built in New York and operated from there, but their captains were often New Englanders.

New England's Ports

Strangely enough, the maritime achievements of the port of New York are an important part of this account of New England and the sea. The main reason is that New Englanders virtually took over New York's maritime operations during this Golden Age. While our chief concern here is maritime New England, New York port must also receive high credit for its role in the flowering of the merchant marine. A fair share of maritime glory should be attributed to both.

Their relative roles are suggested in the title of the annual official report on maritime statistics: *Commerce and Navigation of the United States*. "Commerce" refers to the import and export cargoes: that was New York's sphere of leadership. "Navigation" refers to the ships and the men that carried those cargoes. In that saltier aspect New England's lead was equally impressive. By 1860, New York accounted for 68 percent of the nation's imports and 36 percent of its exports; New England's share was only 11 and 5 percent respectively. But in tonnage "owned" (that is, registered, enrolled, and licensed) New England had 46 percent to New York's 26. In shipbuilding the New England lead was very much larger, at 82 percent to 11 percent; in whaling and fishing the Yankee share was almost a monopoly. In shipmasters, Maine and Massachusetts had 1,902 to New York's 459, while in "mariners" the down-east lead was roughly two to one at 25,389 to 12,141. And many of those seagoing New Yorkers were transplanted New Englanders.

Of course, New York was a single seaport, whereas New England had dozens of ports, ranging downward in size from Boston. New England had thirty-odd customs districts, some of them including several ports. But, as against that, geography protected New York port from any close rivalry. From Sandy Hook, its one entry from the open sea (not counting the back door through Long Island Sound), there were interminable stretches of beach without a single harbor of refuge for anything larger than fishing schooners. Boston, on the other hand, had numerous potential rivals close at hand, from Portland to Providence.

The spectacular success of New York after 1815 was the triumph of natural advantages rather than of native sons. New Englanders captured New York port around 1820 and dominated its business until after the Civil War. Applying a little genealogy to the occupants of New York's countinghouses, shipyards, and quarterdecks, one finds Yankees in most of the important positions. Their attraction to New York was part of their remarkable expansion into many branches of national activity beyond New England's frontier. Motives similar to those that had lured farmers from the stony acres of western New England to the richer farm lands of the Middle West were attracting other Yankees to New York's seaport. Connecticut was the most heavily represented state among the invaders from southern New England. Since Long Island cuts off New Haven and the other western Connecticut ports from the open sea, it is not surprising that their residents took advantage of the rich opportunities so close at hand. Talent poured into New York from all parts of the state and from Rhode Island and southern Massachusetts. Fewer came from beyond Cape Cod, where ample opportunities could be found at home. It seems probable that southern New England's unimpressive level of maritime activity in this period resulted from this "brain drain" of its best talent to New York.

Any list of the leading New York shipping houses between 1815 and 1860 would certainly include six New England firms. Prominent in the China trade were N. L. & G. Griswold (popularly translated "No Loss and Great Gain") from Old Lyme and the Lows from Salem. The Howlands from Norwich were leaders in the Latin American and other trades. A whaling captain, Preserved Fish from New Bedford, handled the whale oil sales at New York, joining with the Grinnells in a firm that ultimately became one of the greatest shipowners of the day. Ranking with them was the great commission house headed by Jonathan Goodhue from Salem and Pelatiah Perit from Norwich, as well as Anson G. Phelps' extensive metal-importing and cotton-exporting concern. Phelps was in successive partnerships with Elisha Peck and William E. Dodge, his son-in-law; all were Connecticut natives. These few names by no means exhaust the list of important transplanted Yankees, whose activities were still often related to their New England maritime background.

The easygoing old Knickerbocker element often resented this influx of New Englanders. At the annual dinner of their St. Nicholas Society they turned their golden rooster's head to the eastward "so that it could crow back at the Yankees." One club member satirized a down-easter as "long legs, hatchet face, skin and bones, slight, pokey, and keen as a briar."

At a somewhat lower level of the Yankee operations in New York were the commission merchants and ship brokers. The commission merchants came down to collect their 5 percent on sales referred to New York from the smaller ports to the eastward. Both ends of these transactions could be retained in New England hands. If a Boston cargo of tea from China, for instance, or a Salem shipment of pepper from Sumatra was to be sold at New York, the commissions were apt to go to a son of the owner, a family friend, or perhaps a junior employee who had moved to New York for that purpose. It was much the same with shipments of domestic cotton goods from Lowell or Fall River, to say nothing of Maine lumber and New Bedford whale oil. Equally lucrative were the possibilities for the ship brokers. It was their business to offer ships, brigs, and schooners from a New England home port for "sale, freight, or charter" and to find as constant employment as possible for the vessels. The ship broker also often acted as an agent or "ship's husband" at a generous commission.

Important as such denizens of the countinghouse were, it was a different type of man — the sea captain — who gave maritime New England its distinctive flavor. Even the British, often self-satisfied in things maritime, paid tribute to the quality of those sea captains. The English shipowner-historian William S. Lindsay wrote that during the first half of the nineteenth century "the masters of American vessels were, as a rule, greatly superior to those who held similar positions in British ships, arising in some measure from the limited education of the latter." Such men were the one adequate common denominator linking the dozens of heterogeneous ports, large and small, between Eastport (close to Canada) and Fairfield (on the edge of New York). Those numerous harbors all belong to our story, yet there is no room to do full justice to each of them. It seems best, though, to present at least a few basic statistics of the thirty-odd customs districts in order to show at a glance their relative performance (see Table 2).

The outlying customs districts of New England varied widely in scope. Many of them, of course, included several active ports. Others, such as Saco, York, and Ipswich virtually died on the vine; yet they lingered on because their sinecure collectorships and surveyorships for Deserving Whigs and Deserving Democrats were so vital a part of the spoils system. In contrast, the New York customhouse in the 1820s was taking in enough in duties to meet the whole running expenses of the federal government! A particularly successful district, in Maine's middle coast, was Waldoboro, with its busy ports of Thomaston, Rockland, Rockport, and Camden in addition to Waldoboro itself. No districts were closed down during this fifty-year period, but two new ones were added: Bangor, Maine, with its lively lumber trade, and Stonington, Connecticut, after it had added whaling to its sealing activity.

Since "navigation" rather than "commerce" was foremost in New England's maritime activity, the figures for vessels "owned" are more

TABLE 2
Statistics of New England Customs Districts

	TOTAL TONNAGE OWNED (Thousand Tons)			SHIPBUILDING (Thousand tons)		EXPORTS-IMPORTS (Thousand dollars)
	1815	*1840*	*1860*	*1840*	*1860*	*1860*
MAINE						
Passamaquoddy	7.4	12.1	25.3	.9	2.9	1,377
Machias	2.4	11.8	34.9	1.9	4.3	105
Frenchman's Bay	5.8	20.4	35.8	1.3	.6	16
Penobscot	20.0	37.1	49.4	1.5	1.8	26
Belfast	—	38.2	80.8	4.2	6.0	70
Bangor	—	—	36.3	—	2.6	238
Waldoborough	19.9	52.9	187.2	12.1	10.9	12
Wiscasset	18.4	13.5	28.2	1.5	.9	61
Bath	22.4	54.0	165.3	7.2	16.8	40
Portland	33.0	56.1	131.8	6.1	5.3	3,442
Saco	5.6	3.4	5.9	.8	—	—
Kennebunk	11.7	7.1	20.4	1.4	5.4	—
York	1.4	1.2	1.5	—	.2	—
NEW HAMPSHIRE						
Portsmouth	29.7	27.4	32.5	2.7	3.8	21
MASSACHUSETTS						
Newburyport	24.9	23.9	31.2	2.8	4.4	170
Ipswich	1.8	3.7	.9	.2	.2	—
Gloucester	9.9	17.1	40.5	.1	4.8	278
Salem-Beverly	35.5	37.0	33.8	.3	.2	2,906
Marblehead	14.6	12.5	7.9	.4	—	32
Boston	137 0	220.2	464.2	7.6	21.1	54,535
Plymouth	21.2	27.5	8.2	2.8	.6	—
Dighton—Fall River	9.7	8.8	16.1	.3	.4	33
New Bedford	24.8	89.1	149.7	1.2	.6	222
Barnstable	10.9	56.6	63.6	1.8	.8	9
Edgartown	.9	8.1	8.8	—	.2	6
Nantucket	14.7	31.9	10.4	.4	—	3
RHODE ISLAND						
Providence	18.5	16.6	19.6	.6	.9	457
Bristol	6.9	15.9	9.8	.7	.3	75
Newport	12.7	10.9	12.3	.4	.2	184
CONNECTICUT						
Middletown	25.9	14.2	16.2	.9	.8	67
New London	13.7	44.8	40.2	1.6	1.0	746
Stonington	—	—	19.6	—	2.5	98
New Haven	13.6	11.5	26.8	.4	1.5	1,239
Fairfield	6.8	16.4	16.3	1.1	1.8	13
TOTAL NEW ENGLAND	581.7	1001.9	1831.4	65.2	104.4	66,481
NEW YORK PORT	278.9	414.8	1464.0	13.3	23.5	371,836
TOTAL U.S.	1368.1	2180.8	5353.9	118.3	212.9	759,288

significant than exports and imports as an indication of its relative maritime importance. The word *owned,* however, should not be taken too literally. *Documented* was technically the more correct word for those vessels, which were registered for foreign trade, enrolled for domestic trade, or licensed, if less than twenty tons, at their hailing port. The cargoes carried by a very large number of Maine vessels appeared in the

Portland, Maine, 1865. *Courtesy Maine Historical Society.*

export-import statistics of many distant ports. An extreme case was the Waldoboro district. In 1860 it ranked fifth in tonnage owned among all the nation's ninety customs districts, directly after the East Coast's "big four" — New York, Boston, Philadelphia, and Baltimore — yet Waldoboro had only $11,000 in imports and no exports at all.

It was characteristic that Boston ranked second only to New York in imports but trailed in exports after the cotton ports of New Orleans, Mobile, Charleston, and Savannah. To attract imports, definite initiative was required, whereas exports found their way to the sea with a call of "come and get it" and with no expense of seagoing energy. (An extreme case was Mobile, which had almost no imports at all.) Portland came next after Boston in total trade; it had an almost even balance between lumber exports and molasses imports, as well as a respectable amount of ownership and shipbuilding.

The three specialties in which New England had a large share of the national total were shipbuilding at Boston and Bath; whaling at New Bedford, after it overtook Nantucket; and fishing at Gloucester,

Boston Harbor, 1857. The clipper in the center is the *Nightingale*. The Hill-Motram engraving. *Courtesy Kendall Whaling Museum.*

after it overtook Marblehead. The sixth really distinctive port was Salem, no longer all that it had been at the turn of the century but still bringing in a heavy total of exotic imports. On the whole, while Maine was making the most spectacular gains in this half-century, southern New England, except for its whaling, remained relatively static, as did the substantial ports of Newburyport and Portsmouth.

Two different factors explain the shifts in port fortunes between the War of 1812 and the Civil War. First, the coming of peace to Europe took away the special advantages the Americans had had as neutrals in the Federalist period. The British and others could now take their exotic cargoes from distant regions and distribute them around Europe. Second, a policy of port consolidation was in progress, with more and more traffic concentrating at Boston and yet more at New York. Even when merchant shipowners did not move to New York, they tended to send their inbound cargoes there because of the broader sales opportunities. In the tea trade, especially, a considerable part of the Boston-controlled cargoes from China were discharged in New York's East River.

Those Yankee expatriates who moved to New York were only one cause of the seaport concentration of this period. The dwindling away of numerous small ports and the stagnation of others were symptoms of a continuing trend, bringing to mind Christ's warning: "Unto everyone that hath shall be given . . . but from him that hath not shall be taken away even that which he hath." While Portland was absorbing the activity of some of the smaller Maine ports, Boston was far more voracious, and even Boston was losing some of its independence in an increasingly close intermeshing with New York. The latter's steadily swelling import statistics concealed the fact that many down-east ships returning from distant ports headed for New York, where their cargoes found a better market. "It is well known," wrote a knowledgeable New Yorker in 1844, "that one-third of the commerce of New York, from 1839 to 1842, was carried either upon Massachusetts account, or in Massachusetts vessels." Samuel Eliot Morison went on to observe that 83 percent of Boston's imports were on local account, that is, purchased abroad by Boston firms. "Manhattan's geographical position was such that all the world poured gold into her lap," he concluded. "Boston's growth resulted from local enterprise."

Distant Seas and Whaling

The "Old China Trade" has been publicized far beyond its quantitive importance. Only a small group of New England aristocrats held control over it and made generous fortunes from this business. As early as 1835, twenty-four ships and two brigs were to arrive at New York from Canton, but only seven went to Boston. By 1860 the score was fifty-three ships for New York and only six for Boston. Despite that imbalance, very substantial profits went into New England pockets, and Boston prospered even if the ships landed their tea in New York. Thomas Handasyd Perkins, Captain William Sturgis, and their family connections enjoyed the early commanding position in the China trade. This continued with John P. Cushing, their Canton representative, until he retired to Boston in 1830, a millionaire. Those interests were then united into the firm of Russell & Co. of Canton, which was founded in 1818 by Samuel Russell of Middletown, Connecticut. At Canton the firm did more business than any other American house. It developed a valuable close relationship with Houqua, the wealthy, generous hong merchant. The Lows, Griswolds, and Howlands, already noted among the Yankee expatriates in New York, were also prominent in the Can-

The Western Factories at Canton, China, *c.* 1840. *Courtesy Mystic Seaport.*

ton trade. A succession of well-connected young men were to become partners with a chance to get rich quickly through the Russell commissions on the trade of the parent houses. One of the Low brothers served in this category, while another commanded some of the Low clippers. Warren Delano from New Bedford was also of this ambitious group. His brother was a partner in the Grinnell firm, and his daughter became the mother of Franklin Delano Roosevelt.

Two particularly interesting nephews of old Thomas Handasyd Perkins served in turn. John Murray Forbes returned home with a fortune that was ample enough to enable him to get in on the ground floor of the Michigan Central Railroad. His brother, Captain Robert Bennett Forbes, was one of the most versatile and able of all the maritime Bostonians. In his lively memoirs, he tells how he missed out on the richest opportunities of a Russell partnership. The firm had for some years been bringing in opium in fast, specially built smuggling schooners. When the Chinese confiscated British opium in 1839, precipitating the Opium War, the head of Russell & Co. announced that the firm would no longer handle opium. Forbes, who had just become a partner, saw his prospective profits diminished. He had earlier argued that opium was really no worse than rum. His name will crop up again in other connections. With the conclusion of that war and the opening of the treaty ports, the center of the tea business moved up to Shanghai. This China trade was to lead to the first of the new large clippers.

The port of Providence was also prominent for a while after 1815. The firm of Brown and Ives in several voyages carried cargoes from Canton or Batavia to Amsterdam. James B. Hedges, in his valuable *The Browns of Providence Plantation,* gives example after example of just how these matters worked financially. In 1816, for instance, the firm's favorite ship, named after the wives of the two partners, *Ann & Hope,* brought to Amsterdam a cargo of Canton goods, chiefly tea, which had cost $207,000; it was sold for some $430,000. After picking up 200,000 Spanish milled dollars, the ship immediately sailed again for Canton and returned with another cargo, which brought a profit of $69,000. One of their other ships was engaged in carrying coffee from Java to Amsterdam. Beginning in 1821, however, the Browns' maritime affairs entered a gradual decline. Finally, in 1838 Brown and Ives sold their last ship, bringing to an end a family maritime activity that had begun in 1721. They shifted their energies to the manufacture of cotton, in which they had already made a start. By 1840 the firm was on the way to becoming one of New England's most important cotton manufacturers. There would be other shifting from sails to spindles, but the change-over by Brown and Ives was the most thoroughgoing.

By 1860, Rhode Island had fallen far from its earlier busy seafaring. Aside from small vessels from the Maritimes, the only arrivals from abroad at Providence were twelve from Britain, eight from the West Indies, and two from Africa. Newport, once one of five leading colonial ports, had a similar dismal record: fifteen from the West Indies, three from South America, two from England, and one from Africa. Bristol had still fewer.

Although Salem never recovered the full splendor of the Derby-Crowninshield period, it kept up a respectable amount of distant prowling after 1815 and even hit upon some new sources of unusual profit. For the next thirty years, Joseph Peabody was Salem's leading merchant-shipowner. For a while, Canton was one of his fields of interest, and he continued in that Salem specialty, Sumatra pepper. In 1830,

The ships *Levant,* built at Medford, 1835, and *Milo,* built at Newburyport, 1811, with an opium clipper, anchored near Hong Kong. Oil painting by unidentified Chinese artist. *Courtesy Peabody Museum of Salem.*

Getting off sandalwood at Dula, Timor, under the eye of the governor, his adjutant, and the shipmaster. Watercolor by Mrs. William Cleveland, the Captain's wife, 1830. *Courtesy Peabody Museum of Salem.*

at Quallah Battoo on Sumatra, the Malays swarmed over his ship *Friendship,* killed some of the officers and crew, and seized the ship. In reprisal, the American frigate *Potomac* was sent to the scene to bombard and burn the town. In the years from 1815 to 1837, Peabody's ship *George* made twenty-one voyages between Salem and Calcutta. Forty-five sea captains started their careers aboard her. A smaller Peabody vessel, the *Leander,* made twenty-six voyages to Europe, the eastern Mediterranean, Africa, and Asia.

The island of Zanzibar, twenty miles off the East African coast, was to be a minor field opened by Salem in the 1830s. The Arab ruler of Muscat, with claims of sorts in East Africa, had shifted his base to Zanzibar. He planned to develop it as an entrepôt and so had thousands of clove trees planted there. Salem vessels soon realized its possibilities, and the result was a commercial treaty. This activity quickly fell into the hands of John Bertram, Salem's last merchant prince. More or less by chance, he secured a large shipment of gum copal through Zanzibar, and Salem learned how to handle the gooey mess. The result was a lasting varnish industry. The cargoes to Zanzibar from Salem included — in addition to the usual rum, tobacco, and gunpowder — unbleached white cotton cloth. This last, with "Massachusetts Sheeting" printed on it in blue, was for years a favorite with the well-dressed natives, who insisted upon this "merikani" in the bazaars. To reap extra profits, Salem started its successful Naumkeag Steam Cotton Company.

On the other side of Africa, along the unhealthy Guinea coast, Salem trade was less formal and centralized. Between 1832 and 1864, nevertheless, there were 558 arrivals from Africa at Salem. Ivory, gold dust, palm oil, and peanuts were brought over in return for tobacco, powder, and 860,000 gallons of New England rum. In 1860, eight ships arrived at Salem from East Africa, along with fourteen barks, eleven brigs, and a schooner from West Africa. In the matter of the slave trade, Salem's hands were apparently clean. One Maine captain, however, was hanged for his part in this outlawed business.

Joseph Peabody died in 1844, and with his death the Calcutta, Sumatra, and China voyages ended. "Although for fifty years thereafter, a dwindling number of Salem firms traded with the Far East," wrote Morison, "Salem ceased to be an important seaport in 1845. That was the very year when President Polk appointed Nathaniel Hawthorne 'surveyor of the port.'" With commerce declining, the post was a sinecure for Hawthorne, giving him time to write *The Scarlet Letter*. He would have less leisure later when President Pierce, who had been a class ahead of him at Bowdoin, sent him to Liverpool as consul.

In 1833, Frederic Tudor took a bold, original step to rejuvenate Boston's East India commerce. A quarter-century earlier, it had been his inspiration to send ice from Wenham Lake, just north of Boston, to warmer climates. He had shown stubborn persistence in creating markets for the ice and developing means of transporting it packed in sawdust. His master stroke came when he sent 180 tons of ice to Calcutta in the ship *Tuscany* and two-thirds of it arrived unmelted! The British in India naturally appreciated this chance for iced drinks and other chilled food, and the trade flourished. The old carrying trade from India to Europe had long since fallen off, of course, with the coming of peace in 1815. American domestic cotton goods had cut off the earlier trade in cheap Indian textiles, just as was happening to the cheap cotton nankeens from China. The ice sales now enabled Americans to continue buying what they wanted from India — jute for gunny sacks, saltpeter, indigo, and linseed. Unlike the China trade that New York was attracting, Boston saw to it that a firm hand was kept on the Calcutta business, which Tudor's initiative had so successfully achieved. In 1857, according to Morison, 96 out of the 112 vessels that loaded at Calcutta for the United States landed their cargoes at Boston, earning an average freight of $20,000.

That was not all of the new business evolving from Tudor's ingenuity. The Boston ice trade expanded simultaneously to major ports throughout South America and Asia, to say nothing of Havana and our own cotton ports. New England, always short of commodities to export, now had a valuable cash crop to offer the world and to give extra employment to its shipping. Virtually every New England village with access to tidewater began to cut ice from its ponds and ship it out. Thoreau, watching the process on his Walden Pond, wrote: "Thus it appears that the sweltering inhabitants of Charleston and New Orleans, of Madras and Bombay and Calcutta, drink at my well." Later the ice cutting spread up to Maine, and toward the end of the century swarms of big schooners would carry off frozen cargoes from the Kennebec.

Bold initiative in distant seas gave little Stonington on the Connecticut-Rhode Island border a unique record in lonesome waters. When the supply of sea otters on the Pacific northwest coast began to diminish,

Dix Cove, Gold Coast, West Africa, with the brig *Herald* of Salem entering in the 1830s. Unsigned oil painting. *Courtesy Peabody Museum of Salem.*

The hermaphrodite brig *Zaine* of Salem, built in Dorchester County, Maryland, 1840, a typical West African trader for small crew, with little draft for entering the shoal rivers and harbors. *Courtesy Peabody Museum of Salem.*

Stonington seafarers turned south to the Cape Horn region in pursuit of sealskins. The catalyst in this trade was Edmund Fanning. In 1797 he made a remarkably successful voyage after sealskins; rounding Cape Horn, his men slaughtered thousands of seals on the barren island of Juan Fernandez. After discovering and naming various other islands, Fanning sailed for Canton, where he exchanged his sealskins for a cargo that realized $120,000 on his arrival at New York. This left him with a clear profit of $53,000 for the voyage. For more than thirty years he devoted himself to propaganda to develop this profitable source. He persuaded New York merchants to put up capital and government officials to send out exploring expeditions. Easiest of all, he found plenty of Stonington seamen eager to carry on the actual work, clubbing the helpless seals to death by the thousands. It was pitiless, brutal, and bloody — but highly profitable. Now as then, in some spots, despite the growing protests, the seals die horribly.

There also happened to be some significant geographic consequences. In 1819, on one of the eighty-odd expeditions which Fanning claimed to have promoted, several small Stonington vessels sailed for the South Shetland Islands, just east of Cape Horn. When distant ice was sighted to the southward of the islands, young Captain Nathaniel B. Palmer was sent down to investigate in the sloop *Hero*. He found that it was apparently continuous ice; thereafter, the name of Palmer Land was long attached to this peninsula of Antarctica. Palmer later commanded clipper ships and packets. Altogether this young captain would become one of New England's foremost mariners. Sealing expeditions on those desolate islands were to continue for decades.

Stonington and Salem were linked in a trade involving dangerous contact with Fiji Island cannibals. In 1829, Captain Benjamin Morrill of Stonington, accompanied by his young wife, set out around the Cape of Good Hope, hoping to find seals in New Zealand. Failing in that project, he decided to sail to Manila and from there to the Fiji Islands, which abounded in *bêche-de-mer* (also known as sea slugs or sea cucumbers), a favorite delicacy of Manila and China gourmets. While gathering these, part of the crew were captured by the Fiji cannibals. Thirteen were eaten; only one escaped. Nonetheless, a half-dozen Salem vessels persisted in this trade until the Civil War. It was worth some $30,000 a year.

The quest for hides for the Massachusetts shoe and leather industry

Drying sheds and boilers for curing *bêche-de-mer,* from which the Chinese make a soup. *Courtesy Kendall Whaling Museum.*

in this period led to one of the outstanding pieces of New England maritime literature. Richard Henry Dana, scion of a prominent Boston family, interrupted his Harvard undergraduate career in 1832 to take a sea voyage for his health. He went not as a passenger but as a foremast hand on the Bryant & Sturgis brig *Pilgrim,* which was bound around Cape Horn to obtain hides in California. Dana's classic *Two Years Before the Mast* records the hardships of the crew in that rigorous service, as well as the crude methods of loading hides in California, then a primitive Mexican province. He came back to Boston on another Bryant & Sturgis vessel, the *Alert,* returned to Harvard, and became a successful Boston lawyer. Later he was to do valuable work in improving the lot of seamen.

The search for hides normally was directed to nearer places in Latin America. In 1843, nearly half of the 311,000 hides imported at Boston came from Argentina and Uruguay. In exchange the Latin Americans took many sorts of offerings from the United States, particularly white domestic cotton cloth. Thus the product of the textile factories of Lowell helped to pay for raw material for the shoe factories of Lynn and Haverhill and the tanneries of Beverly. To handle that flourishing commerce, New England traders were found in most of the foreign ports. At Buenos Aires, for example, the new woolen mills of

Lawrence were beginning to secure raw wool, which would become one of Boston's leading imports. This wool was arriving in amounts about equal to the wool imported from South Africa. Prominent among the New Englanders in South America was William Wheelright from Newburyport, who had a very successful business in Chile, Peru, and Ecuador, and who also established the Pacific Steam Navigation Company under the British flag.

Most profitable and colorful of all New England's far-ranging explorings, statistically and geographically, was the extension of Yankee whaling into distant seas. There had been a substantial development of Nantucket whaling before the Revolution thoroughly disrupted it, and the three postwar decades witnessed a moderate, spasmodic comeback; but during the War of 1812 the vulnerable insularity of Nantucket again cut off whaling. The return of peace, however, led to a lively resumption of the trade by 1818. A few Nantucket whalers had been in the Pacific during the 1790s, but now they began to invade that area in force. At first, the hunting was along the west coast of South America, but soon the whalers moved offshore. The catch, moreover, began to include a fair amount of sperm whales, whose oil and head spermaceti commanded a higher price than ordinary whale oil. As the whalers moved farther out into the Pacific and toward Japan, their roamings brought more and more new islands into the ken of seafarers. Gradually the map became dotted with the names of the captains or ships which had discovered them — or which had been wrecked on them.

There were two especially tragic happenings in the first years of this Pacific expansion. A wild whale charged the *Essex* in 1822 and sank the vessel. Far from land, her crew took to the boats, ran out of food, and turned cannibals. They first ate those who had already starved to death; then, ever more desperate in their hunger, they chose a youth by lot and executed him. The survivors were eventually rescued. The story became a Nantucket classic and also had a wider effect, as it influenced Herman Melville to write *Moby-Dick*. Melville himself in 1841–43 had gone on a whaling voyage in the *Acushnet*. (In recent years, of course, *Moby-Dick* has been captured by the psychoanalysts.) Two years after the *Essex* horrors, the crew of the whaler *Globe* mutinied violently and chopped their officers to death. The mutineers went ashore, where their ringleader was killed, and five of the loyal crew recaptured the ship. They told their story to the American consul at

American vessels whaling in the South Pacific. Lithograph by L. LeBreton, *c.* 1855. *Courtesy Kendall Whaling Museum.*

Valparaiso. Eventually the last two survivors among the mutineers were taken aboard an American warship.

Such episodes did not seem to deter the sending out of more and more whalers. A voyage usually lasted three years. Generally the vessels headed first for the Azores, where they often picked up recruits for the crew, and also at the Cape Verdes. Next they rounded the Cape of Good Hope and looked in at the Bay of Whales in New Zealand. As time went on, they tended to sail closer and closer to Japan, stopped for rest and recreation in the Hawaiian Islands, and eventually pushed up into the frigid waters of the Bering Sea.

After being cooped up for months on end and at times facing danger, the whalemen were apt to be something of a problem when they came ashore. Their behavior had been bad enough at Valparaiso, but it was especially embarrassing when their visits ashore overlapped those of missionaries, who were arriving about the same time in New Zealand and Hawaii. At New Zealand, the whalers would sometimes sail away with the daughters of the Maoris, who would take revenge for such kidnappings on the next missionary brig to come along. In 1820 the brig *Thaddeus* arrived at Hawaii, 163 days out of Boston. Aboard were a band of Yale-trained missionaries and their wives, the advance guard of a group of whom it was later said, "They came to do good, and they did right well." Their descendants eventually more or less owned the islands.

American whaling was almost entirely a venture of New England — and of a fairly limited region of southeastern New England at that. Of the 736 whalers operating in 1846, when the fleet was at its peak, there were only 2 from outside New England, not counting those from Sag Harbor and some adjacent ports on Long Island, which were almost visible from the Connecticut shore. Few groups have wandered to the far ends of the earth and then returned to home ports so remarkably close together. Virtually all the major whaling ports were within a sixty-mile radius of Newport. For a while, whaling centered on Nantucket, but by the mid-1820s it began to shift to New Bedford on the mainland at Buzzards Bay. As at Salem, the shallowness of the Nantucket bar was becoming more serious as ships grew larger. By 1846 more than 400 of the whalers came from Greater New Bedford, including Fairhaven, Dartmouth, Mattappoisett, Sippican, and Westport, all within ten miles of New Bedford itself. At its local peak in 1857, New Bedford alone had 329 ships to Nantucket's 41. For all that, Nantucket has managed to keep its popular reputation as *the* whaling port. Its quaint atmosphere, reminiscent of the 1840s, has retained an appeal to old shipfaring days that New Bedford has largely lost with its expanded cotton mills and more recent electronics industries. In 1846, next to New Bedford with its satellites, came New London with 70 ships. Other whaling ports were Sag Harbor on Long Island, Stonington, Provincetown at the tip of Cape Cod, and Mystic, between New London and Stonington.

Fortunately, a sturdy veteran of the whale fleet has been preserved. The *Charles W. Morgan* was built at New Bedford in 1841. Just a century later, she was brought to Mystic Seaport in Connecticut, where

Drying yard for baleen near New Bedford, Massachusetts. Huge quantities of this springy material were used to make skirt-hoops and corset and collar stays. *Courtesy The Whaling Museum of New Bedford.*

she has ever since been its prime exhibit, with admirers counted in the millions. During the years before 1921, she made thirty-seven voyages and earned more than $1 million. The *Morgan* is a bluff-bowed, full-rigged ship of 351 tons, 106 feet long and 27 feet in beam, originally costing $23,000 plus an equal amount for outfit. Between 1841 and 1865 she made six voyages, with earnings ranging from $44,000 in 1849–53 to $165,000 in 1859–63. During that time the value of sperm oil rose from 88 cents a gallon to $1.61, whale oil tripled to 95 cents, and whalebone quadrupled to $1.53. Thus, even though the size of the whaling fleet reached its peak in 1846, the value of its catch reached higher levels in later years.

By 1860, however, whaling days were numbered. Whale oil, long in demand for lamps and other illumination, was encountering serious rivalry. First the introduction of coal gas for lighting cut into the demand. More serious was the discovery of petroleum in Pennsylvania in 1859, for the new coal oil, or kerosene, was cheaper and more plentiful. It was not only being used domestically but was also exported abroad. In 1863 the United States exported 3,090,000 gallons of sperm and whale oil and only 155,874 gallons of petroleum. A year later the preponderance was reversed to 22,064,000 gallons of petroleum and only 1,267,000 gallons of sperm and whale oil. From that time on, the discrepancy grew wider and wider. Even before 1865 and the disaster suffered by the whaling fleet in the Arctic in a surprise Confederate raid, whale oil was out of the running, already a lost cause.

The Atlantic Trade

Colorful as those far-flung wanderings of New England ships and men might be, cold statistics indicated that the cargoes carried across the three thousand miles of the North Atlantic between Liverpool and New York outweighed all the rest. That primacy dated back to the first days of peace in 1815. The British decided to dump their accumulated Industrial Revolution products in New York rather than in Boston or Philadelphia, and the goods were sold at auction for whatever they might bring. This appealed to the gambling spirit of the American jobbers and shopkeepers, who rushed to New York at the possibility of tempting bargains. By timely legislation and efforts to make life interesting for the strangers within their gates, the New Yorkers managed to make "going to New York" pretty much of a lasting habit.

Jeremiah Thompson, the important Yorkshire woolen representative, at this point took two highly significant steps. Along with three Quaker associates, he announced monthly packet sailings, rigidly on schedule, beginning in 1818, to carry passengers, mail, and fine cargoes. Regular service was thereby secured between New York and Liverpool. This Black Ball line was so successful that additional runs were added to London and Havre. Because local return cargoes were inadequate, Thompson next inaugurated the so-called cotton triangle, bringing cotton up the coast from Charleston, Savannah, and New Orleans and carrying European cargoes back to those southern ports. These developments gave New York port a long lead over its rivals, well before the much-touted Erie Canal linked New York with Lake Erie and the back-country in 1825.

Boston tried to emulate the Black Ball success with its own packet lines in 1822 and 1825, but neither lasted more than a brief time. Return cargoes were the difficulty, as England had little use for northern products. Boston was too far to bring up southern cotton; so Boston packets dropped down the coast to Charleston to load cotton before going to England. The delay involved made the eastbound service unattractive to passengers. In the 1840s a more ambitious packet service between Boston and Liverpool was attempted by Enoch Train. Some of his vessels were excellent McKay yard products, while others were chartered immigrant carriers. This service also failed. The need to go south for cotton made it hopeless to attempt to lure much eastbound traffic from the well-established New York lines.

In 1840 Boston made its one first-rate connection with Liverpool. This was with England's newly subsidized Cunard Line, which began its service to Boston by way of Halifax. For the next few years, Boston received the latest news from Europe by these side-wheelers, which drew a number of distinguished passengers, such as Charles Dickens, for the crossing. Bostonians were very grateful to Cunard and showed it on one occasion, when the harbor was frozen over, by cutting a seven-mile channel through the ice to permit the *Britannia* to sail on schedule. In 1848, however, the pull to New York was strong enough for Cunard to extend its service there, and Boston lapsed into a second-class role.

The only other important regular New England connection with Britain came in 1853, when Portland began seventy profitable years as

Bostonians cutting the Cunnarder *Britannia* out of the ice in February of 1844 to keep her on schedule. *Courtesy M. V. Brewington.*

the winter port of Montreal. In 1845, when railroad connections toward the west were beginning to take form, an energetic Maine lawyer, John A. Poor, went into action. Learning that Boston interests were negotiating at Montreal for a railroad, Poor made a midwinter sleigh ride through a howling blizzard to Montreal to counter their efforts. He was successful. Portland began the Atlantic & St. Lawrence Railroad, and Montreal built the St. Lawrence & Atlantic to meet it at the border. Before these were completed, they were leased for 999 years to the English-controlled Grand Trunk. In 1853 the steamer *Sarah Sands* arrived at Portland with a general cargo and took back the Canadian grain that had come down over the 290-mile new road. In November each year, when the St. Lawrence River froze over, the "English steamers" began to bring their cargoes into Portland to carry back the Canadian grain and cattle. This trade was worth around $1 million a year to Portland. It lasted until 1923, when the government-owned Canadian National took over the Grand Trunk; then politics overcame economics, and the trade went to Halifax and St. John.

By the late 1840s immigration was suddenly becoming big business as a result of the Irish potato famine and political disturbances in Europe. The greatest number of newcomers landed in New York, but Boston and the rest of New England also felt the effects. In addition to those landed in New England, a large number of the others were brought over in Yankee ships. Between 1820 and 1845, some 138,000 immigrants had already entered New England ports. In the next decade 270,000 arrived, making a total of 408,000 for the years 1820–1855. Of that number, 311,000 were landed at Boston and 9,000 in Portland. More than half of these newcomers were Irish, and all had come by sea from Liverpool or other ports. Some 76,000 others had crossed the Atlantic to the Maritime Provinces and had then come down to the Passamaquoddy ports in short, virtually coastal runs. Smaller numbers entered at numerous other New England ports. Liverpool, which had been the leader in the slave trade before it was abolished, profited by that experience in crowding a maximum number of human beings into a minimum amount of shipboard space. Some of the stories of immigrant crossings make very grim reading.

The regular packets absorbed some of the new rush. Enoch Train's Boston line, started in 1844, came on the scene just in time to profit by the new trade, but three of his ships were lost with heavy casualties. The immigration left lasting effects on New York, Boston, and to some extent Portland. In Boston, 35,000 of its inhabitants in 1850 were Irish; in 1860 they were 45,000 of its total 177,000. They found the Democratic party and the Roman Catholic church ready to welcome them, and they soon showed a real aptitude for politics. So far as population went, Boston and Portland received relatively few of the Germans who followed in the wake of the Irish, but Maine-built ships profited well in bringing them over.

While New York had its strong lead in the British commerce, Boston held its own in trade to the Mediterranean and the Baltic. Its busy brigs found business in the ports of both regions, especially in southern France, Italy, and far out in Smyrna. Wines, fruit, olive oil, raisins, figs, and much else were imported. The Mediterranean merchants did not take as much salt cod as formerly, but they showed a partiality toward Lowell cottons and New England rum. Boston likewise maintained its old prominence in the Baltic trade, especially in shipbuilding materials and naval stores.

In addition to those voyages to other continents, New England did a thriving business with Cuba and the Maritime Provinces of British North America (not part of Canada proper until 1867) . These two areas, though under foreign flags, were conveniently close at hand. This commerce had much in common with the coasting trade and its numerous small vessels, most of which came and went often in the course of a year. In 1860 alone, 425 vessels arrived in New England ports from Cuba and 3,550 from the Maritimes.

Cuba at the time was taking over the role which the British sugar islands had played in the colonial period. Jamaica, Barbados, Antigua, and the rest of those islands had fallen upon very hard times. American shipping between 1783 and 1830 was substantially barred from regular trade. The slave trade and, moreover, slavery itself had been abolished. Rising in place of the British islands were Cuba and Puerto Rico, which had alone stood aside from the wave of independence that had swept over Latin America between 1812 and 1825. Numerous planters had flocked in after the revolution in Hispaniola. Also, Spain was relaxing its rigid mercantilist restrictions. By 1818, Cuban trade was open to foreigners, and the Americans were quick to take advantage of this. The Yankees swarmed to Havana, Matanzas, and other ports. In 1860, Cuba and Puerto Rico were the only regions in the world where the United States exceeded Britain in trade.

As far as New England was concerned, molasses, that cheap by-product of sugar production, was a major import along with refined or unrefined sugar. Much of the molasses, in continuation of usual custom, was distilled into rum. Colonial Boston, as Richard Pares emphasizes, had long reeked of rum, and the business still continued there and in nearby Medford and Newburyport. In 1860, New England produced 4,023,000 gallons. Of this total, Massachusetts distilled 3,368,000 gallons; Maine, 452,000 gallons; and Connecticut, 203,000. That amount of rum was surprising for Maine, where in 1851 the well-known prohibitionist, Neal Dow, had pushed through the first dry law in the nation.

The rum was traditional, but Portland was to develop a new, highly profitable alternative use for molasses. Whereas New York was refining expensive "muscovado" brown sugar, Portland developed a method of making sugar of sorts from molasses — a process described as "boiling *in vacuo* and purging with centrifugal machinery." This could produce some eleven grades of sugar, "ranging from nearly white to dark yellow," and naturally selling at a cheaper price than white granulated. With molasses selling at only 15 cents a gallon, a high profit was assured which helped to build up Portland's greatest fortune of the century. John Bundy Brown put into practice the formula which had been developed by a colleague and started his huge Portland Sugar House in 1845. He produced some 250 barrels a day from 25,000 hogsheads of molasses a year. The business, it was estimated, was "raising one and a half million dollars annually," and it kept a whole fleet of brigs and schooners from Matanzas and Cardenas coming constantly. Near Portland there is still a Blackstrap Hill, so called because it was the first land to be sighted by these vessels with their cargoes of "blackstrap" molasses. In 1860 the 269 arrivals brought molasses worth $682,000, which placed Portland third as an importer of that commodity, behind New York and Boston.

Portland more than paid for that molasses with its exports of wood products. These, too, had been traditionally profitable since colonial days. A considerable part of them went to Cuba, particularly staves and headings for molasses hogsheads. With other items of wood manufacture, including boards, ashes, and shingles, the total came to $1,123,000 in 1860.

Even nearer at hand was that other foreign region, which was virtually an extension of the domestic coastal trade area. Nova Scotia, Prince Edward Island, and particularly adjacent New Brunswick had much in common with the state of Maine geographically, economically, and spiritually. Because of the international boundary at Passamaquoddy ("Quoddy") Bay, their trade has produced tangible statistics of a sort completely lacking for the domestic coastal trade. This is particularly true of an exhaustive, 906-page report by Israel D. Andrews, United States Consul in British North America in 1853, that helped to pave the way for the reciprocity treaty a year later. His detailed figures for 1851 would give a fairly accurate picture of Maine's domestic coastal trade except for three items of British North American offerings. One of these items was plaster of paris, or gypsum, "dirty gray cargoes" to "replenish with calcium the tired acres of New England farms." Another was bituminous coal from the mines of Cape Breton Island, Pictou on the lower St. Lawrence, and Cumberland on the Bay of Fundy. The third was grindstones. Aside from these, the comings and goings were very similar to those of Maine's domestic trade. In 1851, for instance, cargoes of flour, cotton manufactures, leather goods, meats, and tea were carried eastward in exchange for fish, potatoes, firewood, and grains.

Incidentally, that same year 1851 saw 2,907 immigrants entering the United States from Quoddy. Apparently, most of them had arrived in the Maritimes from Britain and come down by steamer from St. John to Eastport. The heavy importation of potatoes from the Maritimes that year may have been to meet the demands of the newly arriving Irish. Of the New England ports in the Maritime trade Boston had a long lead in the import dollar value at $2,112,000. This was followed by Quoddy at $565,000, with Portland a distant third.

The Domestic Coasting Trade

In the course of the years, Congress has passed various pieces of legislation designed to aid our merchant marine. None of these, however, has yet to prove so durably beneficial as the Act Concerning the Navigation of the United States of 1 March 1817. Its fourth section made the all-important provision that "no goods, wares, or merchandise shall be imported, under the penalty of forfeiture thereof, from one port of the United States to another port of the United States in a vessel belonging wholly or in part to a subject of any foreign power." Briefly, this meant that foreign flags were ever since barred from our coastal trade. This would be a particular godsend in the "Dark Age" after the Civil War, when foreign flags took over most of the exports and imports. This coastal prohibition has subsequently been extended, in ways which the British and others considered unsportsmanlike, to the trade between East Coast and West Coast ports. Even though foreign vessels might be thousands of miles beyond the territorial waters of the United States in traveling by Panama or Cape Horn, America's coastal prohibition continues in full force. It has also been used to protect the trade with noncontiguous parts of the nation, such as Alaska, Hawaii, and Puerto Rico.

Because of the absence of statistical data a major result of this protection has never been appreciated. For the volume of coastal cargoes, ranging in importance from cotton on down, we have only guesswork; but the coastal trade of the United States in the Golden Age was certainly much more impressive than the foreign. Coastal shipping involved a far greater number of vessels, captains, and crews than did the more spectacular foreign voyages. The daily comings and goings of those coastal vessels make them the really distinctive feature of maritime New England in the "great era" — and, for that matter, long beyond it.

The official data is extremely meager, but it does reveal the far-reaching magnitude and significance of the coastal commerce and, in particular, of the coastal navigation. In one respect, the official figures are specific. A vessel had to be registered for foreign trade, or enrolled or licensed for domestic trade. In the domestic category, fishing was distinguished from the "pure coastal." In 1815 the registered documented tonnage was nearly double the coastal, but gradually the latter was to catch up. In 1860 the coastal tonnage outnumbered the registered by 2,644,000 to 2,545,000. But that was only part of the story. In the statistics of vessels entered and cleared from American ports, the coastal naturally ran far ahead, since each coastal vessel, with its normally shorter runs, was apt to enter port several times a year, while a registered vessel was making only one or two voyages. There was one other consideration, which differentiated American coastwise shipping from the European, where national coastlines were shorter and closer together: an American coastal run from Portland, Maine, to New Orleans (some 2,121 miles), for instance, would carry a vessel from England to 16 foreign countries.

Along the coast, shipping held the transportation field pretty much unchallenged for a long period. It was, of course, simpler and cheaper to send things by schooner than by wagon along the rough roads of the day. Even passengers often preferred to travel by water instead of by stagecoach or horseback. This was especially true of the deeply indented Maine coast, where towns on adjacent fingers of land are sometimes twenty miles apart by road but only a mile by water. The coasting vessels were even able to hold their own against railroads for a long time. American railroad builders were more intent on reaching the western hinterland than in running along the coast. When railroads were first discussed in New England, "it was said that it was useless to contend against a Cape Cod captain, who owned his sloop, and carried codfish and mackerel one way and flour the other; that no road across the country could contend against water transportation."

A basic element in the coastal trade was the country store in the backcountry of a port's sphere of influence. A customer might drive up with a load of salt fish or country produce, sell them after a dicker, and then make purchases from the variegated stock of the general store. When he started back, he might be carrying a scythe, a kettle, a few yards of calico, a barrel of flour, a bag of coffee, and a gallon of rum. Such was the Alpha and Omega of a seaport's commerce in those days. The same customer might well be both the producer of some of the area's exports and the ultimate consumer of the goods collected by the port's merchants from distant regions.

Those vessels that plied New England's coast not only carried a wide variety of things for all sorts of people but also had a good number of passengers aboard. Among the cargoes, the wares imported from beyond the seas would perhaps rank first in point of value and importance. These included the cotton goods of Lancashire, the woolens of Yorkshire, and the ironware of Birmingham and Sheffield. More exotic ports sent coffee, tea, and spices. Generally these cargoes were taken to New York and then transshipped eastward by way of Boston or Portland. Along with the products of Britain's Industrial Revolution came the steadily increasing output of the new industrialism in the United States. Particularly important were the cotton goods of Lowell, the still more recent woolen goods of Lawrence, and the boots and shoes of Lynn and Haverhill — all within a very narrow radius of Boston. This local manufacturing had a double impact on the coastal trade. In addition to distributing the finished products far and wide, local shipping benefited as well by bringing in raw materials, especially cotton from the South.

Still older in tradition was the importation from the southward of flour, upon which New England had depended since colonial times. In 1851 — when Pennsylvania, New York, and Virginia produced respectively 15, 13 and 11 million bushels of wheat — Massachusetts, Rhode Island, and Connecticut raised only 73,000, of which Rhode Island's share was only 49 bushels. Yet the Yankees wanted their white bread, so there was a constant procession into New England harbors of flour-laden vessels from the Hudson, the Delaware, and Chesapeake Bay. New England sent in return salt cod and pickled mackerel. In the same way, the region exported part of its very ample surplus of lumber in payment for anthracite coal. Use of anthracite had begun to spread northward from the Delaware in the 1830s; it competed in New England markets with the bituminous coal from Pictou and Cape Breton in Nova Scotia. In 1822, Boston had received only four coal cargoes from Philadelphia; by 1835 that had risen to 2,631. Yankee ingenuity worked out other ways of paying for what was needed from outside, including exports of paving stones, ice, and baled hay.

The vessels which carried those cargoes fell into three major categories: the very numerous sailing packets, both large and small, linked specific ports; the night boat steamers caught the cream of the traffic on some of the most important runs; and the tramps went wherever business offered and were most prominent in moving certain bulk cargoes, such as lumber, lime, and granite. The boundary lines between those three types were not too rigidly drawn — some coal, for instance, moved northward in packets, while tramps also did their share.

Earliest, most numerous, and most persistent were the coastal packets, which ran on schedules of sorts between specific ports. Sometimes this would mean simply a single sloop or schooner, linking a little Maine community with Portland and bringing in all sorts of cargo for the local storekeepers; the captain would often attend to special errands for some of his friends. At the opposite extreme were the major lines to the cotton ports, with large square-riggers carrying various items southward and returning with cotton for the mills of Lowell.

These new lines had come into existence around 1820, shortly after the Black Ball "square-riggers on schedule" began service between New York and Liverpool. The packets went everywhere, continuing their runs down through the decades at least to the Civil War. Carl Cutler has compiled the names of those that plied the major runs between Boston, New York, Albany, Philadelphia, Norfolk, Baltimore, Charleston, Savannah, Mobile, and New Orleans. From Boston alone there were more than a thousand between the 1820s and 1860s. And those were simply the aristocrats of the packet trade; there were even more on shorter runs. Boston and Portland each had large numbers of local lines.

Each line usually included several vessels, operating under joint management, with sailings at fairly regular intervals, probably once or twice a week. There had to be several vessels to maintain such service, for their runs depended on the whims of the winds. Young Hezekiah Prince, customs inspector at Thomaston, Maine, who recorded many of the comings and goings of the packets between there and Boston, noted on 15 April 1824:

The schooner *Milo*, Capt. Robinson, arrived from Boston this morning. Piper, Varnston and other passengers. . . . Capt. Robinson brought freight for Keith, Cole, Healey, Keegan, Head of Warren and others. He had on board 6 or 7 hhds. rum, 3 or 4 boxes of tea, several boxes of sugar, molasses &c.

But just before Christmas 1825 he wrote:

The schooner *Milo*, John Robinson, has gone ashore in Gloucester Beach during the cold weather last week and the crew and passengers with difficulty escaped to the shore, some of them frozen.

The average time between Boston and New York port was four or five days; between Boston and Philadelphia or Richmond, about two weeks; and between Boston and New Orleans, about twenty-five days. But there was no telling when adverse winds might stretch out these figures or lucky winds shorten them a bit. It has been remarked that "New York was the greatest figure in Boston's coastal trade and Boston was the greatest factor in New York's." So far as sailing vessels were concerned, the run between the two ports was a mean one, for Cape Cod jutted out, with some very tricky sailing between Provincetown and the entrance to Long Island Sound. Nevertheless, some three thousand sailing coasters rounded the Cape each year during this era. Some minor, local sailing-packet services lasted into the twentieth century. The schooners up the Maine coast from Widgery's Wharf at Portland kept contact with the little down-east ports until after World War I, when trucks and improved roads finally offered too strong competition.

The second major category of coasters was the "night boat" driven by steam instead of sail. The service these vessels provided was a continuation of the packets, but steam gave them the great advantage of regularity: one could now predict the time of arrival, in addition to arranging the time of departure. This was a particular attraction to passengers, who became major users of the night boats. They also gave quick, dependable service for the more valuable types of cargo.

Long Island Sound, with its hundred miles of sheltered water, gave the steamboat a valuable opportunity to improve travel conditions between New York and Boston. By land, the distance between the two cities was more than two hundred miles; by sea, the route around Cape Cod was well over three hundred miles. Most of the travel was by stagecoach, but it was a tedious trip. In 1815, for instance, a traveler who left New York by coach at six on Monday morning would spend the first night at New Haven and the second night at Ashland, Massachusetts, arriving at Boston in time for dinner on Wednesday. By water, it was possible to tap the stage route to Boston at numerous points. One could go by water from New York to Providence, for instance, which left less than fifty miles to cover by land. Before 1815, some travelers who were not in a hurry had avoided part of the stage trip by taking packet sloops to, say, Providence, New London, or Norwich; but, of course, their time of arrival was a gamble.

Steam service on Long Island Sound dates from the spring of 1815, when the British withdrew their blockading forces at the end of the War of 1812. The steamer *Fulton* opened the route to New Haven, but the Sound steamers crept eastward from there only gradually. In 1816, when the *Connecticut* was added to the service, New London, at the end of the Sound, became the terminus. A farther extension resulted from the fight against the monopoly which New York State had granted to Fulton and Livingston for all steamboating in New York waters. In reprisal, Connecticut passed a law forbidding steamboats from New York to enter her ports as long as that monopoly remained in force. This led to the substitution of Providence as the terminus of the principal steamers. Long Island did not shelter this extension of the route, and the sea was often very rough off "P'int Judy," as Point Judith was called. Many people had misgivings about this longer route when the veteran Elihu Bunker heroically took the *Connecticut* around the stormy point to Newport and Providence. For the next fifteen years, this 210-mile route to Providence remained the most important of the Sound lines for through travel, because it left less than fifty miles of stagecoaching to Boston. Hartford and several other Connecticut ports acquired steamboats to New York during that time, but not until 1837 did Providence, which had by then a railroad to Boston, lose its primacy in the through traffic.

Once again, little Stonington on the eastern edge of Connecticut close to the Rhode Island border — that prolific breeder of bold mariners — was to come into the maritime foreground as a new rival. New York businessmen built a railroad from Providence to Stonington, where it connected with the Sound steamers from New York. By reducing the water trip, this gave a quicker through connection and avoided the rough water off Point Judith. There was, however, one disadvantage of which the users of Sound steamers were well aware. Because of the longer train ride, the traveler had to be routed out in the gray dawn; going to Providence he might have had a chance to sleep longer. That discomfort would be even more obvious when, in the 1840s, a new service to Allyn's Point (between New London and Norwich), which went on to Boston by way of Worcester, called for even earlier rising.

In 1847 the Fall River Line began its famous ninety-year career, running past Newport to the Massachusetts cotton manufacturing town, which had just completed rail connections with Boston. This involved a train trip only half as long as rival routes, with a correspondingly longer boat trip — and time to sleep. In all those routes, whether by Providence, Stonington, Norwich, or Fall River, the traveler left New York in the late afternoon and was delivered in Boston the next morning. On the return trip, of course, he had the train ride first.

This emphasis on passenger traffic led to the building of more and more elaborately appointed steamers, which more than held their own for years in competition with the railroads for through traffic. Less publicized, but equally important from the economic standpoint, was the fast service given the more valuable freight, where speedy delivery was appreciated. It was significant that a director of one of the lines was Eben Jordan, founder of the great New England department store Jordan Marsh, who fully realized the value of such service.

The night-boat service also spread quickly to the rougher and foggier runs down east from Boston to Maine and beyond. As early as 1822 the steamer *Patent* reached Portland, and by the end of that decade, the century of Boston-Portland night-boat service had begun. Other lines extended to the eastward, particularly the Kennebec run up past Bath to Gardiner and Hallowell, and the Penobscot run which, after stopping at Rockland, Camden, and Belfast, went on up the river to Bangor. Eventually, there was also an "international" service, with steamers from Boston stopping at Portland en route to Quoddy and St. John. Likewise, there was direct steam connection between Portland and New York around Cape Cod. These services were not only well patronized by passengers, despite the rail competition to Portland, but were also valuable in the distribution of cargoes from the southward.

Portland derived lasting, highly profitable benefit from this dependable overnight service. It fitted into the growth of jobbing or whole-

The S. S. *Governor*, typical night-boat of the 1850s, serving between Boston and various Maine ports. *Courtesy Maine Historical Society.*

sale houses, which enabled Portland to serve as an entrepôt between Boston and New York, on the one hand, and the down-east storekeepers, on the other. Some distinguished jobbing houses lasted well into the twentieth century, specializing in textiles, agricultural equipment, hardware, drugs, and groceries. From Portland the wares were distributed by packets along the coast and by wagon (and later rail) to inland communities, some as far as Vermont.

Along with those runs along the Sound and the Maine coast, numerous shorter steamer routes served the area, particularly the Connecticut shore. On the eve of the Civil War, Boston was to receive longer steam service to Philadelphia and Baltimore. Phineas Sprague, a Boston merchant, and his young relative Henry Winsor took the initiative in this improved Boston service. That same year, 1852, a Baltimore group under the leadership of Benjamin Deford, one of the largest tanners in the country, secured a charter for the Merchants' & Miners' Transportation Company. They found a Boston ally in Joseph Whitney, a shoe manufacturer with extensive markets in the southern states. When the Merchants' & Miners' Line dispatched its first vessel, the *Joseph Whitney*, to Boston, at the very end of 1854, "it inaugurated a line built on shoe leather," serving Norfolk as well as Baltimore.

The night-boat runs on the Sound and the Maine coast developed a distinctive type of wooden side-wheeler, with stateroom accommodations for a large number of passengers and increasingly elaborate finish in the main cabins. That style would remain virtually unchanged for the rest of the century. In fact, the night-boat pattern would hold its own after World War I. The little sailing packets maintained service until the Civil War but declined on all but the minor runs after that.

The third main category of coastal vessels might well be called tramps — though "transient vessels" was a more polite term sometimes used. Some of them, like their counterparts on the ocean runs, simply went wherever business offered. They might carry various types of cargo in the course of a year. Many of the others, however, tended to specialize in one of the major bulk trades.

Perhaps the most respectable of the tramps were the vessels, usually square-riggers, which alternated between foreign (registered) and domestic (enrolled) status. The focal points for this business were New Orleans and the other cotton ports. Cotton gave them heavy outbound exports, but far less came from abroad. New Orleans, for instance, in 1860 had exports of $107 million and imports of only $22 million; at Mobile the ratio was $38 million to $1 million. The coastal packets from Boston and New York brought in some of the articles needed from outside, but the tramps also figured heavily. Maine, from the beginning of the century, had been building ships for the cotton trade and naturally did not want them to go south empty. The result was often a triangular trade in which the Yankee vessel took south domestic cargo of one kind or another, then took southern cotton to Liverpool or Havre, and returned usually to New York or Boston with a transatlantic cargo. Some Maine ships did not follow this vague pattern but stayed within the domestic area, bringing cotton northward for the mills of Lowell. In 1850, for example, Mobile shipped 162,000 bales to Great Britain, 111,000 to American northern ports, and 39,000 to France. One of the square-riggers owned by William Lord of Kennebunk brought coal down to Maine from Pictou, carried baled hay and cobblestones south to New Orleans, took cotton to Liverpool, and then returned with a cargo from Britain. But, in addition to the vessels in that lucrative mixture of missions, there were plenty which picked up cargoes wherever they could find them — and sometimes found none.

As for the bulk trades, lumber was foremost among them. Maine was in the process of slashing off the rich heritage that gave it the nick-name "Pine Tree State." This trade, of course, began in colonial times, and along with fish was Maine's primary offering in the field of commerce. In the early nineteenth century, lumbering went on apace, with its chief outlet in Bangor at the head of navigation on the Penobscot. Rapidly approaching its superlative position as the world's leading lumber port, Bangor had 3,376 arrivals in 1860. The port would reach its peak around 1872, before yielding primacy to southern ports. Official statistics, limited to foreign trade, do not give a full picture, for most of Bangor's shipments were coastwise. Part of the cargoes were so-called long timber, consisting either of planks and boards or of heavy timbers which could be sawn into those forms. Along with that went the laths, clapboards, shingles, and other short timber. There were other wood products, not always from pines, such as ship timber, spars, bark for tanning, and the makings of hogsheads and barrels. The little two-masted schooners, which were the principal carriers, not only had their holds well filled but also carried heavy deckloads. Sometimes, when a storm threatened, dozens of them would take refuge in Portland Harbor; and sometimes beaches down the coast would be strewn with laths and shingles from deckloads of vessels that had caught the storms at sea.

Another prime bulk offering from the Maine coast was lime, in constant demand for the plastering of walls and ceilings. Production centered around Rockland, Thomaston, and Rockport, where the limestone was quarried. It was then roasted in great kilns, where thirty cords of wood at a time were burned to extract the quicklime. This was packed into casks for shipment. It constituted a most hazardous cargo, for if water reached the lime, it burst into flames. There was then nothing to do but batten down the hatches in the hope of stifling the blaze. As a last resort, the vessel had to be scuttled, preferably in shallow water where it might be raised again. The lime trade also gave employment to another group of vessels which represented the low point in status — old, wornout sloops or schooners which found their last usefulness in bringing firewood for the voracious kilns. Firewood, some of it coming from the Maritimes, had long been carried in such vessels in the precoal era to stoke the fireplaces of Boston, Portland, and other ports.

Another heavy cargo, granite, came in quantity from Deer Isle,

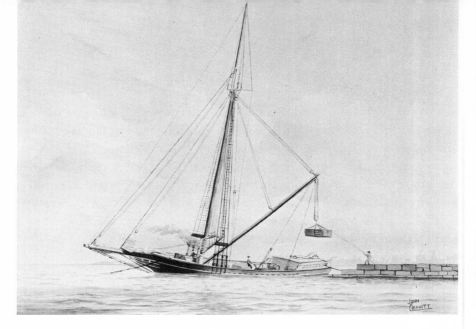

A stone sloop unloading granite blocks. Watercolor by John F. Leavitt. *Courtesy Peabody Museum of Salem.*

The harbor of Rockport, Maine, with ice schooners about to load for southern parts. *Courtesy Capt. W. J. Lewis Parker.*

Stonington, and Vinalhaven off Maine's middle coast. Of this the most valuable and, at the same time, the more difficult to handle were the large granite blocks for post offices, customhouses, and other such structures, as well as heavy pieces for breakwaters. Specialists in handling these awkward cargoes were the big stone sloops of Chebeague, based on that island in Casco Bay off Portland. They had a single big mast and sail, so that it was possible to stow the awkward cargoes inboard. Some of the granite was used simply for paving stones and could serve usefully as ballast.

Ice also sometimes made up whole cargoes. Frederic Tudor, who first shipped ice from just north of Boston, built up an alternative supply from the Kennebec River. The crucial year for ice came in 1860, when the weather in Massachusetts was far too mild for freezing. James L. Cheeseman cut 30,000 tons on the Kennebec that year. Later in the century, the Kennebec ice trade would reach massive proportions.

For vessels carrying those heavy, southbound bulk cargoes of lumber, lime, granite, and ice, one of the principal standbys for return cargoes was coal. Flour was also a possible cargo. The packets, as already noted, sometimes carried coal on the Philadelphia run, and it also often came in tramps. In addition to bituminous from Pictou and Cape Breton, a steady stream of anthracite came from the Delaware. In 1858, for instance, Portland received 36,000 tons of anthracite from Philadelphia for both family and industrial use.

The Fisheries

The oldest of the maritime activities of New England — a major enterprise even before the Pilgrims landed at Plymouth — was the catching of codfish. During the Golden Age, this and other fishing continued on an expanded scale. New Englanders in the cod, herring, and mackerel fisheries accounted for 80 percent of the nation's $5 million catch of those species, with Massachusetts dominating the scene. Over 12,000 Yankees earned their livelihood on the fishing grounds, with as many more employed less directly. New England's whaling brought in a catch worth nearly $8 million in 1860 and employed another 12,000 men. These figures do not include shellfish; in oysters alone, Connecticut had 743 hands engaged and a catch of $610,000. In the size of the crews, New England fishing and whaling were almost identical; in tonnage they were also fairly close. But in whaling the yield was about 60 cents on a dollar of capital; in fishing it was just about double that. Moreover, as we have seen, the year 1860 marked the beginning of the end for whaling, whereas fishing would go on steadily up and up, suffering no major setback until, a century later, Roman Catholics would no longer be required to observe meatless Fridays.

In the first half of the nineteenth century, numerous changes took place in New England's fishing industry. Cape Cod yielded its old prominence to ports along the Maine coast; while in the center, Gloucester overtook Marblehead and established itself as New England's preeminent fishing port. By 1860 its codfish fleet totaled 25,000 tons — ahead of Maine's Penobscot Bay area, Barnstable, Massachusetts, and Frenchman's Bay, Maine. Marblehead trailed far behind, after three other Maine coast ports. Gloucester dominated the mackerel fishery also, ahead of Barnstable, Newburyport, and Portland. Marblehead was already declining when a September gale in 1846 took a toll of eleven vessels and sixty-five men and boys. From that time on, it concentrated more and more on its old "moonlighting" occupation of shoemaking. The Barnstable district included the numerous active ports of Cape Cod, which maintained a very respectable total, particularly in the mackerel fishery. The so-called Plymouth ports of the South Shore below Boston, on the other hand, showed scant gain during this period. Maine had an overall total almost equal to that of Massachusetts, but it was scattered along the coast. Portland gradually achieved rank as one of the fishing industry's leading centers, but Gloucester remained *the* fishing port of New England.

Around the middle of the period, the dried salt cod, which had been a mainstay of trade with the West Indies and the Straits, began to lose its old ascendancy. The cod fishery had, from the beginning of the republic, been the recipient of federal bounties, both to the fishermen and to their vessels, because of the supposed value of their activity as a "nursery of seamen." Gradually, many fishermen came to prefer the more lucrative pursuit of the elusive mackerel, and there were penalties for claiming a codfishing bounty and then going after mackerel. The latter was a seasonal activity, with the mackerel starting early in the spring far to the southward and gradually working north toward the Maine coast. The schools of mackerel were far less dependable than the codfish; they might flock into an area one year and completely desert it

Appleton's Wharf, Marblehead, Massachusetts, *c.* 1840. Unsigned watercolor. *Courtesy Peabody Museum of Salem.*

The heeltappers *Hannah* and *Joseph,* at anchor inside Marblehead Neck. *Courtesy Marblehead Historical Society.*

the next. They were often marketed pickled in brine.

By the mid-1840s, fresh fish began to encroach on the old salted or pickled forms. With the combination of railroads (Gloucester had a branch by 1846) and icing for preservation, the fresh-fish market began to spread across the country. This development brought increased efforts to get the fish speedily to port — vessels began to have wells in their holds to keep the catch fresh. This also led to increased use of Georges Bank, only a hundred miles or so east of Cape Cod, much closer than the Grand Banks, but brutally rough in winter. The Georges fishing grounds, in turn, led to an increased market for the previously scorned haddock as well as for halibut. Far to the eastward in Maine, the seasonal inroads of herring created lively business, eventually resulting in large-scale canning of "sardines."

The use of handlines from a vessel's deck had been the time-honored method of fishing. With mackerel, this involved a process known as "jigging," that is, spreading ground bait on the surface and then counting on the fish going for the hooks embedded in heavy metal sinkers. In the decade before the Civil War, fishing from the deck gave way to going out in dories — which were carried nested aboard — with one or two men fishing from each boat. This became hazardous when, as happened so often on the Banks, fog suddenly shut in.

The type of fishing vessel prevalent at this time also underwent changes. The early little Chebacco boat, so named for the part of Ipswich where it was developed, gave way to the pinky. This too was sharp-ended but had a bowsprit and jib added. Pinkies were very small, only twenty to sixty tons with two pole masts. About 1830 they gradually were superseded by the square-sterned schooners with flush decks, which were only slightly larger but less clumsy. Fast, streamlined "clipper" schooners began to appear in the late 1840s. They could bring their catches quickly to market — *if* they arrived. But the rig was tender, and a tragic toll followed in the wake of every great storm.

Captains Courageous was an appropriate title for Kipling's story of the Gloucester fisherman. Definite actuarial statistics are lacking, but the evidence seems strong that fishing on the Grand Banks or Georges Bank was far more hazardous than whaling or ordinary merchant voyaging. Aside from the risk of dories becoming lost in the fog, there are grim records of encounters with autumnal gales — the 1837 tempest in which seventy-eight men from the Cape Cod fleet were drowned; the

The last working pinky, the *Maine. Courtesy A. M. Barnes.*

Painting of the Great Gale of 1846 on the Grand Banks, in which ten Marble-head vessels sank, drowning sixty-five men and boys. The ship *Samuel Knight* escaped by running before the storm. Oil on panel by William T. Bartoll. *Courtesy Russell W. Knight.*

Fisherman handlining for cod off the Nova Scotia coast. Oil painting by an unidentified artist. *Courtesy Peabody Museum of Salem.*

October gale in 1841, which took eighty-seven men from Cape Cod and destroyed fourteen out of sixteen vessels owned at Pigeon Cove on Cape Ann; the 1846 storm that made so many widows at Marblehead; and the Minot's Light gale of October 1851. Yet, for all that, and despite relatively meager financial returns, there was seldom difficulty in manning the fishing fleet. In southern New England, however, there was safer work in Connecticut oystering, while clams and even lobsters gradually came upon the scene.

Shipbuilding

Almost as ancient as fishing in the maritime history of New England was the building of vessels. The proximity of suitable oak and pine close to the water's edge gave the region an economic advantage over costs in England amounting to some 30 percent. The very configuration of the rocky, indented coastline, especially in Maine, meant that sloops and schooners, if not larger vessels, could be put together almost anywhere. Even though the economic advantages of cheap timber declined after 1830, when it became necessary to cut farther and farther inland, the expansion of American maritime opportunities in the second quarter of the century led to steadily increasing output from the New England shipyards.

Shipbuilding of sorts was scattered along the whole New England coast from Passamaquoddy Bay to Connecticut. It was said of Maine: "There is scarcely a cove on the coast that did not at one time or another contain a building yard." To some extent that is true of the coastal towns to the southward, although shipbuilders were steadily migrating from Massachusetts to Maine because of its more generous timber supply. By 1815 the North River south of Boston was terminating its once remarkable career as a shipbuilding center. Perhaps the most distinctive building port was Essex, close to the fishing ports of Cape Ann, for which it long turned out excellent fishing schooners. The little ports of far eastern Maine also concentrated on that type of small vessel. These smaller communities required little sophisticated designing or elaborate construction apparatus for their building.

Maine's principal contribution was the building of large numbers of substantial square-riggers — brigs at first, then barks, and finally full-rigged ships — for general cargo purposes. If an owner wanted a very special vessel — an ocean packet, for instance — he could get it by paying an extra high price at one of New York's East River yards. But a good sturdy cargo carrier, with a roomy hold, could be turned out on the Kennebec or the middle coast of Maine at a much more reasonable rate. Such vessels particularly met the needs of the cotton carrying trade. Some of the best were "broad, flat-bottomed carriers which could pack 2,000 pounds of cotton for each registered ton" — a more important consideration than speed.

By 1840 the boom was beginning. That year the Maine yards produced 52,000 tons. By 1845 production doubled to 110,000, and in the next ten years it doubled again to a peak of 215,000 tons, more than a third of the whole national total. In 1840 the Waldoboro customs district of the middle coast led the field, but by the 1850s the Bath district, with all the Kennebec yards, was far ahead. During that decade along that one river, Bath itself built 232 vessels and Richmond built 60 — with Bowdinham, Hallowell, and thirty-three other towns, from Augusta at the head of navigation to Phippsburg down close to the open sea, trailing behind. Three-quarters of these were square-riggers, many of them built to replace some of the 600-odd vessels that had been sailed to California with gold-crazy passengers and crew and then abandoned. Bath, endowed by nature with a good, firm, sloping bank just right for shipways, had a long, proud tradition, with some of its family yards producing ships throughout much of the century. Outstanding were the Sewalls, who turned out 105 vessels between 1823 and 1903 for their own use alone, in addition to a number of vessels for other owners. Also prominent were the Houghton and Patten yards.

In the emotions of the 1850s and ever since, the capacious cargo carriers of the Kennebec have been completely overshadowed by the clippers of the great decade of the Golden Age. Writer after writer has sent the *Flying Cloud* around Cape Horn or has meticulously recorded the various speed records in a wealth of detail that, as one maritime historian put it, reads like the *Daily Racing Form*.

The overworked and badly abused word *clipper* simply implied streamlined construction in which carrying capacity was sacrificed to speed, or at least to the hope for speed. It had been applied to the fast little Baltimore schooners and brigs designed to escape from the clutches of the Royal Navy between 1800 and 1815. Except for the emphasis on speed, they had nothing in common with the big China and California clippers of midcentury. The question of which ships merit inclusion in that latter charmed circle has long been a matter of dispute. So much glamour has been built up around them that the word has been used rather loosely. As William H. Rowe put it:

> If an ordinary merchantman had the good luck to make a more than average voyage, she and the magic talisman "clipper" came together and clung to each other like droplets of quicksilver. . . . Then again, even an old apple-bowed hooker that "beat her head three times against a billow and then fell off and sailed around it," is likely to turn up in the sympathetic chronicle of some member of her owner's or skipper's family as a "clipper ship."

Gradually, several maritime historians have established preeminence among the endlessly expanding number of clipper enthusiasts, few of whom are aware of all the facts. These historians include Captain Arthur H. Clark with his topical arrangement, Octavius T. Howe and Frederic C. Matthews with an alphabetical pattern, and Carl Cutler with his

The clipper ship *Dashing Wave,* entering Boston Harbor. Oil painting by William Bradford, 1855. *Courtesy Peabody Museum of Salem.*

delightful chronological account. Such authorities have limited the exclusive club to some hundred-odd vessels that completed the New York-San Francisco run in 110 days or less or made an equally fast passage elsewhere.

The clipper era, roughly from the mid-1840s to the mid-1850s, arose from circumstances which put a premium on speed. First, with the opening of the Chinese treaty ports, came the desire — whether practical or emotional — to be the first in with tea cargoes from Canton or Shanghai. Several big, fast ships, embodying the new streamlined principles, were built for that trade, notably the *Rainbow* and the *Sea Witch.* They were already on hand, to their great profit, in time for the gold rush to San Francisco. Some of the forty-niners went out the hard way overland in covered wagons; some, like the return cargoes of gold, went on the new subsidy liners converging on the isthmus of Panama. But most cargo and numerous passengers went by sea around Cape Horn. At the very outset, large numbers of old vessels attempted that trip, but the needs of the empty market at San Francisco, where things could be sold

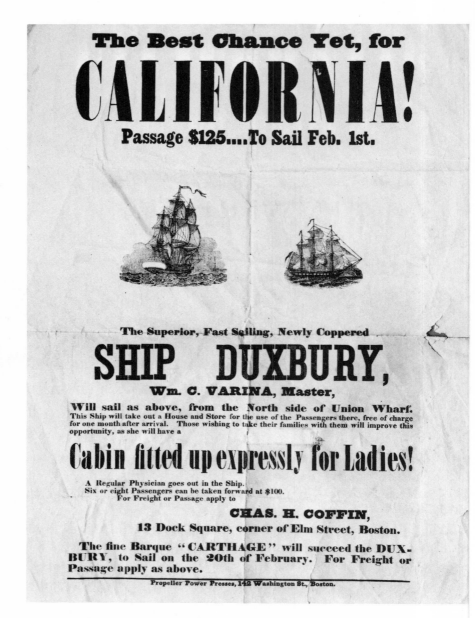

Gold Rush poster advertising the sailing of two vessels from Boston for California, 1850. *Courtesy Peabody Museum of Salem.*

at ten times their prime cost, put a premium on speed. This situation led to a sudden construction of new clippers to capitalize on the opportunity.

The movement was accelerated by an emotional emphasis on speed which can best be caught by reading the shipping news of the *New York Herald* or other journals, particularly in 1851, the *annus mirabilis*. Shipowners, normally tightfisted in all aspects of maritime economy, were so carried away that they spent like drunken sailors in an effort to get the fastest ships, hired the best captains, and finally bet heavily on their ships' speed to San Francisco. All this resulted in producing a great many more of those magnificent vessels — with their "bows turned inside out" and with lofty spars and canvas far beyond normal needs — than the business really warranted. Some of the first clippers paid for themselves, but after two or three years, the story of many was written in red ink.

There was a close rivalry between New England and New York — or, more precisely, between Boston Harbor and the East River — in the building and ownership (registry) of clippers. Of the eighty-two vessels ranked among the select 110-day clippers, Boston built thirty-seven to New York's thirty-two and owned thirty-eight to New York's thirty-nine. But Boston was the starting point for only one-quarter of these fast passages; the rest began at New York. The celebrated 89-day run of the *Flying Cloud* to San Francisco in 1851 demonstrated the shadowy borderline of honors between New York and New England. She started from New York and had *New York* painted on her stern, but she was built in East Boston by a Nova Scotian trained in New York; her captain came from Marblehead; and her senior owner, Moses H. Grinnell, operated from New York but came from Old Lyme, Connecticut.

As for honors in building the best clippers, the contest narrows to two men, both trained in the East River shipyard of Isaac Webb, who had come from Stamford, Connecticut. One was his son, William H. Webb; the other was Donald McKay, the gifted Nova Scotian. In that exclusive group of 110-day passages, nineteen were made by McKay ships and fifteen by Webb's. Webb was the more versatile designer, but primacy among the builders of wooden sailing vessels goes by general accord to Donald McKay. As Samuel Eliot Morison has written, he was an artist and a scientist, an idealist and a practical man of business. "His serene and beautiful character won him the respect and affection of his employees, and made the atmosphere of his shipbuilding yard that of a happy, loyal family." The *Flying Cloud* was the most celebrated of his ships; she made two of the three 89-day runs to San Francisco, the first on her maiden voyage in 1851 and the second in 1854. The third such run was made by the Mystic-built medium clipper *Andrew Jackson* in 1859–60. McKay's *Sovereign of the Seas* also made lasting speed records, as did some of his later ships for the Liverpool-Australia run. His most ambitious effort was the huge, four-masted *Great Republic,* which burned at New York before her first voyage and had to be cut down.

McKay, who had first built some ships at Newburyport before Enoch Train lured him away, had his yard in East Boston. Several other Greater Boston yards also distinguished themselves in the clipper era, notably those of Samuel Hall at Boston, Paul Curtis at Chelsea, and Cudworth & Flint and J. O. Curtis at Medford. Of the clippers built outside Boston Harbor in New England, perhaps the most celebrated was the *Red Jacket,* designed by Samuel Hartt Pook and built by George Thomas at Rockland, Maine; in 1854 she made a record 13-day crossing to Liverpool. The *Phoenix,* built by Thomas Knight in an area still known as Knightville, across the harbor from Portland, made a similar fast run from Savannah and served as a Black Ball packet. The *Dreadnought,* from the yard of Currier & Townsend at Newburyport, became known as the "wild boat of the Atlantic" because of the fast runs — which lost nothing in the telling — by her tough, extrovert skipper, Samuel Samuels.

Although the clipper ship era was glorious, it was over quickly. Vessels built after 1853 felt the impact of what economists call diminishing returns. The San Francisco market, the original reason for speed, had soon become satiated. The repeal of the British Navigation Acts in 1849 had served as a double stimulus, since American-built ships could now be sold in Britain for the first time since the Revolution, and could also bring cargoes to and from China and Australia, with the latter's 1851 gold rush leading to a new boom. Several of McKay's ships were bought by James Baines for his Australian packet line. But by the late 1850s depression set in, accentuated by the 1857 panic.

The weak point of the clipper ships was that about a third of their cargo capacity had to be sacrificed in order to secure their unusual speed. Their lofty overhead hamper and their large crews kept them from competing successfully with more burdensome normal vessels.

Design for the figurehead of the ship *Morning Light*, by John W. Mason, Boston, 1853. *Courtesy Peabody Museum of Salem.*

The clipper *Flying Cloud* in a gale off Cape Horn. Oil painting by James E. Buttersworth. *Courtesy Pennsylvania Museum of Art, Philadelphia.*

McKay's masterpiece, the four-masted ship *Great Republic,* 3,356 tons, built at East Boston, 1853. Oil painting by James E. Buttersworth, *c.* 1853. *Courtesy Peabody Museum of Salem.*

Donald McKay's shipyard in East Boston, about 1855. The ship on the ways is unidentified. Daguerreotype by Southworth & Hawes. *Courtesy Peabody Museum of Salem.*

Loading guano at the Chincha Islands. *Courtesy Mystic Seaport.*

Many wound up bringing Indian and Chinese coolies to the British colonies, where slavery had been abolished, or — a still more unpleasant task — carrying guano from Chile. The later Down-Easters from Maine yards were equivalent to more moderate clippers, relatively fast but capable of carrying more cargo.

The one aspect of shipbuilding in which New England lagged behind New York and some outside regions was the building of steamers, and especially the manufacture of their engines and boilers. These were two separate operations, the machinery being fashioned in ironworks, where New York had a long lead. Even when New England yards built occasional wooden hulls, they were often sent down to New York to have their machinery installed. Boston had two such ironworks, Loring and Atlantic Works. Locomotive works such as those at Taunton and Portland also occasionally turned out marine machinery.

The Civil War

In few wars has there been such an uneven balance of maritime potential as in the American Civil War. The South had long been willing to let the North carry off its cotton and bring in from outside whatever it needed. In 1860 the Bath customs district in Maine built more tonnage than all the southern states from North Carolina to Texas together. Moreover, that Bath-Kennebec district and the adjacent Portland-Casco Bay district together owned almost as much tonnage as those states. As a consequence, New England coastal communities had great potential manpower to build ships and furnish crews for the navy. New England could provide over 2,000 shipmasters to the South's 118 and nearly 40,000 mariners and fishermen to less than 5,000 southerners with this experience. New England not only far outdistanced the South in tonnage owned but also, with five times as many skilled shipwrights, would have no difficulty maintaining its lead.

What made this maritime potential so important was the navy's huge task of blockading the whole three thousand miles of southern coast from Hampton Roads to the Texas-Mexican border. It was not a navy idea. It had come from a soldier — and a southerner at that. General Winfield Scott felt that, as part of his plan to strangle the South, a blockade would hinder southerners from swapping their cotton for British munitions. When Lincoln proclaimed the blockade, the navy was rather appalled by the idea, for it had only a few warships on hand — the rest were off on distant stations. The situation called for improvising some sort of an emergency force until enough regular vessels could be assembled to carry out the blockade duties.

The navy would probably have turned to New England anyway, but it was all the more inclined to do so because so many top wartime jobs at the Navy Department were held by New Englanders. At the head, as Lincoln's secretary of the navy, was one of the most effective men ever to hold that post. The bewhiskered Gideon Welles was a Connecticut journalist who had had pertinent experience as a civilian bureau chief during the Mexican War. At his right hand, as the first assistant secretary of the navy, was Gustavus Vasa Fox, a very able native of Boston. He had served as a regular naval officer until he resigned to manage a big new Massachusetts textile mill. The senior bureau chief was Joseph Smith from the Massachusetts South Shore, a regular naval officer who headed the Bureau of Yards and Docks from 1846 to 1869, an all-time endurance record. An old Connecticut schoolmate of Welles, Andrew Foote, another line officer, headed the new Bureau of Navigation until he was succeeded by Charles Henry Davis. A Bostonian, Davis had edited the *Nautical Almanac* and was the only senior naval officer to hold a Harvard degree. He and Smith were both on the special ironclad board which picked Ericsson's *Monitor.* Still another New Englander was Horatio Bridges, the paymaster general, who had been a classmate of Hawthorne and Longfellow at Bowdoin. One result of this Yankee influence was the wholesale bestowing of Indian names on the new warships, a practice that was not too popular afloat.

Even before new warships could be completed, there was an immediate need for existing vessels. Some of these served as temporary cruisers or gunboats, but New England's particular contribution was in transports. The Civil War was a period of rapid transition in naval development. It was quickly discovered that sail was no longer adequate for first-line action, and the growing importance of steam, with the consequent need for coal, called for novel logistical measures. Blockaders could not keep running north for coal; they would burn it all in transit. Port Royal in South Carolina was therefore captured in 1861 for use as a naval operating base. Little schooners, many from New England, brought down coal from Philadelphia. Two fast coastal steamers ran back and forth with mail and fresh provisions. Other steamers were needed as troop transports, since the North found it expedient, for its amphibious attacks along the southern coast, to move the troops by sea. One transport, the white side-wheeler *Governor,* long a night boat between Boston and Maine, succumbed to the gales off Hatteras. Altogether, the existing New England tonnage rendered valuable service.

There was, however, one striking exception to that usefulness. A navy planner had the brilliant idea that if some old whalers, loaded with stone, could be sunk on the Charleston bar, the port might be closed to blockade runners. Accordingly, some two dozen obsolete whalers were purchased by the navy at New Bedford, New London, and elsewhere and were loaded with rock. (This was virtually the only time when New England stone walls made a profit!) The Stone Fleet was sailed down to Charleston and sunk on the bar. But, in contrast to the hopeful expectations, the ships settled so far into the mud that the channel was deeper than ever.

The "Stone Fleet" whalers, which were filled with rocks and sunk in Southern harbors in a vain effort to prevent blockade-running. *Courtesy Kendall Whaling Museum.*

In addition to furnishing vessels already on hand, the New England coast lost no time in building new warships. Three programs for wooden, unarmored vessels went quickly into construction. New England's shipbuilding potential made it possible to complete their hulls with remarkable speed, though the engines and boilers generally came from elsewhere. New England private yards built eleven of the "ninety-day," 507-ton wooden screw gunboats. Two of these, the *Kineo* and *Katahdin*, built at Portland and Bath respectively, were launched in the first days of October 1861 and, after getting their machinery from New York, were commissioned at Boston Navy Yard in February. They then joined Farragut's fleet in forcing its way past the forts below New Orleans that spring. A second group were the twenty-one New England-built, paddle-wheel double-enders of 900 tons or more. Like the New York ferryboats which preceded them, they could operate in southern rivers without having to turn around. Third, and most impressive, were a group of substantial seagoing cruisers, rated as sloops of war, which slid down the ways at the navy yards in the fall of 1861. Of the fourteen built in New England, three became famous. The *Kearsarge,* built at Kittery-Portsmouth, later sank the Confederate raider *Alabama,* while the *Wachusett,* from Boston Navy Yard, captured the raider *Florida.* The third sloop, the *Housatonic,* also from Boston, was less fortunate; she was sunk by a submarine's torpedo off Charleston, a famous first.

In addition to those wooden vessels, New England turned out a dozen ironclads. The first, the *Galena,* was one of the three types picked by the original ironclad board. Built at Mystic, Connecticut, she was too easily perforated by enemy shot. Maine built one heavy monitor, the *Agamenticus,* and Massachusetts four others. Of the less adequate light-draft class, Maine built one and Massachusetts five. Altogether, including two miscellaneous vessels, the navy yards at Kittery-Portsmouth and Boston built twenty-six ships totaling 36,000 tons and the New England private yards thirty-four ships totaling 29,000 tons.

New England was also called upon for a heavy contribution in manpower — officer and enlisted, deck and engine. The personnel of the small, prewar navy could never have met more than a fraction of the swollen blockade needs in a navy that ultimately expanded to some seven hundred vessels of various sorts. The men who came in as volunteers had had in many cases considerable experience in ship handling, but there was much to be learned. Some of the seasoned prewar veterans could be distributed among the new crews for indoctrination and stiffening, but much improvisation was also necessary. Fortunately, the navy had a ritual and a hierarchy which provided for a certain amount of uniformity in the many aspects of running a ship.

Then and later, the navy would be niggardly in handing out volunteer-reserve rank to officers. In the army, men like N. P. Banks and Ben Butler became major generals straight from civilian life, but, as one congressman put it: "Every man is confident he could command a regiment, but most of them know that they could not command a warship." Consequently, acting-volunteer ranks were limited to lieutenant. (Even in the world wars, lieutenant commander was the highest a nonregular could start.) Some men, accustomed to merchant marine command, did not adjust easily to junior naval status — "Perk" Cressy of Marblehead, who had commanded the *Flying Cloud* on her two, record eighty-nine day runs to San Francisco, was in frequent hot water with authority. As for the volunteer engineers, Benjamin F. Isherwood, engineer in chief of the wartime navy, was asked why he designed such heavy machinery for the new warships. He replied that repair facilities would be few and far between and there was no telling what a green engineer might do to the machinery.

On the quantitative side of New England's personnel contribution, the figures are not as definite as those for shipbuilding, but they do show the enlisted totals up to the spring of 1864. At that time, New England had furnished 30,555 sailors and marines, which was almost identical with the 29,680 "mariners" and fishermen shown in the 1860 census. Massachusetts led with 19,983, followed by Maine at 5,030. New England's contribution came to some 27 percent of the national total. Among officers, 310 were appointed from Maine itself, and another 415 Maine natives were appointed elsewhere, especially at New York. The total for New England was 1,661, mostly deck officers. A large proportion of these officers and men spent their time on generally boring blockade duty, occasionally enlivened by a chase and possible prize money. Others were engaged in the usually frustrating pursuit of Confederate raiders.

New England's maritime contact with the war was not confined to building and manning the hunters. It also provided a painfully large number of the hunted. The South, for lack of resources, was unable to build up much of a combatant navy or a seagoing merchant marine, but it did manage to engage in a spectacular program of commerce destruction. There were only a few raiders — never more than four at sea at a time — but they left a trail of burning northern vessels all the way from Cape Ann out to the Straits of Sunda in one direction and the Bering Sea in the other. Altogether, some two hundred northern vessels were captured, a few by the early privateers but most of them by the regular raiders. About two-thirds of those vessels hailed from New England ports, with Boston and New Bedford suffering the heaviest losses, each with nearly forty victims. In addition to its own losses Maine had built some of the vessels hailing from Boston and New York; altogether, eighty-eight of the victims, almost half the total, were Maine-built.

Whereas rich cargoes on distant runs would later fall victim to the regular raiders, Maine victims were most numerous among those overhauled by the little privateers. The first capture of all was a Maine brig with lime from Thomaston, caught at the Mississippi bar by a towboat with her new letter of marque. Privateering faded out quickly as the blockade tightened. There were even threats in the North of trying the

The U. S. S. *Kearsarge,* which eliminated the C. S. S. *Alabama,* the scourge of Yankee shipping, and to them a pirate. *Courtesy U. S. Navy.*

crews for piracy. Those were the last privateers in history.

The raiding proper, however, dates from May 1861, when the *Sumter,* a medium-sized steamer from the New Orleans-Havana run, was commissioned by the Confederates and placed under the command of the most celebrated of the raiders, Raphael Semmes. While the northerners would denounce the *Sumter* and her successors as privateers or pirates, they were as legitimate belligerents as the forces of Robert E. Lee and Stonewall Jackson. Semmes eluded the Union blockading squadron at the mouth of the Mississippi late in July and took fifteen prizes in the next six months. His first victim was a Bangor ship, the *Golden Rocket,* the first of the many which he would burn:

> The decks of this Maine-built ship were of pine, calked with old-fashioned oakum, and laid with pitch; the woodwork of the cabin was like so much tinder, having been seasoned by many voyages in the tropics, and the forecastle was stowed with paints and oils. The consequence was, that the flame was not long in kindling, but leaped full-grown into the air.

That fate was shared by many a vessel from Maine or Boston. Semmes would naturally have preferred to send them in to be condemned for prize money, but the southern ports were blockaded and the governor of Cuba would not permit prize jurisdiction. Semmes finally disposed of the wornout *Sumter* at Gibraltar in April 1862.

By that time, a much more ambitious aspect of Confederate commerce raiding was well under way. In the summer of 1861, Theodore Roosevelt's uncle, Captain James D. Bulloch, had been sent over to London to persuade the British to build some first-class commerce raiders. Despite the continual protests of Charles Francis Adams, the United States minister, at such unneutral conduct, two of them, the future *Alabama* and *Florida,* were completed at Liverpool and slipped out to sea in 1862, to be armed and commissioned in distant ports — the *Alabama* under Semmes at the Azores, and the *Florida* under John Maffitt at Nassau a few weeks later. The *Florida,* its crew stricken with yellow fever, lay in Mobile for four months and did not go on its first patrol until early in 1863. The *Alabama,* on the other hand, went immediately into action, and in the next two years there were only four months in which she did not take at least one prize. The postwar *Alabama* Claims amounted to $6,500,000 on her fifty-eight victims (two-thirds of which were from New England), while the *Florida's* total score was $3,698,000 (including twenty-four New England vessels valued at $2,200,000) during approximately the same period. Altogether, captures were made by some forty vessels, including minor cruisers and privateers, but the British in 1872 agreed to pay only for damages by the *Alabama,* the *Florida,* and the *Shenandoah.*

The high-water mark of Confederate raiding came in the first half of 1863, just before the tide of war turned on land at Gettysburg and Vicksburg. The *Alabama* and *Florida* found a happy hunting ground where the South Atlantic narrows between the bulges of Brazil and West Africa. Through that bottleneck passed the richest wartime cargoes under the Stars and Stripes, on vessels following the old clipper routes around Cape Horn to California and around the Cape of Good Hope to India and China.

The heaviest of all the claims were those on two Massachusetts ships from beyond Good Hope, burned by the *Florida.* The *Star of Peace* of Boston, recently built at Newburyport, was bound from Calcutta to Boston with a cargo that included saltpeter for duPont gunpowder. The claims on her loss came to $480,000, just ahead of the $453,000 on

Confederate commerce-raider *Sumter*, under Capt. Semmes, taking the whaler *Eben Dodge* of New Bedford, February 8, 1862. The *Dodge* was burned, but the crew were set ashore. *Courtesy Kendall Whaling Museum.*

the tea cargo of the veteran *Oneida* of New Bedford, inbound from China. Almost as valuable was some of the general cargo on the Cape Horn run — a continuation of the original California clipper pattern, with scores of individual shipments. Semmes described one of these veritable department-store cargoes in the *Anna F. Schmitt,* built at Kennebunkport and bound from Boston to San Francisco. She had, he wrote, "ready-made clothing, hats, boots, and shoes. . . crockery, china-ware, glass, lamps, clocks, sewing machines, patent medicines, clothes-pins, and the best inventions for killing bedbugs." By no means all the ships intercepted there were carrying cargoes of such value; some were reduced to ladings of guano or coal. After taking nearly thirty prizes, with claims totaling nearly $4 million, in what Semmes called "the great Brazilian highway," the two cruisers left the area and headed in opposite directions, the *Florida* early in June for New England and vicinity, the *Alabama* a month later for African and Asiatic waters.

The Confederate bark *Tacony* preceded the *Florida* into New England waters and created a real panic in twelve days of mid-June, even

raiding the Gloucester fishing fleet. For some time the northern mercantile interests had been clamoring for protection against the raiders.
Now that cry reached a crescendo. Nearly forty Union warships were at
one time hunting the *Tacony,* so her commanding officer burned her
and shifted operations to the schooner *Archer,* bringing the war to its
closest contact with the New England coast. Boldly entering Portland
Harbor, he seized the revenue cutter *Caleb Cushing,* but she depended
on sail and the wind died down. Union troops and guns were put
aboard the Boston and New York steamers, which chased her. The
cutter's ammunition could not be reached because the lieutenant captured on board had hidden the key. The *Caleb Cushing* was therefore
blown up and the crew imprisoned. The *Florida* was also in that general
area, taking a few prizes.

The *Alabama,* in the meantime, was heading for distant eastern
seas. Off Cape Town, while crowds watched from the shore, she seized
the Boston bark *Sea Bride,* thereby winning lasting appreciation; a
century later the Malays of Cape Town were still singing "Here Comes
the *Alabama.*" Then, after one of her few long rests in port, she pro-
ceeded farther east. South of the Straits of Sunda, between Java and
Sumatra, she captured and burned the bark *Amanda* of Bangor, Maine.
Shortly after that, following his thrilling capture of two New York clippers, Semmes wrote of the terror inspired by his raiding:

> A very gratifying spectacle met my eyes at Singapore. There were twenty-
> two American ships there — huge Indiamen — almost all of which were
> dismantled and laid up. The burning of our first ship in those seas, the
> *Amanda* off the Straits of Sunda, had sent a threat of horror through all the
> Yankee shipping far and near and it had hastened to get out of harm's way.

Semmes returned to Europe and put into the French port of Cherbourg
to repair. On 19 June 1864 the *Alabama* was sunk by the pride of Kittery, the cruiser *Kearsarge.* The long-standing indignation at her "pirate" raiding was reflected on a souvenir plate brought out at Boston:
"Built in an English yard, of English oak, manned by an English crew,
armed with English guns, and sunk in the English Channel." Then, on 7
October, the *Florida* was located in the harbor of Bahia, Brazil, by the
Boston-built *Wachusett,* whose commander, frustrated by the constant
unneutral acts of the Brazilians and others, rammed and seized her and
carried her off.

Though the two main raiders had been put out of the way, two others inflicted considerable damage during the last year of the war. In August 1864 a very fast, London-built, former blockade runner, renamed the *Tallahassee,* followed the bold example of the *Tacony* and the *Archer* with a successful raid in New York and New England waters. Her captures ranged from a New York immigrant packet to little, lumber-laden Maine schooners. There were even Confederate plans to have her join in a wild raid to burn some of the Maine seaports. The consul at St. John, New Brunswick, sent down a warning, and some of the land-based Confederate guerrillas were captured when they tried to rob the bank at Calais.

The third of the "big three" Confederate raiders, the *Shenandoah,* undertook the task of destroying the northern whaling fleet in the Pacific. At that time, the Bering Sea was one of the standard whaling grounds, and Captain James I. Waddell found the New Bedford fleet there late in June 1865. On the first ship he encountered, he saw a San Francisco paper with the telegraphic announcement that Lee had surrendered but that General Johnson was still at large with an army in North Carolina. On the strength of that flimsy evidence he burned eighteen of the whalers — eight in a single day. He described that final sorry bonfire, just four years after Semmes burned the first Maine ship in the Gulf: "The heavens were illuminated with the red glare, presenting a picture of indescribable grandeur while the water was covered with black smoke, commingling with fiery sparks. Discharges on board often resembled distant artillery." Then he hastened for England, fearing that he might be held as a pirate if a Union cruiser caught him. The total claims of the *Shenandoah* victims were almost as high as those for the *Alabama.*

The major impact of the Confederate raiders had been psychological. They did not seriously affect the military conduct of the war beyond drawing away numerous cruisers which might have tightened the blockade. Only one Union vessel in a hundred that sailed in foreign trade during the war was captured. The real damage was done by the fear of capture, reflected in war-risk insurance rates, which ran as high as 8 percent at the height of the scare in 1863. This meant that a merchant had to pay $800 more to insure $10,000 worth of cargo shipped under the American flag than under a neutral flag. Semmes had noted the drastic effects of that scare at Singapore. In order to keep business for their ships, many northern shipowners used the Union Jack as a flag of convenience to save them from the raiders. This so-called flight from the flag reached drastic proportions as the war progressed. The tonnage shifting to British colors climbed from 71,000 in 1861 to a total of 921,000 tons, or about a thousand ships, by the end of the war. The celebrated *Flying Cloud* was "sold British" in 1862. About three hundred more vessels, including some of the finest ships in the American merchant marine, switched to other flags. Carl Cutler lists seventy-four clippers transferred to foreign flags between 1861 and 1865. Fifty-five of these vessels were New England-built, and forty-four were owned there. Boston had a striking share, having built thirty and owned thirty-four. In contrast, New York had built only eleven and owned twenty-two.

New England emerged from the conflict with only about half of its prewar registered tonnage. Vessels burned by the raiders were of course lost for good, while those which had shifted to other flags were never allowed to return to American registry. Boston, the principal victim, saw its registered tonnage fall from 414,000 tons in 1860 to 54,000 in 1865. At New Bedford the prewar tonnage of 141,000 shrank to 63,000. In terms of percentage New York escaped a bit more easily, dropping from 838,000 to 471,000. And as compensation for those losses in "navigation" New York had its continuing gains in exports and imports — a trend that would be maintained strongly throughout the century.

The war's end brought maritime New England's golden age to a close, although future generations of Yankees would find new ways to carry on old traditions of seafaring greatness.

IV

The Dark Age, 1865–1914

THE end of the Civil War in 1865 marked the beginning of the Dark Age for the American merchant marine in deep-water commerce. Shipping registered in foreign trade declined from 2.5 million tons on the eve of the war to 1.5 million tons six years later. In 1853, at the height of the clipper-ship boom, the tonnage of the American merchant fleet was about 15 percent greater than Great Britain's; by the end of 1866 it had fallen behind by over 30 percent. In the immediate prewar years American vessels had carried about two-thirds of all American foreign commerce. At war's end they carried less than one-third, and by the end of the century, less than 10 percent. The position of American vessels in general world trade was equally dismal.

As an important maritime center, New England bore the brunt of this decline. Many a Yankee youth with his heart set on following his father to sea had to look shoreward instead for his living. Only the coasting trade still offered an opportunity for a career in sail. Some New Englanders became steamboat men, while others swallowed their pride and earned a livelihood building, handling, and caring for yachts owned by the summertime sailors who had begun flocking to the New England coast.

Foreign Commerce

"It is a curious fact," stated the *American Sentinel & Times* of Bath in January 1867, "that at the present time there is not a single new merchant ship or steamer building at any of the numerous shipyards of either New York, Brooklyn, or Jersey City, and only two, it is said, in all the yards of the country." This seems to have been a garbled version of a report to the U.S. Commission of Navigation concerning shipyards in New York City and Boston. Had the Bath editors stepped outside and looked around their own city, they might have seen at least some of the twenty-seven vessels to be launched by Bath shipbuilders in 1867. But perhaps the editors took too literally the New England belief that only a full-rigged ship really counted as a merchant ship.

The immediate cause for the depression in American shipping was the raiding by Confederate cruisers. Not only had they destroyed many vessels, but their presence at sea had also inflated insurance rates and discouraged foreign shippers from using American vessels during the war. The effect had been to drive hundreds of owners to register their vessels under foreign flags. While some had been sold to foreign owners, others remained under American control, but after the war shipbuilding interests insisted that all these vessels be prohibited from returning to American registry. This would not be the last time that shipbuilders and shipowners opposed each other.

A rise in shipbuilding costs of at least 50 percent and the difficulty of obtaining skilled labor sharply limited the construction of replacements for these vessels. Labor rates in European and British North American yards had always been lower than in the United States, generally, but American management and the skill and energy of the American workman had nearly offset the advantage. Now the shift to iron in Europe and particularly in Great Britain and the use of cheap wood in Canada further decreased the cost of foreign-built vessels. Still another problem was the high American tariffs on imported copper, iron, hemp, canvas, and other materials required in constructing ships. In 1870, Representative John Lynch of Maine, chairman of the House Committee of Merchant Marine and Fisheries, recommended that these materials be admitted duty free and that a subsidy be granted to American sailing and steam vessels engaged in foreign trade. Much discussion ensued, but no action, for the western states, which dominated the federal government after the Civil War, were little interested in maritime affairs. Not until 1894 were Lynch's recommendations concerning tariffs adopted, and Congress never did approve a general bounty for American foreign shipping.

Another problem stemmed from the fact that Great Britain, the only major rival of the United States in maritime affairs, had used the Civil War to break up the regular and long-established American channels of trade. Nearly all the steerage passenger business on which American shipping depended greatly as well as the freight and first-class passenger business was being done by foreign steamers. The latter had been accomplished, seemingly unnoticed by the government of the United States, by the introduction of regulations, especially by Great Britain, bearing purposely and extremely hard on the passenger trade of American vessels. In January 1867 the *Portland Price Current* brought out another reason for the condition of the American merchant marine. "There is an utter destitution of system in the officering of our vessels, and the want of accountability in both officers and men which is rapidly deteriorating the whole merchantile marine of the country." Few of the officers were properly trained for their calling; they "came up like topsies." The owners suffered in the returns they should have received from their vessels and the underwriters suffered losses. The latter protected themselves by raising insurance rates, but neither they nor the owners made any attempt to have laws enacted and enforced to try to bring in a better class of men in all grades of the merchant service. It was not until 1898 that masters and chief mates of American sailing vessels of over 700 tons were required to have licenses for which they had to pass examinations. "Things have come to such a pass that not many young men of intelligence and character will continue in our merchant service," the article continued. "Numbers of them will make a voyage or two then abandon the service in disgust. Why? Because it has become the receptacle for the refuse of almost every nation upon the earth."

Shipbuilding and shipowning interests clashed again over the issue of "free ships." At the end of the Civil War only American-built vessels could be registered as American, with minor exceptions. Under a "free ship" policy, shipowners would have been able to obtain low-cost iron ships abroad; but shipbuilders, labor interests, and the navy combined to block any change until well into the twentieth century. At last, by the Ship Registry Act of 1914, any foreign-built vessel could be registered as American for foreign commerce; but by then the ubiquitous British tramp steamer, with its sturdy steel hull and triple-expansion engines, had taken over most of the routes formerly controlled by Americans in the days of sail. Steam's advantage was especially strong after

1869, when the opening of the Suez Canal provided a shortcut to Asia.

Despite the lack of a government subsidy, a group of Boston merchants formed the American Steamship Company in 1865 to compete with Great Britain's well-established Cunard Line, for which Boston was a major port of call. George W. Jackman, Jr., of Newburyport built two wooden, screw-propelled steamers for the company at a cost of $400,000. Named the *Ontario* and the *Erie,* the new steamers measured about three thousand tons, had three decks, and carried full ship rigs. For the *Ontario's* launching in November 1866, Newburyport's shops closed and special trains brought crowds from near and far. It was a gala occasion and a grand success: the vessel broke three twelve-inch hawsers, uprooted several trees, and stuck in the mud of Carr's Island in the Merrimack River. The *Erie's* launching during the following spring was more sedate. The *Ontario* made three transatlantic voyages, and her performance was said to be the equal of any Cunarder of the day. But no line, no matter how fine its vessels, could compete successfully against the heavily subsidized Cunarders. The *Ontario* lost so much money that she was soon laid up, along with the *Erie,* which never did go into her intended service. They were sold for $256,000 each in 1869.

A reduction in its mail subsidies led the Cunard Line to curtail much of its Boston service in 1868. Successful American sailing ship service, however, and the promise of grain by the Boston & Albany Railroad for return cargoes persuaded Cunard to restore regular service after April 1871. Other British lines also ran into Boston, and their steamers gradually came to dominate the foreign trade of Boston and other New England ports. In 1880 a total of 332 British steamers took cargoes out of Boston, and by 1910 over three-fourths of New England's foreign trade was carried in British bottoms.

Despite this preponderance of foreign vessels in its overseas trade, several ports within the region continued an active maritime life. Boston, together with its satellite waterfronts in Charlestown and East Boston, remained the nation's second busiest port (behind New York), although its $200 million worth of foreign commerce in 1910 amounted to only 6 percent of the country's total. Portland, Hartford, and Providence witnessed small but significant activity in foreign trade. Two other New England seaports, Bangor and Passamaquoddy, together boasted a foreign trade of over $6 million, but almost all of it was conducted by rail and other land transportation with Canada.

The Boston waterfront about 1890, with the Nantasket steamboat *Twilight*. Note the square-riggers and schooners moored across channel. *Courtesy William A. Baker.*

Immigrants landing in Portland, Maine, from S. S. *Oregon,* 1884, wash drawing by Fr. Goth. *Courtesy Peabody Museum of Salem.*

Boston's greatest import in the decades before World War I was raw wool from England and Australia for the mills of Massachusetts. The city was, in fact, the world's second largest wool market. Egyptian cotton fed other mills, while hides and other animal skins from India and South America came in for the state's tanneries. Undoubtedly the city's most interesting "imports" were its immigrants, averaging between 30,000 and 50,000 each year during the last decades of the nineteenth century and reaching a peak of over 100,000 on the eve of World War I.

Much of New England's trade during the period brought cargoes of wood pulp and fish in from the Canadian Maritimes in exchange for a wide variety of American products. A small but increasingly profitable trade in bananas marked the rise of the United Fruit Company (with headquarters on Long Wharf), one of Boston's most influential shipping firms during the first half of the twentieth century. Hartford specialized in the importation of raw and waste silk, mostly from France, while British steamers brought into Providence a variety of cargoes including cut stones and pearls. Significantly, the region was now importing raw materials rather than finished products, in contrast to earlier periods in its history.

New England's export trade amounted to little more than a third of its imports in value; and some ports, such as Hartford and Providence, exported next to nothing in return for their extensive imports. Cured leather from the tanneries of Massachusetts ranked first among the region's exports, along with bacon and ham, lard, and cattle. Boots and shoes dominated the meager list of finished products, for most of New England's manufacturers as late as 1910 found ready markets within the nation's borders. One fact had not changed: England was not only the region's greatest source of imports but also its leading foreign market.

Despite the dismal position of New England commerce during the Dark Age, the region's deep-water maritime interests were kept alive in at least two important ways. A number of New England shipowners sent their vessels to other parts of the United States in search of exportable cargoes, bringing back cargoes to ports outside of New England as well. Although owned in New England, these vessels rarely returned to their home ports. A Boston firm, William F. Weld & Co., in fact, owned the nation's largest merchant fleet during the latter part of the nineteenth century, but its Black Horse house flag, proudly flying from more

Deck view of the ship *Ice King*. Pencil sketch by Mrs. Marina L. Sargent, the Captain's wife, on a voyage from Sumatra and Java to Boston, *c.* 1879. *Courtesy Peabody Museum of Salem.*

than fifty square-riggers, was seldom seen along Boston's waterfront. John S. Emery's fleet specialized in the West India, African, and Australian trades, while the Charles Hunt Company was prominent on South American routes.

Despite initial post-Civil War difficulties, shipbuilding was New England's other main contact with deep-water commerce during the last decades of the nineteenth century. With the general rise in shipbuilding costs after 1865, the wooden shipbuilding industry gradually died out in the ports south of New England and became concentrated in the north, primarily in Maine. The increase in size of ships forced the closing of Medford's yards on the shallow Mystic River, but builders at East Boston and Quincy turned out a few for a number of years. Although many ports in Maine were active shipbuilding centers, the greatest concentration of yards was at the Kennebec town of Bath. There, for instance, the firm of Goss & Sawyer (later the New England Shipbuilding Company), built mainly on contract, while the Sewalls and other family firms built principally for their own use. Many yards in other towns constructed vessels primarily on contract, although when business was slow, they built a few on speculation and sailed them to Boston or New York for a market.

In spite of the increased cost of materials, most of which came from outside Maine, the state's shipbuilders were able to turn out relatively inexpensive ships for the deep-sea trades because of the excess labor supply. Generally speaking, the state was not affected by the clipper-ship boom; its builders continued to launch conservatively designed vessels in which carrying capacity was more important than speed. The population was relatively stable, and there were no competing industries; the labor supply was ample and unorganized. Although a few of the yards in the smaller ports worked from sun to sun, with two hours off in the middle of the day, most operated on a ten-hour basis. The rates of pay were about 25 percent or more lower than in the large urban areas to the south.

The principal product of the Maine shipyards from the end of the Civil War to the 1890s came to be known as the Down-Easters. These were large ships, ranging for the most part from two hundred to three hundred feet in length, of good model and excellent finish. They were the highest development of the wooden square-rigger. Unlike the earlier clippers, which had borne romantic names, a large number of the

The Down-Easter *A. J. Fuller*, built at Bath, Maine, 1881, under all plain sail. *Courtesy Bath Marine Museum.*

The famous ship *Henry B. Hyde*, 2,463 tons, built at Bath, Maine, 1884. Oil painting by W. Preston, 1891.

The Atlantic Works shipyard in East Boston, the steamship *City of Bangor* at left. *Courtesy Hart Nautical Museum, M. I. T.*

Down-Easters were named for their managing owners or builders, thus preserving a list of the men prominent in the last days of American deep-water sail. In appearance the Down-Easters resembled the earlier clippers, but they often had more sheer. Forward they had a curved stem with little decoration, while the stern was either rounded or had a light counter with an elliptical transom. At and below the load water-line they were much fuller than the clippers, and it might be stretching the definition to call them even medium clippers. Their ends were well formed, however, and they carried large cargoes. On the whole, the sail plans of the Down-Easters were relatively smaller than those of the clippers of the 1850s, but their large size gave them the power to carry sail in heavy winds, and many made passages nearly as fast as those of the extreme clippers. The *Henry B. Hyde,* built at Bath in 1884 by John McDonald in Flint & Chapman's yard, is considered by many the finest of the type.

No iron full-rigged ships were built in New England — and only three in the entire country — although the Atlantic Works of East Boston did construct the iron brig *Novelty,* a bulk molasses carrier, in 1869. The only steel square-riggers built in the United States were constructed by the Sewall Yard at Bath between 1893 and 1902. There were nine all told, none of which bore a resemblance to the wooden Down-Easters. The first was the 310-foot *Dirigo,* launched on 3 February 1894. She

The steel ship *Dirigo*, almost ready for sea. It was built by Sewall at Bath, Maine, 1894. *Courtesy Bath Marine Museum.*

The steel bark *Kiaulani*, built by the Sewalls at Bath, Maine, 1899. *Courtesy Bath Marine Museum.*

was essentially a British four-masted barque of her day, having been designed by J. F. Waddington of Liverpool, and all her plates and shapes were fabricated near Glasgow and sent to Bath by steamer. Seven other four-masters were slightly enlarged versions of the *Dirigo* but built of American steel. In spite of their rig, the Sewalls always referred to these vessels as ships since they had three square-rigged masts. The Sewalls' last steel square-rigger was the 226-foot bark *Kaiulani,* built for San Francisco owners in 1899.

Although the Sewall yard closed down in 1902, New England boasted two other major steel-shipbuilding yards at the turn of the century, the Fore River Ship & Engine Company at Quincy, Massachusetts, and the Bath Iron Works Ltd. on the Kennebec in Maine. Several

firms made iron and steel hulls, engines, boilers, and other ship machinery. Fore River grew out of a machine shop set up by Thomas A.
Watson, a founder of the Bell Telephone Company, who had retired
from that venture in 1881 to a farm on the banks of the Weymouth
Fore River in Braintree. Bored with the life of a gentleman farmer,
Watson hired a young machinist, Frank O. Wellington, and after several failures they built a fifty-horsepower compound marine engine
which led to several orders for both engines and yachts. In 1884 the
partners organized the Fore River Engine Company.

Barely weathering a prolonged depression in the yacht business
during the 1890s, the firm won a contract shortly after the blowing up
of the U.S.S. *Maine* in 1898 to build two torpedo boats for the navy.
Soon after, the yard built its first steel vessel, the lightship *Diamond
Shoals.* A contract to build the 3,000-ton cruiser *Des Moines* made expansion necessary, and the partners purchased a site at Quincy Point.
Among the vessels built during the company's first years in the new yard
were the seven-masted schooner *Thomas W. Lawson* and the battle-
ships *New Jersey, Rhode Island,* and *Vermont.* The Fore River Ship
& Engine Company, as it was renamed, soon became one of the nation's
three major shipbuilding yards. Supported until 1902 entirely by Watson's own resources, it needed financial assistance to carry out its expanded construction program, and control passed into the hands of
Boston interests. In 1913 it was taken over by the Bethlehem Steel
Company.

In its early years the Bath Iron Works was also dependent on the
financial resources of one man, General Thomas W. Hyde, who upon
his return from the Civil War purchased a small iron foundry, where he
developed the famous Hyde windlass and other marine machinery. In
1889 Hyde bought the defunct Goss Marine Iron Works and organized
the Bath Iron Works Ltd. to continue his manufacture of ship's machinery and to enter the shipbuilding field.

The company's first contract was for the wooden-hulled steamer
Cottage City; Hyde subcontracted the hull and concentrated on building her 1,400-horsepower, triple-expansion engines and four boilers. Like
the Fore River yard, the Bath Iron Works prospered on naval contracts,
building two gunboats and the armored ram *Katahdin* during its first
five years, along with the Sound steamer *City of Lowell.* A disastrous
fire in 1894 destroyed nearly all of the company's wooden shops, and

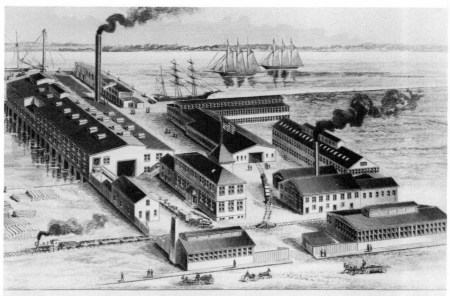

WORKS AT BATH, MAINE.

The Bath Iron Works, Bath, Maine, *c.* 1900. *Courtesy William A. Baker*.

The Boston-Bangor steamer *Camden,* built at Bath, Maine, 1907. Oil painting by Antonio Jacobsen, 1915. *Courtesy Peabody Museum of Salem*.

Bath's entire south end was saved only by an eighteen-inch blanket of snow. Contracts for small yachts and lightships saw the yard through the hard times that followed, and by 1900 brick shops had replaced those lost earlier. During these years the Bath Iron Works built five of the navy's fastest torpedo boats and, even more significant, the nation's first oceangoing tramp steamer. Thereafter, Bath built both naval and merchant vessels, including the steamers *Camden* and *Belfast,* both powered with Parsons steam turbines, for the Boston & Bangor Steamship Company.

Thus through shipbuilding did some New Englanders retain their main contact with deep-water commerce after the Civil War. When the crisis of World War I once more called the nation to a role on the high seas, New England would be ready to carry its share of the burden.

Coastal Commerce and Navigation

Although the period 1865–1914 was the Dark Age for New England's foreign commerce, it was a booming era for coastwise trade, from which foreign competition was barred. Sailing vessels carried heavy freight along the coast at rates competitive with the railroads. To most New Englanders living along the coast, however, it was the ubiquitous white passenger steamer that symbolized the region's continuing relation with salt water.

Apart from the town-to-town runs, steamboating in New England fell into two categories, the lines running out of New York on Long Island Sound to Connecticut and Rhode Island and those running down east out of Boston. In addition were three major direct services: between Boston and New York around Cape Cod, between Portland and New York, and between Boston and Canada's Maritime Provinces. Sound steamers generally connected New York City with one or another of New England's many railroads. Steamers into Bridgeport served the Housatonic Valley, while New Haven had its own lines to New York. Major landings along the Connecticut River became ports of call for Sound steamers on their way to Hartford in the post-Civil War period, while smaller vessels calling at the minor landings connected with the big boats at Saybrook. Groton on the Thames, Stonington, and Providence were particularly important points of connection with through trains to Boston.

All the Long Island Sound lines had their share of enthusiastic patrons, but in song, story, and fact there was nothing quite like the Fall River Line. Changes in its corporate ownership were confusing, and its Narragansett terminus moved from Fall River to Newport, to Bristol, and back to Fall River; but its reputation for regularity, safety, and fine boats was unsurpassed. In the late 1890s, when the New York, New Haven & Hartford Railroad Company consolidated the major Long Island Sound steamboat lines into the corporation that eventually became the New England Steamship Company, all the services were managed by personnel of the Fall River Line. From 1874, when records were first kept, until operations were suspended in 1937, only one passenger lost his life among the nearly 19 million carried.

The Fall River Liner *Pilgrim,* placed in commission in 1883, marked a conspicuous advance in safety at sea. She was the first American vessel built with a double hull of iron which, with six watertight bulkheads, gave the hull ninety watertight compartments in all. Her machinery and boilers were enclosed in a metal casing that extended to the hurricane deck. The *Pilgrim* was lighted by electricity and was equipped with probably the first electrically operated, automatic fire alarms and watchman's time detectors. She was also the first vessel to carry a crew especially trained in lifesaving techniques. These standards, maintained and improved through the years, culminated in the great 455-foot *Commonwealth,* built in 1908, which could carry 1300 passengers, a crew of 262, and over 100,000 cubic feet of freight. Propelled by paddle wheels, as were all the Fall River Line boats, the *Commonwealth* had a speed of about eighteen knots.

From the corporate point of view, down-east steamboating from Boston was considerably simpler than the tangled web of Long Island Sound companies. On the other hand, physical conditions were much more difficult, for the Gulf of Maine in a strong northeaster was not quite suitable for steamboats designed and built for smoother waters.

The Boston-Portland run was one of three principal routes to the coast of Maine. With origins well before the Civil War, the Portland Steam Packet Company operated a number of well-loved vessels along the run for many years. Perhaps the best known was the steamer *Portland,* built at Bath in 1890 by the New England Company with boilers by the Bath Iron Works and engine from the Portland Company. She

The S. S. *Providence,* built at Quincy, Massachusetts, for the Fall River Line to Boston. Oil painting by Antonio Jacobsen, 1915. *Courtesy Peabody Museum of Salem.*

The shipyard of the New England Company at Bath, Maine, *c.* 1890. *Courtesy Bath Marine Museum.*

The ill-fated steamer *Portland,* passing Portland Head Light. Oil painting by G. M. Hathaway. *Courtesy Peabody Museum of Salem.*

The S. S. *Kennebec,* in the Boston-Gardiner service, at wharf in Richmond, Maine. *Courtesy William A. Baker.*

gave her name to the famous storm of November 1898 when she sank off Cape Cod with the loss of all 176 passengers and crew.

Another service ran between the Kennebec River ports and Boston. The Kennebec Steamboat Company operated vessels as far as Gardiner and Hallowell, with smaller steamers running up to Augusta. Service was normally suspended during the winter months because of ice though an effort was briefly made at the end of the nineteenth century to provide a winter boat. The company's *Star of the East,* a 244-footer which had been in service since 1866, was rebuilt as the *Sagadahoc* in 1889 and was joined by the Bath-built *Kennebec* in the same year.

Penobscot Bay and the river had their own direct route to Boston, with Bangor, Belfast, and Rockland the major ports of call. Begun before the Civil War, the service went through several reorganizations in the postwar years before it was taken over by the Boston & Bangor Steamship Company in 1882. The *Katahdin* and *Lewiston* gave many years of dependable service, as did the *City of Bangor* and the *City of Rockland.* The latter wooden side-wheelers were replaced by a pair of steel-hulled, turbine-driven, triple-screwed steamers built by the Bath Iron Works, the *Camden* of 1907 and the *Belfast* of 1909. For a brief few years Bar Harbor also had direct connection with Boston, as did Machias and Eastport. But for the most part the coast east of Penobscot Bay relied upon smaller lines working out of Rockland, which was served by rail as well as steamer connections with Boston.

Strictly speaking, the steamer runs from New England to the Maritime Provinces were part of American foreign commerce, but they in fact began as extensions of coastwise services. In 1860 backers of the Portland Steam Packet Company helped found the International Steamship Company, which operated between Boston, Portland, and ports in New Brunswick and Nova Scotia. For a time the same group ran another line from Portland to Halifax and St. John's, Newfoundland. Still another service linked Boston and Yarmouth until after the outbreak of World War I.

A consolidation of major significance took place in 1901 when Charles W. Morse, a native of Bath, combined the Portland Steam Packet Company with several other major lines out of Boston to form the Eastern Steamship Company. Morse had already amassed a fortune by cornering the ice market in New York before he turned to banking and shipping. His ambition was to control coastal shipping from Maine

The S. S. *State of Maine,* built at Bath, Maine, 1881, for the Boston, Portland, Eastport to St. John service. Oil painting attributed to Antonio Jacobsen, 1915. *Courtesy Peabody Museum of Salem.*

The Boston–New York steamer *Harvard,* built at Chester, Pennsylvania, 1906. Oil painting by Antonio Jacobsen, 1906. *Courtesy Peabody Museum of Salem.*

to Texas (he was known for a time as the "Admiral of the Atlantic Coast"), and he came very close to achieving his goal. In 1906 he purchased the Metropolitan Line on the New York-Boston run and was challenged by the New Haven Railroad's Merchants Line. Morse retaliated with two magnificent 23-knot steamers, the *Harvard* and the *Yale,* which covered the 330-mile route around Cape Cod in fair weather or foul in fifteen hours. When he tried to buy out the New Haven's Long Island Sound lines, President Theodore Roosevelt was so worried about the possible consequences that he persuaded the railroad's executives not to sell. Although Morse was jailed in 1910 for bank fraud, after his release he managed to resume his controversial career for ten more years.

Boston and later Providence also became terminals for long-distance coastwise steamers linking New England directly with Philadelphia, Baltimore, and Savannah, among other Atlantic ports. Both passenger and freight service were provided. The Merchants' & Miners' Line and Sprague, Soule and Company, both founded before the Civil War, were the principal houses involved. F. W. Nickerson & Company of Boston organized a Boston-Savannah Line in 1869 which was incorporated in September 1882 as the Boston & Savannah Steamship Company. At various times other lines connected Boston and Providence with several southern ports. In addition to these regular freight lines, cargo steamers of a number of companies brought cargoes from various Atlantic and Gulf coast ports; a few companies operated from the Pacific coast around the tip of South America until the opening of the Panama Canal in 1914.

Interwoven with this web of steamer lines were literally hundreds of sailing coasters of varying sizes plying New England waters during the years between 1865 and 1914. Although a few large sloops and even some brigantines sailed as coasters, the fleet was composed principally of schooners ranging in size from 50-foot two-masters to the 395-foot seven-masted *Thomas W. Lawson*. Photographs can convey only the static situation when twenty or thirty large, coal-laden schooners might be anchored in Holmes Hole (now Vineyard Haven) awaiting a favorable wind. Gone forever are the sounds — the creaking blocks, the slatting sails, and the chuffing of hoisting engines when all tried to leave at the same time as the wind came fair from the southwest. There was then a great race across Nantucket Sound and around the Cape to Boston and Portland, for the last vessel to arrive might have to wait a week or two for her turn to unload at the wharf.

Following the Civil War, the growth of the cities and towns of New England created an almost insatiable demand for lumber for the construction of dwellings, shops, and factories. The lumber came largely from Maine, where Bangor and Stockton Springs were important shipping ports, and from the southern states. Some of the best southern oak and hard pine went to Maine for the building of more schooners to carry lumber and other commodities to the big cities.

It was the growing market for bituminous coal, however, that created the greatest demand for schooners in increasing numbers and size. New England's waterpower no longer sufficed to operate all the new mills and factories, which now turned to coal for fuel. As the network of railroads expanded, more coal was also needed for their operation. Coal provided gas for illumination and household cooking, but the general shift to electricity during the period required even more coal for the central generating plants. Another shift which added to the electrical load was that from horsecars to electric cars on street railway systems. Finally, the general growth of the population meant that more anthracite coal was required for heating dwellings, stores, and business offices.

While many schooners sailed exclusively in the coal trade, going south light, others looked for a southbound cargo. Maine ice from the Kennebec River and from countless natural and manmade ponds provided one important return. From a total of about 30,000 tons shipped in 1860, the ice business grew to nearly 30,000,000 tons in 1890. By 1910 the business was practically ended, however, because the monopolistic operations of Charles W. Morse had led to the rapid development of artificial ice machines. During the heyday of the business, large icehouses practically lined both banks of the Kennebec from Richmond to Hallowell and dotted the Maine coastline.

Before the days of Portland cement, a very special material for making plaster was the lime burned in the kilns of Thomaston, Rockland, and Rockport and shipped in casks in tight little two-masted schooners. When a schooner's seams got too weary for this exacting trade, she often carried lumber out of Bangor; and it was said that when she grew too old for even that, she was put to work carrying building stone. But the last is a bit of an exaggeration, as some schooners were specially constructed for the trade, with large hatches and an uncommon spacing

Windbound schooners in Portland harbor, *c.* 1900. *Courtesy Peabody Museum of Salem.*

Ice schooners ready to load at the Independent Ice Company's storage house. *Courtesy Capt. W. J. Lewis Parker.*

The stone schooner *Annie & Reuben,* of Stonington, Maine, loaded with granite blocks. Note the stone boom on her deck load. Watercolor by John F. Leavitt.

The five-masted schooner *Governor Ames,* built at Waldoboro, Maine, 1888. *Courtesy Hart Nautical Museum, M. I. T.*

of masts. A good example was the two-master *Annie & Reuben,* launched at Bath in 1891, which sailed the coast for about fifty years.

The production of granite for a variety of uses was an important business in Maine for years, and abandoned quarries may be found from Blue Hill to the islands of Casco Bay. In Massachusetts, Quincy and Rockport were important granite-producing centers. Some fine large sloops were developed for the trade out of Rockport, and others sailed from Chebeague Island in Casco Bay.

Another well-known building material — brownstone — was quarried at Portland, Connecticut, and shipped out in a variety of craft via the Connecticut River and Long Island Sound. It may still be seen here and there in most large New England cities, but it was particularly favored for the façades of dwellings in what is now midtown New York, the famous brownstone fronts.

At first, two-masted schooners carried almost all of the coastwise cargoes. As late as 1864 only 39 three-masted schooners were documented, but the growth of the coal trade after the war stimulated the construction of the larger vessels. There was a practical limit to their size, however; the largest was the 920-ton *Bradford C. French,* launched by David Clark at Kennebunkport in 1884. The year 1879 saw the first four-masted schooner, the converted steamer *Weybosset,* and 1880 the launching at Bath by Goss & Sawyer of the first schooner built as such, the 996-ton *William L. White.* About 460 of the type had been built when the last four-master was launched in 1921. The largest was the Bath-built, 2,015-ton *Frank A. Palmer* of 1897.

To reduce the size of the sails required on the largest of the four-masters, the obvious move was to add a fifth mast. The first schooner so rigged, the 1,764-ton *Governor Ames,* was built at Waldoboro in 1888. She was dismasted on her maiden voyage, and it was ten years before another five-master was launched. In all, fifty-six five-masted schooners were built, all but four of them in Maine. The largest, the 3,138-ton *Jane Palmer,* was built at East Boston in 1904; she was originally intended to have six masts.

The inevitable step to six masts had been taken with the launching in 1900 of the *George W. Wells,* by John J. Wardwell at Camden, Maine. She was followed in two months by the slightly larger, Bath-built *Eleanor A. Percy.* In 1901, when they were the only six-masted schooners in the world, they collided on a summer night off Cape Cod;

although damaged, both made port safely. Only nine wooden six-masters were built, all in Maine and seven by Percy & Small at Bath. The last and greatest was the Bath-built *Wyoming* of 1909; of 3,730 tons measurement, she loaded on one occasion at Newport News a total of 6,004 tons of coal.

Only three steel schooners were built in New England. In 1902 the Fore River Ship & Engine Company built the world's only seven-masted schooner, the *Thomas W. Lawson,* and the six-master *William L. Douglas* followed the next year. The Sewall yard launched the five-masted *Kineo* at Bath in 1903.

Even while the sailing colliers were increasing in number and size, there were signs pointing to the end of their usefulness. Between 1869 and 1874 the Reading Railroad Company, a large owner of anthracite mines, had built a fleet of 14 iron steamers to transport its coal to New England, mainly to Boston. In 1880 it was noted that each vessel of this fleet made between thirty and thirty-five trips a year. Hence the total amount of coal delivered was between 450,000 and 500,000 tons —a quantity that might have required the services of from 150 to 250 schooners, which averaged little better than a dozen trips a year.

All but one of these steam colliers was still in service in 1902, but after 1874 the Reading turned to the construction of tugs and barges, an example followed by the owners of several other large anthracite mining companies. Many fine down-east square-riggers were cut down and ended their days on the ends of towlines, while large wooden barges fitted with abbreviated schooner rigs were built for the coal trade. The first steam colliers for the bituminous coal trade did not appear until 1907, when the New England Gas & Coke Company put the *Everett, Malden,* and *Melrose* in service.

Up to the end of the nineteenth century, the operating of a schooner was largely a community enterprise with many persons holding shares. A share was usually considered to be 1/64, but in some cases a person might own as little as 1/256; a managing owner rarely held more than 5/64 in any one schooner, but he might be managing the affairs of several at a given time. The excellent financial returns of most of the sailing colliers eventually attracted much capital from Massachusetts and important investors throughout the country, leading to fleet operations. In spite of this trend toward big business, each new schooner continued to be financed separately by shares, with the exception of

The six-masted schooner *George W. Wells*, built at Camden, Maine, 1900. *Courtesy Peabody Museum of Salem.*

The schooner *Thomas W. Lawson,* on the ways, Fore River Ship and Engine Company, Quincy, Massachusetts, July, 1922. *Courtesy Hart Nautical Museum, M.I.T.*

The coal barges *Lonestar* and *Oakland* under tow by the tug *Underwriter*, 1888. All three could and did spread sails with a fair wind. *Courtesy Hart Nautical Museum, M. I. T.*

those owned by the Coastwise Transportation Company of Boston. This company was formed in 1903 by Captain John G. Crowley, who had had his first command in 1877 at the age of twenty-one and nine years later was sailing his own three-master out of Taunton, Massachusetts, an important center in the bituminous coal trade. The company prospered and turned to steam colliers in 1910–11.

An unusual fleet was that managed by William F. Palmer, a Boston schoolteacher who decided in 1899, at the age of forty-one, to enter the shipping business. He had studied naval architecture while teaching in Taunton and subsequently designed all but two of the fifteen schooners he operated during the first decade of the twentieth century. Most of them were five-masters, the last of which was launched in 1908. An unusual series of marine disasters haunted the Palmer fleet throughout its history, thirteen of the vessels being lost at sea through collision, fire, shipwreck, and even submarine attack.

In design and construction the post-Civil War coastal passenger steamboats were developments of the prewar boats, growing larger and providing more amenities as the years passed. Side paddle wheels continued as the favored form of propulsion for the passenger boats, while screw propellers became fairly common for the smaller freighters. Above a relatively shallow hull — there was a draft restriction at one end or the other of most runs — the superstructure outline swept out to enclose the paddle wheels, forming a spacious deck for freight and some of the passenger accommodations. The overhang of this deck was supported by diagonal braces from the hull, which helped, not always successfully, to break the force of the waves. Not until the early 1880s did builders begin to sheathe over these struts to form watertight sponsons. At about the same time, heavy girders and bracing were incorporated in the main hull structure to replace the prominent external trusses, known as hog frames, which were always in the way, particularly on the freight deck.

Prior to the Civil War it was common practice for the down-east lines from Boston to employ steamboats originally built for Long Island Sound runs. After the war, boats were built specially for the runs out of Boston. These tended to have somewhat deeper hulls, which improved their seaworthiness and also affected the arrangement of passenger accommodations. Throughout the steamboat era in New England, the purchaser of a passage ticket was entitled to a berth in the ladies' or gentlemen's cabin. These were essentially dormitory spaces; stateroom accommodations were available at an extra charge.

Although the arrangement of passenger spaces varied somewhat from boat to boat, that of the 256-foot *Kennebec* built at Bath in 1889 was typical. Aft on the main deck was the ladies' cabin, a large compartment in the center of which was a steam radiator, flanked by great mahogany sofas upholstered with dark red plush. Along each side were 5 "apartments," each containing 6 berths, the entrances to which were hung with green and white figured curtains of raw silk. On the lower deck, forward of the boiler room, were the dining room and the gentlemen's cabin, fitted with 177 berths. Freight was carried on the main deck forward of the machinery space.

The main companionway leading from the main deck up to the saloon divided at the top to port and starboard. On the bulkhead over the landing was a heavy French plate mirror set in a massive frame of gilt and bronze, "a handsome piece of furniture." The saloon was a large compartment with sixty staterooms along each side, each fitted with two berths. It was decorated with cherry-stained pilasters, alter-

nating with light buff panels and a narrow horizontal strip of fancywork
in gilt and soft purple. The arched roof was a dome that projected
above the hurricane deck, and the sides of the projection were fitted
with figured glass panels. The carpet on the saloon deck was a light-
figured Axminster, and the easy chairs and sofas were of mahogany
upholstered with dark red plush. Three electric chandeliers illuminated the saloon, but oil lamps were provided for emergency conditions.
On the hurricane deck were the pilothouse and the officers' quarters.

In contrast to the large paddle-wheel passenger steamboats, the
ordinary freight boats and many of the general-purpose boats on runs
where speed was not important were propeller-driven. Because of its
space advantage, however, they had the same type of overhanging main
deck as the paddle steamers. Right after the Civil War, the machinery
in most of the propeller-driven boats consisted of two cylinders, taking
steam at boiler pressure, connected to one shaft; each cylinder and its
mechanism was considered as one engine. During the 1870s and 1880s
the expansive force of steam began to be utilized, first in compound
engines, in which steam from a high-pressure cylinder is exhausted to
a low-pressure cylinder, and then in triple-expansion engines employing three and sometimes four cylinders. When the large, screw-
propelled passenger steamboats such as the *Richard Peck* were built,
they were fitted with triple-expansion engines driving twin screws.

The majority of paddle-wheel steamboats were fitted with the simple, economical, and long-lasting working-beam (commonly but erro-
neously called "walking-beam") engines. Such engines turned the
paddle wheels at about twenty revolutions per minute. Paddle-wheel
propulsion had the advantage of developing immediate full power
astern, a definite aid in crowded waters when many landings had to be
made on a tight schedule.

The coastal steamships on long exposed runs, such as those operated
by the Merchants' & Miners' Line, had regular seagoing hulls without
the overhanging main deck of the steamboats. Built primarily for the
carriage of freight, the immediate post-Civil War ships had limited
passenger accommodations, often just a single long deckhouse. By the
1900s provisions for passengers were quite extensive, with perhaps two
levels of deckhouses above the main hull. Up to the turn of the century,
most of the coastal steamships and a few of the steamboats running down
east from Boston were fitted with sails for use in emergencies. The

Long Island Sound steamboats dispensed with sails quite early.

As for the sailing coasters, two basic hull forms were employed after the Civil War. One was a true coaster type having a relatively shallow hull capable of carrying large deck loads; the ends were short, sharp, and well formed. The other hull type can best be described as that of a typical deep-sea, medium clipper ship having great depth of hull. Many of the shallow-hulled coasters were fitted with center-boards; even the first five-masted schooner, the *Governor Ames,* had one. In large schooners the centerboard was a substantial item, being from twenty to thirty feet long and six to eight inches thick. Wooden centerboard cases eventually develop leaks, however, and when this happened on the large schooners, the boards were removed to the detriment of sailing qualities.

As the sailing coasters gradually lost the freighting business to steam, they turned almost exclusively to bulk cargoes, and the well-formed hulls of the 1860s and 1870s were displaced by straight-sided deep vessels having short entrances and runs. The four-, five-, and six-masted schooners had this almost standard form; they varied only in dimensions and in the small trademarks of individual designers. Under certain conditions the large schooners were quite fast, but their small crews — one-half to one-third the number required on a square-rigger of equal tonnage — construction, and rig did not permit hard driving. Small crews were feasible, as from about 1885 on it was common prac-tice to install a donkey engine and boiler for weighing anchor and hoisting sails. A schooner so equipped had nearly half a day's advantage, when getting under way, over one which depended on the brute force of the crew. From the practical point of view, the development of the small coasting schooner ended in the middle 1880s, although many con-tinued to be built up to World War I. The development of the big schooner ended about 1910, when steam vessels were constructed for the bituminous coal trade.

Fisheries

Any mention of New England fishing immediately brings to mind the bankers out of Gloucester, schooners designed to fish from Georges (originally St. George's) Bank out to the Grand Banks of Newfound-land. The main catches of the New England fishing schooners were cod,

halibut, and mackerel, the first two taken with trawl lines set from
dories, while mackerel, a schooling fish, was caught with seines. In 1891
the first modern, ketch-rigged fisherman, the Essex-built *Resolute,*
joined the Gloucester fleet to experiment with the English method of
beam-trawling, that is, dragging a net along the bottom. Because of
frequent damage to her gear and the low prices for the catch, she was
rerigged as a schooner the following year after only four trips and employed as a dory fisherman.

Gloucester, though the leader of the fishing industry, was far from
alone, for schooners operated from most of the ports of Massachusetts
and Maine. Boston had a sizable fleet and was the great marketing
center. About half the seafood products shipped from Boston were consumed in New England, about one-fifth in New York State, and the
remaining three-tenths in Philadelphia, Baltimore, Washington, and
points south and west. Fresh seafood was shipped in boxes or barrels
well covered with ice, while the rest was dried, pickled, frozen,
or canned.

The history of the New England fishing schooner is currently under
revision, being stripped not only of myth and romance but also of some
long-cherished "facts." The reputations of some Gloucester skippers
for hard driving which resulted in frequent loss of life apparently
came from their efforts to live up to the stories written by James B.
Connolly, author of *Out of Gloucester* and other yarns. And instead of
an orderly improvement in size, speed, and general qualities, changes
came about by whim and economics, and progress varied considerably.

The basic New England fishing schooner, from the end of the Civil
War to the middle 1880s, was of the so-called clipper model, which resembled the then-popular schooner yacht in form but had a deep struc-
tural keel in place of the centerboard. The bow was long and sharp,
and the stern was wide with heavy quarters; the freeboard was
relatively low. The clipper-model fisherman carried a lot of sail and
was very fast, a quality important in a vessel trying to get iced fish to
market. Older schooners were still employed in the salt fish trade, in
which speed was not necessary.

But by the 1870s it was already apparent, from the heavy loss of
vessels and lives, that something was wrong with the design of the clipper schooner. Caught by a squall under full sail or tripped in heavy seas
because of its fine bow and full stern, the schooner could not recover

from a large angle of heel and either capsized or swamped. During the next decade Captain Joseph W. Collins, a former Gloucester fisherman who had joined the U.S. Fish Commission, began a campaign for better and safer fishing schooners. In 1884 the noted Boston designer and builder Dennison J. Lawlor built an improved, deeper schooner which he named the *Roulette* and which proved to be fast and weatherly. Toward the end of that decade Edward Burgess designed the *Fredonia,* a vessel so successful that the Fredonia model remained popular well into the 1900s. Thomas F. McManus's Indian-headers and B. B. Crown-inshield's *Rob Roy* represented still further improvements.

New England fishing schooners were built in just about every conceivable location, from a well-established shipyard to a fisherman's backyard that might be a fair distance from the water. In the latter case, neighbors with many yoke of oxen and a liberal supply of "grease" in the form of New England's favorite liquid refreshment, rum, moved the vessels to tidewater with surprising ease. Whenever the building of fishing schooners is mentioned, however, one small town comes first to mind — Essex, Massachusetts, far up a small winding river. There the families of Adams, Burnham, James, Oxner, and Story built a large percentage of the fishing fleet, as had their predecessors since a shipyard site was set off by the town in 1668.

Steam power was first employed in the New England fishing fleet in the menhaden fishery out of Boothbay Harbor, Maine, about 1871, and by 1888 there were fifty-five steamers operating in this business. The menhaden being inshore fish, only short trips were necessary, for which steam (and later the internal combustion engine) was quite suitable. Because of the speed of the large schooners in getting iced fish to market, steam was slow to be adopted in the offshore fisheries. In 1905, however, the Fore River Ship & Engine Company built the 136-foot, steel steam trawler *Spray* from plans obtained in England by a Boston group. She was so successful that four more were built in 1910–11 and another four in 1912–13. While cod, halibut, and mackerel continued to be the important fish, the successful introduction of trawling meant that other species were more readily available in the markets.

From the end of the Civil War to the introduction of the internal combustion engine in the early 1900s, New England saw the final development of many fine small sailing craft for the inshore fisheries, including those for herring, lobsters, and oysters. The various type names

The knockabout fisherman *Helen B. Thomas,* built at Essex, Massachusetts, 1902. *Courtesy Hart Nautical Museum, M. I. T.*

Fishermen under construction at Essex, Massachusetts. *Courtesy Peabody Museum of Salem.*

Friendship sloop, lobstering about 1884.

are almost a geography lesson, but because most were employed along a fair extent of the coastline, there was considerable overlapping. At the western end of Long Island Sound were shoal-draft New York sloops, which also operated as catboats, and Bridgeport had some fine sloops for oystering. New Haven and Fair Haven had the flat-bottomed sharpies said to have been developed from large dugout canoes, and on the Connecticut River were "drag boats" for shad. Farther east was the Noank sloop, a more seaworthy development of the New York sloop.

Rhode Island is best known for the two-masted, keel Block Island "cowhorn," but there were also Newport catboats, and the so-called Providence River boat was employed all over Narragansett Bay. On the Massachusetts coast were the No Man's Land boat, the Cape Cod cat, the Kingston and Hull lobster boats, various dories between Boston and Cape Ann, and the large Gloucester sloop boats. New Hampshire had the so-called New England whaler and the Isles of Shoals boat, which seems to have been known at nearby Newburyport as a shay.

The best known of the small Maine fishing boats today is the Friendship sloop, which is having a strong revival in the world of yachting. Almost forgotten, however, is her predecessor, the Muscongus Bay centerboard sloop. Other small fishing boats employed along the Maine coast, starting in the west, were the Hampton boat of Casco Bay, the

Crotch Island pinky, the closely related Monhegan and Matinicus boats, peapods in considerable variety, and two sizes of double-ended Eastport pinkies, or Quoddy boats.

In addition to the sloops around Bridgeport and the sharpies at New Haven, there were some fine centerboard schooners employed in the Long Island Sound oyster fishery; they were basically of the Chesapeake Bay model. Steam power was introduced in the oyster business about 1876. The oyster beds off the Connecticut shore covered many thousands of acres, and the business was pursued as with dry land crops, with regular planting, cultivating, and harvesting. The empty shells from one season's crop were planted in beds to which the spawn could adhere. Copper wastes entering the Sound from the many brass factories on the rivers in the western part of the state turned the oysters green, so that it was necessary to dredge and replant them in cleaner waters to eliminate the color before marketing them three or four years later. Often the replanting was done in beds off the north shore of Long Island. An alternative solution, prohibiting the factories from polluting public waters, made little headway.

The many shallow bays and salt ponds of Cape Cod also produced oysters; Wellfleet was an important center for the business. Many of the Cape Cod oyster schooners were keel vessels employed in the mackerel fishery during the summer, but there were also a number of centerboard schooners. The early schooners of the latter type were brought from the Chesapeake, but during the 1880s some were built at Essex, Massachusetts.

While fishing implies the presence of water, the digging of soft clams from one end of New England to the other depended on its temporary absence. Clams could be dug along almost every part of the shoreline as the tide receded, and small boats of many descriptions served to transport diggers to productive offshore flats uncovered at low tide. Clams were important primarily as bait for other fisheries. The hard-shell variety, the quahog (or whatever local spelling one prefers), were taken by long-handled rakes from small boats in shallow bays and off beaches seldom if ever uncovered at low tide.

Another type of fishing that depended on the tide was trap, or weir, fishing, which was important during this period from the tip of Cape Cod along the shore to eastern Connecticut. The traps were formed by securing nets to an outline of poles driven into the soft bottom. Fish

Oystering in Long Island Sound; at left, a steam dredge; at right, New Haven Sharpies.

guided in through a narrow entrance at high tide were harvested at low tide. Many an unwary yachtsman came to grief in these traps on dark nights. Along the Maine coast similar methods were used to trap large schools of herring.

We cannot leave the inshore fisheries without mention of two other New England delicacies, the bay scallop and the lobster. Scallops were taken by dredging in shallow bays and harbors; the important grounds ranged from Niantic Bay around the shores of Cape Cod. Lobsters were once so plentiful along the rocky ledges of the Maine coast that one Vinalhaven fisherman reportedly caught nine hundred in one day, mostly picking them up by hand. By the turn of the century, lobsters were generally trapped in underwater pots, a method that continues to this day.

At the end of the Civil War the depleted New England whaling fleet, owned mainly in New Bedford, was in no position to compete with the growing petroleum industry. Because of high prices there was a brief revival immediately after the war, but the price of oil soon fell, and only the demand for bone kept the remaining fleet at sea. The main whaling grounds of this period were the Bering and Arctic seas, and many New England-owned whalers outfitted on the Pacific coast; at one time in the 1890s, more were sailing from San Francisco than New Bedford. In 1871 thirty-four whalers were crushed in the Arctic ice, and 1876 saw the loss of twelve more. After several other disasters, auxiliary steam whalers were built, the first being the *Mary and Helen,* built at Bath in 1879 for William Lewis of New Bedford. The first steam whaler, however, had been the *Pioneer,* a converted transport, which sailed from New London on 4 June 1864 and returned on 18 September 1865, yielding $151,000 net.

As might be expected in a dying industry, relatively few new sailing whalers were built. A few of these were schooner-rigged, and some fishing schooners were converted for the business. The last vessel specially built for whaling was the brigantine *Viola,* launched in 1910 at Essex, Massachusetts, by John James & Son. She sailed from New Bedford on 5 September 1917 and disappeared without a trace.

Danger at Sea

With the great increase in coastwise traffic after the Civil War, both sail and steam, improved marking of the coastal channels was slowly carried out. The modern yachtsman familiar, for instance, with the many buoys and beacons in Hingham and Quincy bays off Boston Harbor probably does not realize that few of these aids to navigation existed before 1885. In that year the Boston Marine Society petitioned the Congress for a harbor light on Pemberton Point in Hull and for buoys to mark the channels to Hingham, North Weymouth, Quincy Point, Weymouth, and other sections. It was noted at the time that over a million passengers were carried annually by steamers to and from Hull, Nantasket Beach, Downer's Landing, and Hingham and that large quantities of coal, lumber, granite, and fertilizing materials were transported in sailing vessels through the various channels of these bays. Many other busy waterways along the New England coast were also in need of buoys. Lacking them, shipmasters and pilots sailing in these waters learned their trade the hard way, often with disastrous results if the bottom was rocky. They had to depend on an intimate knowledge of currents, reefs, and sandbars, with only landmarks, easily obscured by rain and fog, for guidance.

The early American lighthouses were equipped first with tallow candles and later with groups of simple oil lamps; there was no method

Boon Island Light House, Maine, marking one of the off-shore lights on the New England coast. Oil painting by Clement Drew, 1878. *Courtesy Peabody Museum of Salem.*

of differentiating one lighthouse from another, but they were so few that this was not important. Weak though they were by modern standards, any light was a great boon to seamen. About the time of the War of 1812, crude lenses were added to some of the lighthouses, and the Argand lamp came into use. A major advance came in 1841, when the first French-made Fresnel lens in the United States was installed in the Navesink Highlands Light at the entrance to New York Harbor, and ten years later Nantucket's Sankaty Head Light was similarly equipped. Because of their superiority Fresnel lenses were installed in all lighthouses during the next few years.

With few exceptions the major light stations on the New England coast had been established long before the Civil War. These were improved from time to time, and in a few cases the towers were rebuilt after the war. One of the new stations was the Block Island Southeast Light, built in 1875. Another was on The Graves off Boston Harbor, which had been marked by a bell buoy since 1854. The growing use and improvement of the North Channel through Broad Sound brought about the lighting of these dangerous rocks in 1905. The important lighthouse on Race Rock at the eastern entrance to Long Island Sound, the scene of many disasters, was not lighted until 1879.

Further aids to navigation along the coast for both night and day sailing were the light vessels. The first in America was built in 1823 to mark Carysfort Reef off the coast of Florida, and the second was moored off Cape Hatteras in 1824. At the end of the nineteenth century, New England waters had sixteen lightships, eight of which marked the channels through Vineyard and Nantucket sounds around Cape Cod. Difficult as it was, the convenient channel for the southbound ice and lumber schooners and the northbound coal schooners lay through those sounds, for the only alternative was to sail far offshore around the poorly charted Nantucket Shoals. In the boom year 1883 nearly twenty thousand vessels passed the Cross Rip light vessel in Nantucket Sound; the yearly average during the 1870s and 1880s was about thirteen thousand.

There were times, however, when none of these aids to navigation could be seen, when the navigator's worst enemy — fog — came "on little cat feet." Cannon and hand-rung bells had long been employed as fog signals; the latter were used in a few cases even into the early twentieth century. Air whistles and horns operated by hand or horse-power were tried in the early 1850s; later, steam and hot-air engines were employed for power. In October 1865 at New Haven, Connecticut, extended tests were made with bells, steam whistles, the "steam gong," or double whistle, and the air-operated reed Daboll trumpet. Further tests were conducted in other places, principally to check the phenomenon of "ghosts," or silent areas. In one case a vessel grounded one-eighth of a mile from a siren which was barely heard, if at all, on board but was clearly heard fifteen miles away. By the early 1870s, mechanical fog signals had been installed at most of the major New England light stations. Bells, mechanically rung, were used on many minor coastal, harbor, and river stations and retained in service until comparatively recent years.

The first practical system for wireless telegraphy through the atmosphere was devised in the 1890s by the Italian Guglielmo Marconi. In 1901 the first wireless station in America was established on Nantucket. Four years later its operators received word from the South Shoal lightship of a serious leak. Its crew became the first mariners rescued by

Perkins Island Light and Fog Signal, Kennebec River, Maine. *Courtesy William A. Baker.*

Marconi's invention. In 1909 the Nantucket wireless station helped save over fifteen hundred passengers and crew aboard the liners *Republic* and *Florida,* which had collided south of the island. Earlier schemes for utilizing the conductance of water were not neglected, and in 1905 the Boston Marine Society urged the U.S. Lighthouse Board to put into use the invention of the Submarine Signal Company for conveying warning sounds through the water.

In spite of all these aids to navigation, vessels were wrecked and the U.S. Life-Saving Service came to the rescue. This famous service was an outgrowth of the activities of the Humane Society of Massachusetts, which was organized on 6 January 1786 and incorporated in 1791. Its first effort to aid shipwrecked mariners was the erection in 1787 of huts on Marshfield and Nantasket beaches and on Lovell's Island in Boston Harbor. By 1841 the society had sixteen lifeboat stations along the coast of Massachusetts from Martha's Vineyard to Newburyport. The first federal lifesaving station in New England was established at Watch Hill, Rhode Island, in 1850, and other stations followed. Until 1871 the boats were manned by volunteers when in service, and from 1854 on keepers were appointed to care for the equipment. During all this time the service was under the control of the U.S. Revenue Marine Bureau.

In 1871 the Congress appropriated $200,000 to put the Life-Saving Service on a secure and permanent basis and authorized the Secretary of the Treasury to employ crews of surfmen at such stations for such periods as might be found necessary. Then began a long period of building and equipping stations. For New England, one station in Rhode Island and nine stations for Cape Cod were authorized in 1872; in the following year five new stations were established in Maine, one on the New Hampshire coast, five more in Massachusetts, and another for Rhode Island. Other stations were added from time to time as their need was demonstrated. In 1878 the Congress passed an act establishing the Life-Saving Service as a bureau separate from the Revenue Marine Bureau. Gold and silver medals were authorized for those who risked their lives saving others.

The basic feature of the service was the nightly patrol from sunset till dawn in fair weather and foul. Where stations were close to each other, as on Cape Cod, patrolmen from adjacent stations met at half-way shelters, exchanged identifying tokens, and retraced their steps; at isolated stations there were specific boundaries for each patrol. If a patrolman spotted a wreck, he burned a red flare called a Coston light, to assure those on board that aid was at hand and then hurried back to his station to arouse his comrades. A specially built surfboat weighing about a thousand pounds and mounted on a carriage was then hauled — by horses, if available, or by the men — along the beach to the place of the wreck and launched. At times three or four capsizings occurred before the surfboat was able to reach the wreck and take off the crew. When the surf was too heavy to permit launching, a breeches buoy was rigged, if possible, to rescue the shipwrecked crew one at a time through the surf.

After the Life-Saving Service had done its duty and a storm had subsided, the wreckers, legal or otherwise, took over. The term was somewhat unfortunate, as it was the job of the legal wreckers to try to salvage a wrecked vessel and its cargo. Many ships were successfully gotten off with cargoes intact, but at times the cargo had to be removed in lighters before attempts could be made to salvage the hull. Local inhabitants, however, often left little for the legal owners of a ship and cargo, particularly when a ship broke up and her cargo was scattered along the beach. Although frowned upon by the law, such wrecking

Launching the Plum Island Life-Saving boat into the surf, Plum Island, New-buryport, Massachusetts. *Courtesy Peabody Museum of Salem.*

activity was considered a respectable occupation in many seaside communities. On Cape Cod and elsewhere there are oral traditions of "mooncussers" — those who cussed on clear, moonlit nights when they could not show false lights to lure ships on shore, where they would be waiting to strip the vessels as soon as they hit.

Of the thousands of shipwrecks on the New England coast — and there are said to have been over 3,000 on the outer beach of Cape Cod alone — the greatest number lost at one time occurred during the *Portland* Gale of 26–27 November 1898. In all, 141 vessels were wrecked during this storm and over 456 lives lost. Not only did this gale wreck vessels, but at many points the shoreline was changed, even to the opening of a new mouth for the North River in Plymouth County, Massachusetts, an alteration that would have been a boon to shipbuilders on the river had it occurred one or two centuries earlier. Only slightly less destructive was the gale of 25–26 November 1888, when 15 vessels were wrecked between Scituate and Boston. Some old seamen have said that this gale was stronger than the *Portland* storm.

During both these storms and on countless other occasions, Hull's famous lifesaver, Captain Joshua James, was active. Holder of seven gold and silver medals, Captain James was awarded his first in 1850 as a volunteer for the Humane Society. In 1889, at the age of sixty-two, he was appointed keeper of the new Point Allerton Station of the Life-Saving Service, the age limit of forty-six being waived because of his reputation. During the 1888 gale he and his crew were said to have rescued 29 men in twenty-four hours from five vessels that met disaster, and during the thirteen years he served as keeper they reportedly saved 540 lives and over $1 million worth of vessels and cargo. Captain James died on 17 March 1902 as he stepped ashore from a practice run in the surfboat; in February 1970 the main building of the new Coast Guard station at Hull was dedicated in his honor.

Along with better aids to navigation and the Life-Saving Service came the dredging of various harbor and coastwise channels, the creation of harbors of refuge, and, after many years of debate, the Cape Cod Canal. While many of the improvements of New England harbors consisted mainly of dredging natural channels and building breakwaters to protect wharves and anchorages, Boston Harbor received two new main channels. By 1892 the main channel through the Narrows between Georges and Lovell's islands had been dredged to a depth of twenty-seven feet. Between 1892 and 1905 the United States Army Engineers dredged what is now known as the Broad Sound South Channel to a depth of thirty feet. The Broad Sound North Channel, the present main channel into Boston Harbor, was dredged between 1902 and 1916.

A proposal in 1882 to build a breakwater and create a harbor of refuge at Rockport on Cape Ann led to a serious menace to navigation that still traps the unwary. Construction was started in 1885 on what was to be a 9000-foot-long breakwater, but by 1894 only 200 feet of the superstructure was completed. The closing of the Cape Ann granite quarries led to suspension of the work in 1912 after about $1.5 million had been spent. Only about 6000 feet of foundation had been laid and about 600 feet of superstructure completed. No provisions were made to secure the latter, and some of it has tumbled down.

Of all the channels along the coast, perhaps the most difficult was that around Cape Cod into Nantucket Sound. The Monomoy and Nantucket shoals in this region were the ones that turned back the *Mayflower* in 1620. There were two channels around Monomoy Point — the so-called Monomoy Passage through Pollock Rip Slue and Butler's Hole, with a deep-water channel joining the two; and the Main, or South, Channel between the Monomoy and Nantucket shoals. The Monomoy Passage was the shorter but more difficult, as the Slue and Butler's Hole were only about half a mile wide with minimum depths of about twenty-seven feet. Proposals were made early in the twentieth century to improve this passage for the large coal schooners and many steamers then using the route. The dredging of a channel was started in 1912 and continued to the beginning of World War I.

The difficulties connected with sailing around Monomoy Point made the possibility of a canal across Cape Cod an attractive proposition. The advantages had been noted by Samuel Sewall in 1676 and the General Court of Massachusetts in 1697. The subject came to life again in 1776, when the General Court appointed a committee to determine the practicability of a canal with two double locks at each end and two bridges. The federal government investigated the possibility of a canal in 1818 and 1824 but took no further action. In 1860 the General Court appointed another committee, which reported favorably on a canal, pointing out that 10,000 vessels sailed around the Cape annually and that in seventeen years there had been 827 marine disasters in the region. In 1883 the Cape Cod Ship Canal Company began the project but ran into financial difficulties. Later the Boston, Cape Cod, and New York Canal Company, backed by August Belmont, received a charter to build and operate a toll canal, and work was resumed in June 1909. The final cut of a sea-level canal was made on 4 July 1914, and on the thirtieth the canal was opened to vessels drawing less than fifteen feet. Subsequent improvements still did not attract sufficient vessels to make the operation profitable, however, and the canal was taken over by the federal government during World War I.

The New England Playground

The sea was no playground to those who wrested their daily living from it, but to city dwellers the ocean was quite attractive on a summer day, and after the Civil War more and more took advantage of New England's great asset. As had the Indians for centuries, people flocked from their inland homes to seaside resorts to battle the "no see 'ums" and the larger mosquitoes and to partake of clams, oysters, and lobster, although they left no great shell heaps to match those of the Indians. In this summer movement to the sea, urbanites were aided by the spreading railroads, the trolley-car lines, and of course the steamboats. Among prized possessions today are the elaborate brochures published by various transportation companies extolling the virtues of this or that locality and its hotels.

On Long Island Sound most of the cities had some kind of seaside amusement park which was easily reached by a trolley-car line or small steamer. Summer colonies grew along the many beaches, and a considerable number of wealthy New Yorkers constructed elaborate summer establishments along the banks of the lower Connecticut River. Many now famous but long-gone hotels catered to those who came by steamer for a night, a week, or even a month. Religious camp meetings were held at Tylerville, a musical seminary flourished for a time at East Haddam's Upper Landing, and the Opera House at Goodspeed's Landing just below featured the best Broadway and Metropolitan talent. This activity was blighted for a time in the 1870s when a plague of malaria followed the building of the Connecticut Valley Railroad. Even families in modest circumstances and the militia joined the trek to the sea. One of the old-time summer residents has told of starting out as a boy in the 1890s at 4:00 A.M. in a carriage behind a sleepy horse for the eighteen-mile trip from Colchester to a cottage at Niantic, where the Connecticut National Guard then went and still goes for its summer encampment.

Providence was the center for a large fleet of excursion steamboats in the 1870s, 1880s, and early 1890s. Daily trippers arriving by railroad joined the local inhabitants on the steamers, which sailed every half-hour loaded to the guards. Bullock's Point, which became Crescent Park, and Rocky Point were popular spots for clam chowder and other seafood; both also featured roller coasters, merry-go-rounds, and the like. Other chowder places were Field's Point, Boyden Heights, Riverside, Vanity Fair, Pleasant Bluffs, and Mark Rock. Some steamers sailed to the quieter resorts on the lower part of Narragansett Bay. At Newport the curious boarded two-horse sightseeing wagons for tours past the houses of the fashionable rich, while the drivers recited the latest scandals. The majority of the Newporters rarely emerged for their drives until late in the afternoon, when the last of the trippers had sailed for home. As many as fifty thousand excursionists patronized the Providence River and Narragansett Bay steamboats on a Sunday or holiday. Some of the more hardy trippers, willing to brave a bout of seasickness, took a steamer out to Block Island. Service there two or three times a week during the summer from Providence was started in the 1870s, with daily service beginning in 1895. The island also had steamer connections with New London and Norwich.

Martha's Vineyard, a whaling center in the eighteenth century, became a popular summer resort by the 1860s. The Methodists had established a summer campground there in 1835 at Cottage City (later renamed Oak Bluffs). To handle the summer visitors, a three-foot-gauge railroad was completed in 1874 from Oak Bluffs through Edgartown to Katama; the latter faded out as a resort about a decade later. In 1892 a big hotel at Oak Bluffs burned and along with it the railroad's pier. The last trains ran in 1896. The main business of Nantucket shifted in the mid-nineteenth century from whaling to summer visitors, and it too had a narrow-gauge railroad for their convenience. This line was opened in 1881 from the town of Nantucket to the south-shore resort of Surfside and reportedly carried thirty thousand passengers during that summer. Extended to Siasconset in 1884, this railroad passed out of existence in 1910.

Steamboat service from the mainland to these islands was provided by two companies at the close of the Civil War, one from New Bedford and the other from Hyannis. In 1872, a railroad extension was completed to Wood's Hole, which then replaced Hyannis as a terminus. The companies merged in 1886 as the New Bedford, Martha's Vineyard & Nantucket Steamboat Company. This in turn became part of the New Haven Railroad system in later years.

Boston's big summer beaches were — and still are — Nantasket on the South Shore and Revere to the north. A look at certain sections of any of many towns around the shores of greater Boston Harbor, however, betrays their beginnings as summer colonies; even the outer islands were well settled. To be among the elite in Boston after the Civil War, one had to have a summer house at the shore, or go to the White Mountains, or stay at one of the fashionable hotels — say, the Old Colony House at the head of the harbor in Hingham; or the Atlantic, or Pacific, or Rockland Houses on the lower end of Nantasket Beach; or the Hotel Pemberton on Windmill Point in Hull. The latter, one of the fabulous hotels of the era, was a three-story wooden building of over a hundred rooms, surrounded by wide, triple-deck piazzas; its roof line showed a variety of gables, towers, and minarets. The establishment was complete with wine vaults, an illuminating-gas plant, billiard tables, and "a bar of generous proportions." There were two band concerts daily, and on every Wednesday and Saturday evening there was a brilliant display of fireworks.

Most of the patrons of these hotels sailed from Boston on the boats of the Boston & Hingham Steamboat Company. Set up in 1831 as a general transportation company, it gradually became a line for summer commuters and excursionists. Patrons of the Nantasket Beach hotels, in the years right after the Civil War, went over by stage from Hingham; there were also stages from Hingham to Scituate and Marshfield. By the early 1880s there was a channel for steamboats up the Weir River to the back side of lower Nantasket Beach, and a railroad had been built from Hingham along the beach to the Hotel Pemberton. In 1881 the Boston & Hingham Steamboat Company divided into two separate companies, but they merged again nine years later as the Nantasket Beach Steamboat Company, with the beach as its principal port of call.

In 1854 Samuel Downer of Dorchester purchased a large tract in Hingham, including Crow Point and Otis Hill, on which to build an oil

The S. S. *Gen'l Lincoln, c.* 1886, in the Nantasket Beach–Boston service, a typical protected-water passenger steamer. *Courtesy Hart Nautical Museum, M. I. T.*

refinery. It was said that he had refused to join in an oil business with a young bookkeeper from Cleveland named John D. Rockefeller because he did not approve of the latter's ruthless methods. The site proved unsuitable, however, and beginning in 1870–71 he turned Crow Point into a pleasure park, which he named Melville Gardens after his wife. Downer provided Melville Gardens, the most famous picnic-resort in the harbor, with all manner of means for summer enjoyment — groves, shaded walks, ponds for rowing, bath houses, bowling alleys, shooting galleries, croquet lawns, billiard halls, a bear pit, a monkey cage, a dancing pavilion, a café, and a clambake pavilion where eight hundred persons could partake of clams "cooked in the genuine and unmodified manner of Rhode Island." Very special were twenty electric lights to illuminate the gardens at night. Downer occasionally brightened the quiet summer Sundays with what he called lay sermons for the visitors to the Gardens. On the tip of Crow Point he built the Rose Standish House, a luxurious summer hotel, and three wharves; the Hingham Yacht Club now occupies the site.

The New York Yacht Club squadron off Newport, Rhode Island, 1872. *Courtesy Hart Nautical Museum, M. I. T.*

Crow Point epitomized the family day-resort so popular all along the coast at the turn of the century. Steamboats made frequent trips to and from Boston, band music floated out over the water, and merry throngs filled the Gardens for years.

After the *Portland* Gale of 1898 destroyed the steamboat wharf in Hingham's inner harbor, the boats of the Nantasket Beach Steamboat Company never again negotiated the winding channel between the islands. They continued, however, to land commuters and others at Crow Point; from there the inevitable trolley-car line provided transportation to other parts of the town.

Bostonians bound north for Revere Beach had no steamboat service to their pleasure spot. They could only cross the harbor on a ferryboat which connected with the trains of the Boston, Revere Beach, & Lynn Railway, a narrow-gauge steam line, later electrified. There were, however, other steamboat lines from Boston that offered excursionists their choice of Plymouth, Provincetown, Salem and Beverly, or Gloucester. A drive along New England's coast from Boston to Portland takes one through numerous other famous summer colonies, many of which were well established before the Civil War — those on Cape Ann, on New Hampshire's Hampton and Rye beaches, and on Maine's York and Old Orchard beaches, to name but a few. Along the Maine coast east of

Portland, until the coming of the automobile, only the towns with steamboat service had a sizable influx of summer visitors. By the turn of the century there was quite a network of local steamboat lines running down rivers from railroad terminals or connecting with the main steamboat lines to Boston.

Each of these resorts — and every other spot along the coast — had its enthusiastic supporters, who returned year after year and were far from bashful in extolling the virtues of their favorite. A typical fan was Joseph W. Smith of Andover, Massachusetts, who wrote in 1887:

> There is no resort on the whole Atlantic coast that Biddeford Pool is second to as a summer watering place. I speak from my own experience, and my readers will pardon me if my enthusiasm runs strong in this direction. Having visited various sea-shore resorts from Maine to Florida, I find that there is something lacking in them that gives to life the pleasures and joys that I find at the Pool. Although the hotels do not compare with those at Cape May, Long Branch, Newport and Nantasket, in splendor and fine appointments, yet they are all kept on a good principle, and one is very sure to get what he pays for. Those who seek a quiet retreat, away from the turmoil and bustle of the city, cannot fail to find at the Pool that quiet and rest they need; and those who are fond of deep-sea fishing, boating and bathing, are sure to find a place that has no superior in this direction.

Two unusual resorts grew from this summer rush to the sea — Newport and Bar Harbor. Social life at Newport started in colonial days; apart from certain hot springs attended as medical resorts, it is probably the country's oldest summer resort. Its growth after the Civil War came from the service of the Fall River Line and the spread of yachting. The waters off Newport were ideal for sailing, the town soon became the destination for cruising New Yorkers, and the New York Yacht Club began holding its annual regatta there. This interest in the town led to the building of fine summer residences along the ocean and to the development of the famous Ten Mile Drive on which to show one's self, horses, and carriages. Regardless of their size, sumptuousness, and corps of servants, these summer residences at Newport were simply "cottages" to their owners. Matrons vied with one another in giving dinner parties for which, if short of male guests, they could draw on personnel at the Naval War College, which had been established at Newport after the close of the Civil War. With all the parties, driving, yachting, and naval activities, Newport was a gay place.

In contrast to long-established Newport, what was to become Bar Harbor was known only to the native farmers, fishermen, and seamen until 1844, when Thomas Cole, founder of the Hudson River school of painting, visited Mount Desert Island. Other artists, sportsmen, and yachtsmen followed; the first long-term summer boarders came in 1852. Steamboat service was disrupted during the war, but afterward the earlier vacationers returned with their families, establishing a pattern followed by their children and grandchildren.

William Cullen Bryant described the future town of Bar Harbor in 1869:

> The Village of East Eden, while possessing a charming lookout over the bay, is without one feature of beauty. It is built upon a treeless plain, and consists for the most part of a group of small white houses, rapidly extemporized for the accommodation of summer boarders. Every structure, with the exception of a few cottages erected by wealthy gentlemen of Boston, stands without trees, garden or any other pleasant surroundings.

In addition to describing the town, this quotation reveals a bit of its nomenclature: the permanent residents owned "houses," while the summer folk, the rusticators, had either "camps" (if plain and un-sheathed inside) or "cottages" (if sheathed). As at Newport, some of the "cottages" were rather elaborate.

Up to 1884 the only convenient way of reaching Mount Desert Island involved a considerable trip by boat. Portland and Rockland were the main ports of embarkation, but in 1882 a service was established from Bangor. In 1884 a railroad extension was completed from Bangor through Ellsworth to Mount Desert Ferry, on Hancock Point, from where it was only a short ride on the steamer *Sebenoa* or her successors to Bar Harbor. The daytime, all-Pullman Bar Harbor express from New York began service in 1887.

Mount Desert Island at first attracted people of individuality who liked getting up for a 7:00 A.M. breakfast, who wanted nothing more than to walk, fish, or go on picnics, and who enjoyed intelligent, literate fellow guests. For the few who might complain, a standard rejoinder was "You came for a change, didn't you?" These "boarders" were the families of clergymen, college professors, and the like. Then came the "cottage" builders, who wanted and eventually obtained the typical re-sort trimmings — a water supply, electricity, tennis courts, golf courses,

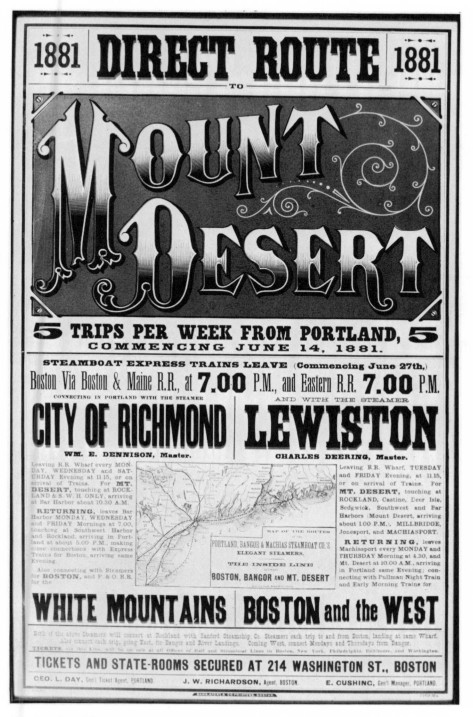

Poster advertising coastal service from Mount Desert to Boston and the West, via the "Steamboat Express Trains" in 1881. *Courtesy Benjamin W. Labaree.*

Bar Harbor, Maine, *c.* 1900. Note the summer hotels and the pinky second from left. *Courtesy William A. Baker.*

yacht races, and clubs. Some boarders became cottagers, and some cottagers built camps on Blue Hill Bay to get away from the rigors of cottage life. In spite of these changes, special manners and customs were preserved through the years. Thus in 1878 an observer wrote:

> There is much life and gaiety in the season at Mount Desert and the visitor will find the same varied society usually seen at watering places; the bad element excepted. There is much sociability amongst the people at the hotels and less regard is paid to the strict conventionalities that prevail at many summer resorts.

The final group to come to Mount Desert Island during these years were those fleeing the complications of cottage life at Newport. These refugees, of course, built equally sumptuous cottages at Bar Harbor.

In catering to the summer visitors, the natives piled up considerable profits, for in addition to work in the summer, the cottages required caretakers during the winters, and there were always odd jobs in opening them each spring. As might be expected, relations between the rusticators and the natives varied from social snobbery to a careful appraisal of qualities. The natives were too busy during the summer to worry about their treatment by the summer folk, but they stored up all the gossip and intrigue for their own social times during the winter; they would never admit to knowing anything during the summer season.

Yachting

The degree of leisure and wealth so essential to the development of yachting was not attained by the citizens of the Atlantic seaboard until after the first third of the nineteenth century, and even then there were not many nautically minded sportsmen who could take the needed time. On the other hand, many seaside residents, owners of small craft employed in commercial pursuits, often used their boats for a pleasant afternoon sail. Thus quite early there was a distinction between yachting and boating.

No people were ever more advantageously situated for enjoying the ocean than those who dwell on the Atlantic seaboard of the United States north of the Virginia capes. The shores of Maine present one of the most interesting marine areas to be found on the North American continent; the deeply indented coastline and numerous islands afford an endless variety of scenery. Moving south, there is good yachting and boating between Cape Ann and Cape Cod, where the waters are generally smooth in summer and harbors are available every few miles. South of Cape Cod is Nantucket Sound, a large, semienclosed body of water, full of shoals through which the tide rushes with considerable speed. The winds here are fresher than those north of Cape Cod. Next comes Buzzards Bay, with fresh, even strong, winds unbroken by islands; at times it can be too rough for pleasure-sailing in small craft. Many consider Narragansett Bay a sailor's paradise, as winds can be strong while the numerous islands prevent a buildup of waves. The waters directly south of Narragansett Bay have been since 1860 the most favored spot on the coast for yacht racing. The winds off Newport are usually fresh and constant, and the tidal currents are moderate, so that little advantage can be had by one familiar with the waters over one who is not.

About twenty miles west of Narragansett Bay is the entrance to Long Island Sound, an expanse of water over one hundred miles long with an average width of fifteen miles. Winds are lighter on the Sound than on the bays to the eastward, and on some racing days in midsummer they are practically nonexistent at the western end. New York harbor was also once a fine place for sailing, but the growth of commercial traffic finally made pleasure boating anything but pleasant. (Although New York is not properly within the limits of this survey, the activities of New York yachtsmen on Long Island Sound and waters farther east are so important that some developments in New York yachting must be included.)

As with many other things, the course of American yachting was interrupted by the Civil War. When peace came and money was more plentiful, sport of all kinds was more popular than in the country's earlier days, and yachting came in for its share of the general prosperity. At the close of the war Cape Cod formed a natural division between types of yachts. To the north of the Cape, yachtsmen favored staunch, seagoing craft. To the south, centerboard skimming dishes predominated because of the influence of New York, where anchorages available to yachts were quite shallow.

Some fine, large schooners, both centerboard and keel, suitable for long-distance racing were built for New York yachtsmen right after the Civil War. On 11 December 1866 two of them, the *Fleetwing* and the *Vesta,* with the older *Henrietta,* sailed from New York in a race to England for a stake of $30,000. The *Henrietta* won, sailing 3,106 miles in 13 days, 21 hours, and 55 minutes. The building and racing of large yachts in match races for high stakes continued until nearly 1880. The capsizing of the large centerboard schooner *Mohawk* in July 1876 with the loss of five lives, while she was riding at anchor off Staten Island with her sails set, had a strong deterring effect on the building of such vessels. Other factors influencing the decline of the schooner were growing interests in polo, horse racing, and smaller, sloop-rigged yachts.

In the smaller classes, "sandbaggers" were the common type — sloop-rigged craft in which stability to carry a press of sail was obtained from a number of sandbags, which had to be shifted to the weather side at each tack. Length overall was the only measurement for rating such boats. A typical sandbagger measured twenty-one feet both on deck and on the waterline, carried about eighteen hundred square feet

Sandbaggers off New London. *Courtesy Mystic Seaport.*

of sail, and had a crew of nine heavyweights, usually professionals, who were the moving spirits behind eighteen hundred pounds of sandbags. Such a boat was capable of high speed in smooth water with the proper breeze, but if the wind lightened during a race, the sandbags and sometimes a few of the crew went over the side. The type died as soon as shifting ballast was prohibited, but professionalism in yacht racing continued for many years.

In 1864 the two young Herreshoff brothers, John B. and Nathanael G., began a yacht-building business at Bristol, Rhode Island, and by 1872 they had turned out many successful sloops and schooners. In 1872 Nathanael, the younger brother and the designer, brought out the thirty-seven-foot sloop *Shadow*, which was not beaten for sixteen years. She was the first yacht built on what was later known as the compromise model, combining the breadth of the American centerboarder with the depth of the English keel type.

The sloop yacht *Shadow,* designed and built by N. G. Herreshoff, 1872. *Courtesy Hart Nautical Museum, M. I. T.*

Most of the progress — or at least change — in American yacht design can be attributed to two factors, the defense of the *America*'s Cup and changes in measurement rules. In July 1857 the Royal Yacht Squadron Cup, won by the schooner *America* in 1851, was given by her owners to the New York Yacht Club as a perpetual challenge cup. The simple deed of gift, revised and made more complicated in 1882, led not only to important yacht racing but also to strife of the bitterest kind.

The first two matches for the *America*'s Cup, seen from this distance in time, were farces. An English yachtsman, James Ashbury, opened negotiations for a match and was finally granted one race over the New York Yacht Club's course off New York Harbor in 1870. Ashbury's schooner *Cambria* finished tenth against a fleet of seventeen American yachts. The schooner *Magic* won, and the *America*, completely rebuilt and rerigged, placed fourth. Ashbury built a new schooner, the *Livonia,* for a second try in 1871. This match was a bit more sporting: it was set up as the best four out of seven races, with the

Livonia meeting only one boat in each. The New York Yacht Club, however, named four schooners as defenders, both light- and heavy-weather types, and reserved the right to select one on the morning of each race according to the weather. The defending schooner *Columbia* took the first two races but lost the third to the *Livonia;* the defender *Sappho* won the fourth and fifth races, which ended the match.

The measurement rules of the period, together with time-allowance tables, were devised in order that yachts of different sizes and types might race together. From the end of the Civil War to 1882 several rules were employed in the United States: the length-times-breadth rule, a cubical-contents rule, and a mean-length rule. In none of these was sail area measured; and shallow, wide, overcanvassed yachts were favored. In Great Britain, on the other hand, the measurement rule at that time favored long, narrow, deep craft with large chunks of outside ballast. The majority of English racing yachts were rigged as cutters, with a boomed but loose-footed gaff mainsail, a topsail, and three triangular headsails; the bowsprit could be brought in on deck. The American sloops, in contrast, had a gaff mainsail whose foot was laced to a boom, a topsail, and usually one but sometimes two triangular headsails set on a fixed bowsprit.

After several disasters involving American sloops, a few yachtsmen in this country became interested in the English cutter, claiming that the type was a better sea boat than the American sloop. In 1881 the Scottish cutter *Madge* came to the United States. Forty-six feet long overall, she had a beam of only seven feet, nine inches, and a draft of nearly eight feet, a plank-on-edge cutter of the extreme type. She was so uniformly successful in races against American sloops that many yachtsmen were converted, and arguments between "cutter cranks" and supporters of the American sloops continued for nearly twenty years. The only sloop to uphold American honors was the Herreshoff-built *Shadow,* which, as we have seen, had a compromise type of hull.

When a challenge for the *America*'s Cup came in 1884 naming two ninety-ton cutters, the *Genesta* and the *Galatea,* the New York Yacht Club realized that there were no sloops or cutters of equal size available as defenders. After many discussions, the compromise sloop *Priscilla* was built for New York interests, while a Boston syndicate built a compromise cutter designed by Edward Burgess and named the *Puritan.* There is some evidence that in designing the *Puritan,* Burgess was greatly influenced by a model of an improved *Shadow* cut by Nathanael Herreshoff. The *Puritan*'s hull was wider and shallower than that of a true cutter, and she was fitted with a centerboard; her rig was that of a cutter except that the mainsail was laced to the boom. Despite items in the New York press warning "brick sloops" and "bean boats" to stay east of Cape Cod, the *Puritan* won easily over the *Priscilla* in trial races and over the *Genesta* in the Cup match in September 1885. Burgess designed two more Cup defenders of the same type — the *Mayflower,* which defeated the *Galatea* in 1886, and the *Volunteer,* which successfully defended the Cup against the *Thistle* in 1887.

The year 1882 saw a new yacht measurement rule, adopted by the Seawanhaka Corinthian Yacht Club of New York, that measured sail area as well as length. Although many yachtsmen objected, the rule was in general use by 1890. About that time a new class of sloops (rating 46 feet, under the Seawanhaka rule) was formed at New York, and for the 1891 season Nathanael Herreshoff built for Edwin D. Morgan the now-famous *Gloriana,* which held first place in that class throughout the year. In the popular mind, two features accounted for her success — a short waterline relative to overall length, and a long, pointed forward overhang. Both were superficial results of other innovations, yet the bow so impressed the average yachtsman that many craft, even some catboats, were rebuilt with the *Gloriana* bow to make them faster.

No less sensational but far more important for the future of small craft was another 1891 Herreshoff creation, a half-decked sloop of twenty-five-foot waterline and seven-foot beam named the *Dilemma.* She had a canoe-shaped hull of easy form and long overhangs. Power to carry sail was obtained from a two-ton, cigar-shaped bulb of lead attached to the lower edge of a deep steel plate that was bolted to the keel, the so-called fin keel. The *Dilemma* proved nothing concerning the vital problems of conventional yacht design; she simply evaded them. Everything that tended to produce room for accommodations in the yacht was eliminated, but for day sailing and racing nothing was better for speed and ease of handling. Herreshoff designed and built the vessels that successfully defended the cup five times between 1893 and 1920, and he incorporated many of his ideas into such famous defenders as the *Columbia* and the *Reliance.*

Following the 1901 *America*'s Cup match, it became fairly apparent that in large yachts the limit to which everything could be sacrificed

The sloop yacht *Gloriana*, designed and built by N. G. Herreshoff, 1891. *Courtesy Hart Nautical Museum, M. I. T.*

to speed had been reached. The design features of the Cup yachts were reflected in the moderate-sized classes, and generally speaking, an unsatisfactory type of racing boat was being developed. In the smaller day racers there was developed a type as bad as the old sandbagger — the so-called scow, which had a short, bluff waterline when upright but a long, narrow shape when heeled. An extreme example was the sloop *Outlook,* built in 1902, which measured 52 feet, 7 inches on deck with a waterline length upright of only 20 feet, 10 inches; her breadth was 16 feet. When heeled she was in effect a canoe about 50 feet long and 8 feet wide. The hulls of such craft were so shallow that they had to be strengthened by trusswork above the deck.

The greatest racing yacht of this general type was Herreshoff's defender of 1903, the *Reliance,* a wide, shallow-hulled type with a deep keel. Measuring 90 feet on her load waterline, she was 143 feet, 8 inches long on deck and carried 16,160 square feet of sail — over 2,000 square feet more than her competitor, Sir Thomas Lipton's *Shamrock III.* Although she was not a true scow, her form was such that when heeled

The Cup-defender sloop *Reliance,* built by N. G. Herreshoff, 1903. *Courtesy Hart Nautical Museum, M. I. T.*

with her lee rail awash she had an effective sailing length of 130 feet. A Boston-built candidate for the 1901 match, the Crowninshield-designed *Independence,* was a true fin-keel scow that proved to be structurally weak and generally unmanageable, although she gave evidence of exceptional speed at times.

Then in 1903 the New York Yacht Club adopted a measurement rule, devised by Nathanael Herreshoff, that took account of displacement as well as length and sail area. This marked the end of the scow type except in certain localities where special classes raced. By 1905 the rule had been widely adopted by other clubs and was generally known as the Universal Rule. In 1913 the New York Yacht Club accepted another challenge for the *America*'s Cup from Sir Thomas Lipton, the yachts to be seventy-five feet long on the load waterline. In subsequent negotiations it was agreed that the yachts would be measured under the Universal Rule. Three candidates were built for the defense of the cup — the *Resolute* by the Herreshoffs; the *Vanitie,* designed by William Gardner of New York and constructed by George Lawley & Sons at Boston; and the *Defiance,* designed by George Owen of Boston and built by the Bath Iron Works. The *Resolute* was ahead in the trial races and the *Shamrock IV* had reached Bermuda when the outbreak of World War I forced an indefinite postponement of the match. The *Shamrock IV* continued on to New York, where she was laid up.

Yachting under sail in the United States was developed by men who were essentially seamen: they loved the sea and built their yachts as a means of controlling and commanding its power. There was, however, another phase developed by men commercially interested in steam navigation; this was steam yachting. While a few steam yachts had been built before the Civil War, they did not flourish until the 1880s. In a way, steam yachting was akin to the "cottages" of Newport and Bar Harbor. Luxuries could be had afloat without the inconveniences and discomforts of the sailing yacht.

Most of the steam yachts built soon after the end of the Civil War were defective in that they were built from models carved by men familiar only with sailing forms. The results were often grotesque. In company with the sailing yachts, their hulls were shallow with little freeboard, and they had long trunk cabins with many windows, which were not only dangerous in rough water but seriously impaired the strength of the hull. In the larger steam yachts the builder first had to provide large rooms with elaborate furniture and fittings, a great weight of plumbing, marble steps and baths, and similar inappropriate luxuries, and then move the whole at fifteen to eighteen knots. The elaborate owner's quarters left little room for machinery, coal, and crew accommodations. Steam yachts built to these requirements were unsuited for the open sea.

Many American yachtsmen imported steam yachts from Great Britain which were well built, simply furnished, and seaworthy. On the other hand, their rooms were small and arranged for cruising in a damp climate, and they did not have the speed necessary to run from New York to Newport in a day. A large number were spoiled after arriving in the United States by having their quarters remodeled. In time a distinctive American type was evolved, suitable for summer use on Long Island Sound and up the east coast as far as Bar Harbor, but mainly for the short run to Newport. Such steam yachts also served as houseboats in the vicinity of New York City, picking the owners up in

Typical small steam yacht, the *Navarch*, in Boston Harbor, built, 1892. *Courtesy Hart Nautical Museum, M. I. T.*

the afternoon, taking them up the Hudson, into Long Island Sound, or outside Sandy Hook, and returning them to the city the next morning. Some were employed only in a commuting service, carrying the owners between home and office.

The Herreshoff Manufacturing Company was organized primarily to build steam yachts, and its Hull No. 1 was delivered in 1868. This was a launch for which the company built the engine and boiler, while the hull was constructed elsewhere; for subsequent yachts the company built both hull and machinery. The Herreshoffs perfected a light, compact compound engine and a coil boiler, also very light and compact. This machinery was installed in hulls of good form and of special construction, considerably lighter and stronger than common practice. The company gradually extended its business into larger engines and hulls but constructed few really large steam yachts. Its 94-foot *Stiletto* of 1885, which was capable of a speed of 22 knots, became the first torpedo boat in the United States Navy in 1887. The company later designed and built several torpedo boats.

A few owners of steam yachts were interested in speed, and a few long-distance races were held; but there was little point in them, since once a yacht had made a trial run, her speed was known. The fastest American steam yacht was the 130-foot *Arrow* of 1902, whose hull and machinery were designed by Charles D. Mosher, who specialized in light boilers and fast launches. The *Arrow* was owned by Charles R. Flint and was said to have made 39 knots with her two 2,000-horse-power, quadruple-expansion engines. George Lawley & Son's of Boston also turned out some fast steam yachts and torpedo boats. Their *Cigarette* of 1905, designed by Swasey, Raymond, & Page of Boston, was a well-known fast commuter of the period.

The use of steam launches and yachts was somewhat limited by the law that required a licensed engineer to operate them. Few yachtsmen held licenses, hence they had to employ engineers. The development of the internal combustion engine, however, completely changed the picture of yachting under power, as such engines could be operated by anyone. Power yachting was thus opened to the less wealthy, and the sport grew. At first suitable only for small boats and somewhat erratic in operation, the gasoline engine was considered quite reliable by the beginning of World War I and was being installed in craft as long as eighty feet. Powerboat racing in turn aided the development of the gasoline engine. While some large square-rigged and schooner-rigged yachts had been built with auxiliary steam plants, such plants took up much useful space. The gasoline engine and its fuel tanks could be tucked out of the way; hence it was an ideal auxiliary propulsion system for all sizes of sailing yachts when the wind failed.

Retreat from the High Seas

From the end of the Civil War in 1865 to the outbreak of World War I in August 1914, vessels flying the flag of the United States in foreign commerce practically disappeared from the seas. Replacing them gradually was an immense fleet, both sail and steam, engaged in the protected coastwise trade, which included the trade around Cape Horn between the Atlantic and Pacific coasts. In this trade, sail slowly disappeared as steam-propelled vessels improved, for one of the latter replaced two, three, or more sailing vessels.

New England maritime traditions changed considerably as even the coastwise trade gravitated to the bigger ports and as shipbuilding and ship operating were replaced by manufacturing. Only in some of the schooner trades was the old practice of shareholding in vessels continued until 1914, and even in these the shareholders were no longer exclusively the inhabitants of coastal towns but included investors from various parts of the country. Many New Englanders' only connection with the sea was a ride on an excursion boat or a passage by steamer to and from some vacation spot in Maine, but the railroads and then automobiles offered serious competition to some of these services.

It remained for yachting to preserve some of New England's maritime traditions. The fine finish and spit-and-polish of the large sailing and steam yachts which filled the harbors in summer brought back memories of the great clippers, while the successful defenses of the *America*'s Cup recalled the days of commercial rivalry on the oceans when American sailing vessels were supreme. But even in the smallest dory with a rag of a sail, a youngster was master of his vessel, learning some of the self-reliance that had been so much a part of the Yankee tradition.

V

The Twentieth Century

DURING the half-century or so since the outbreak of World War I, New England has continued to drift further away from its maritime heritage. As late as 1880 New Englanders owned well over one-third of the nation's merchant tonnage, but by the 1950s their share had fallen to about 4 percent. Shipments from the region continued to drop throughout the century, until by 1967 less than 1 percent of the nation's exports left from New England ports. The fact that oil for Canada enters at Portland, Maine (and goes right through on the pipeline) has inflated the region's import figures. Excluding this oil, less than 6 percent of American imports entered New England harbors.

As in the Dark Age before it, the most recent chapter in New England's maritime history would be still more bleak were it not for the fact that coastwise commerce has held up somewhat more firmly. Above all, the trend toward recreational boating has reached boom proportions in the decades since World War II. More than ever, New Englanders and other Americans are using the sea not to earn a livelihood but to assuage for a few summer weeks the tensions of the urban society in which they struggle to exist through most of the year. As for the memory of days now gone of New England's maritime greatness, they are preserved only among the collections of marine museums and in the minds of old men.

Foreign Commerce and Shipbuilding

At the outbreak of World War I in August 1914, only about 10 percent of the foreign commerce of the United States was being carried by the American deep-sea merchant marine. But as German merchant ships were quickly driven from the seas and a substantial part of the merchant navies of Great Britain and her allies was devoted to the support of military operations, the United States regretted its dependence on the vessels of other nations. Shipping rates skyrocketed, and shipowners enjoyed high earnings. To establish a permanent American merchant marine, the Congress passed the Shipping Act of 1916, which created the U.S. Shipping Board with authority to form one or more corporations for the purchase, construction, charter, and operation of merchant vessels in the commerce of the United States. But before the objectives of this act could be accomplished, the United States entered the war.

In view of these shipping conditions, it is not surprising to find that American shipyards were humming long before the Congress declared war on Germany on 6 April 1917. A large number of the vessels under construction were for British companies, but others were for American owners to be employed in trades that had not seen Old Glory for years. The majority of the new vessels were of steel, but the construction of large wooden schooners, in the doldrums since about 1910, was revived for what proved to be its last gasp. On 11 July 1917, President Woodrow Wilson requisitioned all steel vessels then under construction in the United States.

Because of the great expansion of shipbuilding, both merchant and naval, occasioned by the war, the United States was for a few years the world's greatest shipbuilder. Merchant shipbuilding was controlled by the government-owned U.S. Shipping Board Emergency Fleet Corporation, formed on 16 April 1917, just ten days after this country entered the war. When the armistice was signed on 11 November 1918, the production of ships was just getting under way.

Four New England shipyards contributed to the steel merchant shipbuilding program, both under the requisitioning and under contract. The Fore River Yard of the Bethlehem Shipbuilding Corporation at Quincy, Massachusetts, had nine ships requisitioned and built six under contract. The relatively new Texas Company at Bath had eight ships requisitioned, while the Atlantic Corporation at Portsmouth, New Hampshire, and the Groton Iron Works in Groton, Connecticut, turned out ten and nine respectively under contract. In the wooden shipbuilding program, yards all along the Maine coast delivered a total

Boston T-Wharf before World War I. Note sloop in left foreground. *Courtesy William A. Baker.*

of twenty-nine vessels, while yards in the rest of New England built another thirty-six, not including schooners built for private accounts.

The designs for the Shipping Board's steel vessels were as simple as possible, and in their construction considerable prefabrication was accomplished by the larger shipyards. Steel plates and shapes were rolled, bent, and punched and much of the machinery was manufactured by inland plants, allowing the shipyards to concentrate on the assembly of the ships. The enormous production of the wartime shipyards proved that shipbuilding in the United States was a matter of economics, not of technical ability.

During the war the talents of New England's two major, privately owned steel shipyards — the Bath Iron Works and Bethlehem's Fore River Yard — were concentrated on naval construction. From 1917 through 1920 the Bath yard completed fourteen destroyers. Bethlehem's yard turned out thirty-six destroyers in a little over two years

Wooden steamship and yard of L. H. Shattuck, Newington, New Hampshire, 1918. *Courtesy William A. Baker.*

The U. S. S. *Lexington*, built at Fore River Yard, 1921–27. *Courtesy Mariners Museum, Newport News, Virginia.*

and in addition built twenty-three submarines. In 1917 the yard took a contract to build a battle cruiser, which after complete redesigning was commissioned in 1927 as the aircraft carrier *Lexington*. The *"Lex"* (with her sister ship, the *Saratoga)* was the backbone of the navy's air wing until she was lost in the Battle of the Coral Sea in May 1942. In addition to this program and the merchant ships, the government authorized the construction of three additional plants to be operated by Bethlehem. The first was a yard in the Squantum section of Quincy, which built thirty-five destroyers from the hard winter of 1917–18 to December 1919. The U.S.S. *Reid* (DD-292) was completed by this yard in forty-five and a half working days. The second plant, which was for the construction of boilers, was located in Providence, while the third, intended for the manufacture of turbine material, was to have been in Buffalo, New York. The Electric Boat Company at Groton was involved in the construction of the submarines at Quincy, while the New London Ship & Engine Company, also at Groton, built submarine tenders. The Boston Navy Yard built storeships and oilers, while the Portsmouth Navy Yard constructed only submarines.

In 1918 America's foreign trade was about two and a half times greater than in 1913, yet American-flag vessels carried only 22 percent, simply because the nation did not have enough ships. In 1920, when the country's foreign commerce reached its pre-World War II peak of about three times the 1913 figure and the war-built ships were available, the percentage jumped to nearly 43. With the coming of peace there were the inevitable readjustments in world trade. The great demand for ships to carry military cargoes was gone; foreign shipping returned to the old trade routes; and as the European countries rebuilt their economies, new and more efficient ships appeared. The result was a worldwide oversupply of ships. American ships carried about 32 percent of the country's foreign trade in 1926, and the average from then until 1939 was about 35 percent.

The Merchant Marine Act of 1920 provided for the establishment of American shipping services on a number of routes considered essential. Privately owned ships were to be employed, but where this was not possible, the chartering of government-owned vessels was allowed. Because of inadequate subsidies, the small incentive for private investments, and the high cost of replacing essential ships, little was accomplished. The Congress authorized a construction loan fund of $125 million, but in view of the high costs and the fleet of ships on hand, however unsuitable they were, merchant shipbuilding could not be justified. The Washington Disarmament Conference of 1922 curtailed naval construction, and the American shipbuilding industry was in a depressed state from 1922 to 1928. In the latter year a new Merchant Marine Act, commonly called the Jones-White Act, provided for ten-year mail contract subsidies, with rates varying according to the size and speed of the vessels employed. Because of the 1929 business depression, the mail contractors were able to build only 31 combination passenger-cargo vessels by 1933. No cargo ships at all were constructed under the provisions of the 1928 act, and between 1927 and 1935 only 8 ocean-going dry-cargo ships were launched from American yards. In contrast, 853 were built during the same period in the United Kingdom alone.

The depressed state of American shipbuilding in the mid-1920s forced the closing of the Bath Iron Works in 1925 after thirty-five years of operation. The plant was sold under foreclosure to a group of used-machinery dealers in spite of the efforts of local people to reopen the business. The new owners gutted the yard of machinery and equipment, and the wharves and building berths fell into a dilapidated condition. In the middle of 1927, what was left of the property was sold to a company that intended to use the former machine-shop building for making wood-pulp products. Instead, through the efforts of William S. Newell, Archibald M. Main, and Joseph A. MacDonald, the Bath Iron Works Corporation was organized in October 1927. It leased the yard and obtained enough equipment to build the twin-screw diesel yacht *Vanda* for Ernest B. Dane of Brookline, Massachusetts.

Many fine yachts followed the *Vanda,* including J. P. Morgan's 343-foot, turbine-propelled *Corsair IV*. A fleet of five diesel yachts was built on speculation, but their sale was seriously hampered by the business depression that began with the stock market crash late in 1929. The last of the five, the *Aletes,* remained at the company's pier until May 1941, when she was purchased by the United States Navy for about a fifth of her cost and turned over to Great Britain for use as a submarine patrol boat. Although the bottom had dropped out of the yacht market, the yard's continuation was assured when it received in 1931 a contract to build the U.S.S. *Dewey,* one of the first class of destroyers built since the World War I program.

During the 1920s Bethlehem's Fore River Yard, with the U.S.S.

The steam yacht *Corsair,* built by Bath Iron Works, 1930 — not the largest but one of the finest afloat during the last days of the great yachts. *Courtesy Bath Marine Museum.*

The S. S. *Veragua,* of the United Fruit Company, built at Fore River Yard, 1932. *Courtesy Mariners Museum, Newport News, Virginia.*

Lexington as a backlog, had better luck. Following the delivery of the tanker *Wm. Boyce Thompson* to the Sinclair Navigation Company in 1921, however, it was not until 1925 that the yard received its next contract — two ferries for the City of Boston. Limited naval construction was resumed in 1927 with a contract for the 10,000-ton cruiser *Northampton*. Under the stimulus of the Jones-White Act, the Fore River Yard built the 605-foot passenger liners *Mariposa, Monterey,* and *Lurline* for the Oceanic Steamship Company (better known as the Matson Line) and the 415-foot refrigerated ships *Antigua, Quirigua, Veragua* for the United Fruit Company. The U.S.S. *Farragut,* delivered in 1934, was the first American destroyer built since World War I. The award of a contract in January 1933 for the building of the cruiser *Quincy* marked the beginning of a long naval construction program. Early in the 1920s the Bethlehem Steel Company purchased two of Boston's oldest shipyards, the Atlantic Works and the Simpson Dry Dock Company. The former yard was closed in the early 1930s, but the latter is still in operation as a repair yard.

The Merchant Marine Act of 1936 recognized that the United States should have a merchant marine sufficient to carry its domestic water-borne commerce and a substantial portion of the water-borne export and import foreign commerce; sufficient to provide shipping service on essential routes; capable of serving as a military and naval auxiliary; and composed of the best equipped, safest, and most suitable types of vessels, constructed in the United States and manned with a trained and efficient citizen personnel. A new agency, the U.S. Maritime Commission, was organized to carry out the purposes of the act and to take over the functions of earlier agencies as well as those of the Postmaster General relating to mail contracts. The means to be employed included construction-differential subsidies, additional subsidies to offset aid granted by foreign countries to their shipping lines, construction of vessels for chartering, crew training, and the prescribing of minimum working conditions for all officers and crews on ships receiving operating subsidies.

With the outbreak of World War II, Great Britain again needed ships and turned to the United States for them in the summer of 1940. Two shipyards were organized, one on the east coast and one on the west, to build 30 ships each. The British furnished a simple design for a sturdy, ten-knot cargo ship of about 10,000 tons deadweight fitted

The S. S. *Augustus P. Loring,* a Liberty ship built at the New England Ship-building Company, South Portland, Maine, 1944. Photograph by John Loch-head. *Courtesy Mariners Museum, Newport News, Virginia.*

with a triple-expansion reciprocating engine and coal-burning, fire-tube boilers. Similar ships had been built for years in British shipyards, and they were suitable for many trades. When in late 1940 the Maritime Commission was instructed to undertake an emergency building pro-gram of 200 ships, later increased to 312, this British design, slightly modified to meet American requirements, became the famous Liberty ship. By the end of the war, fifteen shipyards had delivered 2,580 basic Liberty ships and 130 adaptations, in addition to the first 60 constructed for Great Britain.

The east coast shipyard that built the 30 ships for the British was organized by two established shipbuilding firms as the Todd-Bath Iron Shipbuilding Corporation. Its new facilities at South Portland, Maine, were a departure from accepted shipyard practice, as the vessels were built in shallow basins from which they were easily floated at a certain stage of completion. At the end of the British contract the company was reorganized as the South Portland Shipbuilding Corporation, and a so-called West Yard was erected where ships were built and launched in the normal fashion. Under this corporate structure, 20 Liberty ships were built in the East Yard basins and 19 were launched from the ways

The New England Shipbuilding Company, South Portland, Maine, December, 1941. *Courtesy Mariners Museum, Newport News, Virginia.*

The U. S. S. *Nicholas* (DD-499), built at Bath Iron Works, 1941–42. *Courtesy Mariners Museum, Newport News, Virginia.*

in the West Yard. Reorganized again as the New England Shipbuilding Corporation, the firm delivered 112 more Liberty ships from the East Yard and 93 from the West. The only other new steel shipyard in New England was that of the Walsh-Kaiser Company, originally the Rheem Manufacturing Company, at Providence. This yard completed 11 Liberty ships before turning out 32 twin-screw, shallow-draft transports.

Under the Maritime Commission's program, wooden shipbuilding was revived in Maine. It was not, however, a return to sail or even to wooden steamships, but only to ship-shaped, 134-foot, seagoing barges of 1,500 tons deadweight. Yards at Belfast, Camden, South Gardiner, and South Freeport produced altogether thirteen barges.

During World War II the Bath Iron Works Corporation repeated the role of its predecessor and built only destroyers. Production at Bethlehem's Quincy Yard ranged from landing ships to a battleship but was concentrated on cruisers and aircraft carriers. Bethlehem also operated a shipyard in nearby Hingham which turned out landing craft, destroyer escorts, and high-speed transports. The Walsh-Kaiser Company, in addition to Liberty ships and transports, built 21 frigates, all of which were delivered to the British. The Electric Boat Company at Groton and the Portsmouth Naval Yard at Kittery, Maine, built between them two-thirds of the nearly 300 submarines that saw active duty with the United States Navy during World War II. In addition, 36 of the boats which the Bethlehem yard built during the 1920s were still in service, primarily as training vessels at the big submarine base at New London (actually in Groton, just upriver from Electric Boat). Altogether, seventy-seven New England organizations produced vessels, or at least some type of floating equipment, for the Navy Department, War Department, and Coast Guard — items ranging from rubber rafts, garbage lighters, and tugs to transports, submarines, and aircraft carriers.

Commercial ship construction was resumed at Quincy in 1948, when Bethlehem received a contract from the Texas Company for four 595-foot, 28,000-ton-deadweight tankers. Their designation as supertankers rapidly became meaningless with the growth of tanker size and capacity. Quincy's contribution to the growth reached its peak with the delivery in 1962 of the 892-foot, 106,500-ton-deadweight *Manhattan,* which in 1969 became the first commercial ship to traverse the famed Northwest Passage. Most of Bethlehem's tanker construction during the

1950s was for foreign owners. Also in 1948, the Quincy Yard received a contract to design and build two 632-foot passenger liners for the Mediterranean service of the American Export Lines; when delivered in 1951, they were named the *Independence* and the *Constitution*.

During the Korean conflict of the early 1950s, the U.S. Maritime Administration sponsored the construction of a group of forty-five high-speed cargo ships, the Mariner class. The class was designed at Quincy and five ships were built there, three of which were named for New England states — the *Old Colony Mariner,* the *Nutmeg Mariner,* and the *Pine Tree Mariner.* Between 1961 and 1963 Bethlehem constructed six dry-cargo ships for the United States Lines. In addition to a number of destroyers and frigates, the Quincy Yard built two nuclear-powered surface ships for the United States Navy, the cruiser *Long Beach* and the frigate *Bainbridge.* While the frigates of World War II had been relatively slow, lightly armed, escort vessels, the postwar frigates were of the type formerly designated destroyer leaders.

At the end of 1963, for various financial and labor reasons, Bethlehem ended its operations at Quincy, and the facilities were sold to the General Dynamics Corporation: The yard was reopened a few months later as a subsidiary of that corporation's Electric Boat Division at Groton, but it later became a separate division specializing in surface ships and early in 1970 was designated the Quincy Shipbuilding Division. Since World War II the Electric Boat Division has been practically a private navy yard, building submarines for the United States Navy; here were built the world's first nuclear-powered vessel, the *Nautilus,* and many of the Polaris submarines. The Portsmouth Naval Shipyard has also continued as a major builder of submarines. And Bath-built destroyers retain the respect of naval personnel, although political considerations have cost the yard a share in new construction programs. In the late 1960s Bath constructed three large container ships for the American Export Isbrandtsen Lines. These 582-foot ships were the largest ever built on the Kennebec.

While all this construction benefited one aspect of New England's maritime activities, shipping itself steadily declined. In the years since the end of World War II, the percentage of the foreign commerce of the United States carried in American-flag vessels has fallen to an even lower level than that reached before 1914. From a high of 57.6 percent at the end of the war, it fell to 25 percent in 1955, and by early 1970 it

The S. S. *Manhattan,* designed and built at the Quincy yard, Bethlehem Steel Company, the first tanker through the North West Passage, 1969–70. *Courtesy Bethlehem Steel Company.*

The S. S. *Boston* of the Eastern Steamship Line. *Courtesy Mariners Museum, Newport News, Virginia.*

had dropped to only 6 percent. Though the actual volume of commerce was larger than in earlier years, fewer of the modern, large, high-speed cargo ships, such as those of the Mariner class, were needed to carry it. In the spring of 1970 the only American-flag cargo ships bringing foreign cargoes to Boston were those of the Farrell Lines, and they came only once a month. With the increasing popularity of air travel in postwar America, soon the only passenger liners to call at Boston were a few cruise ships and an occasional vessel in the Mediterranean run. The American merchant marine as a whole was in a condition similar to that which had led to the creation of the Maritime Commission in 1936 — old and therefore expensive to operate and maintain. Seventy percent of the freighters, 90 percent of the bulk carriers, and 50 percent of the tankers were more than twenty years old. In 1970 — after years of talking (but no action) and of disputes among the shipping industry, labor, and the federal government — the Congress authorized a new merchant shipbuilding program to raise the amount of the country's participation in its foreign commerce to about 30 percent.

Coastal Commerce and Navigation

After World War I, coastwise shipping operated under entirely different conditions from those faced by the ocean shipping. Companies in the coastwise shipping business received no construction or operating assistance other than the long-standing law that reserved that trade for American-built and -operated vessels. In 1929 the coastwise fleet comprised 715 vessels: 89 combination passenger and freight ships, 408 freighters, and 218 tankers. (The corresponding numbers in foreign commerce were 79, 469, and 111, for a total of 659.)

Because of the mounting shipbuilding costs between the two world wars, coastal cargo ship operators were limited largely to older vessels and those constructed under the Shipping Board's program during the first war. Small freighters built on the Great Lakes and brought to salt water via the Welland Canal and St. Lawrence River proved quite useful. The tanker segment of the coastal fleet received the greatest number of new ships constructed without government assistance during the interwar years. From 1923 to 1939 a total of seventy-seven tankers measuring 2,000 gross tons or more were built in American shipyards, two-thirds of them during the last four years of the period.

A few new ships were built for the passenger and freight services out of Boston. The year 1924 saw the completion of the *Boston* and the *New York* for the summer run of the Eastern Steamship Lines between Boston and New York through the Cape Cod Canal. Later in the decade, four fine steamers were built for the company's services to the Maritime Provinces in the summer and its Boston-New York run in winter. While the *Boston* and the *New York* followed typical Sound-steamer practice in having considerable overhang, the four later boats — the *Evangeline,* the *Yarmouth,* the *Acadia,* and the *St. John* — looked like small ocean liners. The Merchants' & Miners' Line had five new vessels built between 1923 and 1926, and the Savannah Line also added new ships during the early 1920s.

The New England steamboat services were considerably disrupted during World War I, when many vessels were sold or chartered to the federal government as in earlier wars. Those that survived or were re-established after the war faced the growing competition of motortrucks for the transportation of freight and of the private automobile for general travel. Longshoremen's strikes added to their difficulties. Passenger service between New Haven and New York ended in 1918, when the *Richard Peck* was transferred to the New Bedford run, following the loss of the steamboat *Maine* on Execution Rock at the western end of Long Island Sound. Freight boats continued to serve New Haven for a few more years, but they and the passenger boats serving Hartford, New London, and New Bedford were gone by the middle 1930s.

The old rail and steamboat routes connecting Boston and New York via Fall River and Providence kept going a bit longer. The famous Fall River Line ended operations in July 1937 for a variety of economic reasons, but the Providence service lasted until early in 1942, when the *Arrow* and the *Comet* (formerly the *Belfast* and the *Camden* on the Boston-Bangor route) were taken by the federal government for war service. The direct Boston-New York run through the canal ended in November 1941, when the *Boston* and the *New York* were requisitioned; later they were sent to England but were sunk en route by German torpedoes in September 1943.

By the 1918 season the best boats of the Eastern Steamship Lines had gone to war. The *Bunker Hill* and the *Massachusetts* from the Boston-New York run had been converted to mine layers, in which capacity they served the United States Navy until early in World War II.

The former was reconverted to a cargo ship in 1941, while the latter, sunk by Japanese bombs at Pearl Harbor, was salvaged to become a gasoline engine repair ship. To maintain the Boston-New York service, the *Belfast* and the *Camden* were transferred from the Boston-Bangor route; they in turn were replaced by the old paddle steamers *City of Bangor* and *City of Rockland* from the Kennebec River run to Bath and Gardiner. This left the Kennebec ports without steamboat service to Boston until the formation of the Kennebec Steamship Company, which purchased the *City of Rockland* and began operating her in 1921. Her stranding on Dix Island in the lower Kennebec on 2 September 1923 marked the end of about a century of nearly continuous steamboat service between the river ports and Boston. The similar service to the Penobscot ended in 1935, as did the run between Boston and St. John, New Brunswick.

In 1926 Boothbay Harbor, by then well established as a summer resort, finally obtained direct steamboat service from Boston, when the Eastern Steamship Company put the *City of Bangor* and the *Brandon* on the route. These boats operated six days a week during the 1926 and 1927 seasons, stopping at Portland each way. The *City of Bangor* made the final Portland-Boston trip in September 1927, after which she was tied up at an East Boston wharf until she sank under a heavy load of snow in December 1933. Beginning in June 1928, the *Brandon* operated between Boothbay Harbor and Portland until Labor Day of the same year, when the service ended permanently.

The fates of local steamboat runs in New England followed the same general pattern. Service between Boston and Gloucester, which had begun in 1844, finally ended in 1927. The Boston and Gloucester Steamboat Company ended its operations in September 1925, but in March 1926 the Massachusetts Bay Steamship Corporation began a daily freight service between Boston, Gloucester, and Provincetown, employing the converted submarine chaser *Governor Prence*. In July 1926 this company resumed daily passenger service between Boston and Gloucester with the steamboat *Monhegan*. On 18 December a three-alarm fire destroyed the company's Boston office and freight shed, together with freight shipments intended for the *Monhegan*. Severe financial losses crippled the line, and the *Monhegan* made her last sailing in January 1927.

Improved road and motor transport ended the near-isolation of

The S. S. *Naushon*, of the New England Steamship Company, running from New Bedford to Martha's Vineyard and Nantucket; built at Fore River Yard, 1929. *Courtesy Mariners Museum, Newport News, Virginia.*

many of Maine's seacoast towns and their dependence on steamboat services. Typical of the general decline and ending of most of the shorter steamboat runs along the Maine coast was the fate of those to Boothbay. The Augusta, Gardiner, & Boothday Steamboat Company connected those three towns and intermediate ports, employing the *Islander II* and the *Virginia,* until 1926. The *Virginia* was the last steamboat to operate between Bath and Boothbay, making her final run under other ownership in 1941. Between 1907 and 1930 the little *Winter Harbor* made two trips a day, six days a week, winter and summer, from Wiscasset to Boothbay, carrying mail, passengers, and freight. The successful low bid for the mail contract by a trucking firm in 1927 brought about the end of this run. The *Winter Harbor* was tied up to an unused wharf at Wiscasset, where she slowly went to pieces. The *Newcastle* performed a similar mail service between Damariscotta and East Boothbay until the late 1920s.

Longer runs fared no better. The Portland-Rockland-Lubec-Eastport service ended about 1926, but those from Rockland to Brooklin and Bar Harbor managed to keep operating until April 1934. Several of Maine's islands, however, still have boat service, although in the minds of many the present diesel-propelled craft are poor substitutes for the graceful steamers of the past. The Camden-Islesboro-Belfast run has been replaced by an auto ferry from Lincolnville Beach. The *North Haven* and the *W. S. White* were the last steamboats to operate from Rockland to Vinalhaven and the nearby islands. The *White* was the first to be taken in 1942 for government service, while the *North Haven* made her final trip on 30 May. They were replaced late in July 1943 by the 65-foot, diesel-propelled *Vinalhaven II,* operated by the Vinalhaven Port District. The state of Maine now operates auto ferries on this and other routes from Rockland.

Mail, passenger, and freight service to Monhegan, formerly operated from Boothbay, is now based at Port Clyde, which reduces the length of the open-water part of the run. Summer tourist services are still provided from Boothbay, which is also the base for runs to nearer islands and to Bath. From Portland the Casco Bay Line, employing a variety of steel, diesel-propelled craft, still serves the nearby islands on a daily basis throughout the year and in summer provides daily service to Bailey Island.

The last of the little Maine steamboats is the *Sabino,* which was built at East Boothbay in 1908 as the *Tourist.* She received her present name when purchased by the Popham Beach Steamboat Company in 1922 for the run from Bath to the mouth of the Kennebec River. From 1927 to 1958, when she was laid up, the *Sabino* plied among the islands of Casco Bay. Purchased in 1961 by James Corbin of Salisbury, Massachusetts, she was hauled out and lovingly restored. Rechristened and relaunched in 1967, the *Sabino,* hailing from Newburyport, carried steamboat buffs on excursions up and down the Merrimack.

A bit of the maritime spirit of the past was revived in 1937, when the Seaboard Navigation Company was organized by several enterprising young men from various parts of Maine to operate a freight service from Boston to Penobscot River ports. Their first vessel, the converted trawler *Penobscot,* began operating in April 1938, by which time space had been rented on Commercial Wharf at Boston and on wharves at Rockland, Bucksport, and Bangor. An attempt to increase southbound cargoes by chartering the steamer *Stratford* to run a feeder service, carrying sardines from Eastport and Lubec to Rockland, was frustrated by a poor sardine season. Late in 1938 a second converted trawler, the *Kennebec,* was obtained and put in service on 10 December, but she made only two trips to Bangor before ice closed the river for the winter.

It was intended that these two vessels would carry potatoes south to Middle Atlantic ports, where they would load canned goods for Boston and then take general freight back to the Penobscot. The lack of tourist business in Maine during the 1938 recession year, curtailed northbound cargoes, unsettled market conditions that affected the potato trade, and a truck strike in Boston early in 1939 contributed to the abandonment of the Penobscot run. Attempted tramp operations were foiled by the refusal of Boston longshoremen to handle cargoes loaded at non-union ports, and the company was forced to end operations in 1939.

During the 1920s and 1930s the last of the prewar coasting schooners and those built in the war years fought a losing battle with steam, motor transport, and the elements. Prewar experience made it easy to predict the future. Successful voyages during the war years had earned fantastic profits, and in 1920 the freight rate for coal by schooner from Norfolk to Boston was three dollars a ton. By 1921, however, the rate had dropped to one dollar a ton. Some of the larger schooners, such as those operated by Crowell & Thurlow, managed to obtain coal charters throughout the 1920s, but they were slowly driven from the trade by the steam colliers. The last coal cargoes delivered by sail to New England were transported in the smaller three-masted and two-masted schooners to little ports tucked here and there in Maine.

The last important cargo available to the sailing coasters was lumber, and the Florida building boom of the mid-1920s saw the gathering of quite a fleet. A few schooners were employed in the fertilizer trade from South America, and salt from the West Indies and phosphate rock from Florida were occasionally carried. Starting about 1927 a number of schooners — about twenty-five at one time — found employment in transporting creosoted railroad ties from the southern states to Boston and New York.

The business depression of the early 1930s struck hard at the sailing fleets. In 1931 the New England Maritime Company, owner of one of the largest active fleets, went bankrupt, and the sale of nine of its schooners brought only $13,425. The four-master *Charles D. Stanford,*

The schooners *Hesper* and *Luther Little* at Wiscasset. Derelicts and power stations have replaced the once busy wharves. *Courtesy Marine Department of Economic Development.*

built in 1918 for $100,000, was sold in 1931 for only $5,000. Many schooners were laid up to await better days; they could be found along the waterfronts of the larger ports and in many of Maine's coves.

Most of the schooners that went into lay-up during the early 1930s never sailed again. Typical of such vessels are the four-masters *Hesper* and *Luther Little,* which have been subjects for tourists' cameras at Wiscasset since 1932. The 210-foot *Hesper* was launched from the yard of the Crowninshield Shipbuilding Company at South Somerset, Massachusetts, in 1918; and her first owners, Rogers & Webb of Boston, were able to employ her in some of the lucrative wartime trade. After at least two transatlantic voyages to Lisbon with coal, she settled into the coastwise trade and carried coal and lumber until 1928, when she was laid up in the harbor of Rockport, Maine. Later moved to Portland, she was sold at auction in June 1932 for six hundred dollars. On 1 September 1932 she arrived at Wiscasset at the end of a towline and since then has slowly gone to pieces; her masts were cut down in 1940. The *Luther Little,* built by the Reed Brothers at Somerset in 1917, also was employed in wartime trade before entering the coastwise trade, in which she sailed until the mid-1920s. In June 1932 she too was auctioned and taken to Wiscasset; at this writing her lower masts are still standing.

Sail was finally driven from the coastwise trade by the regular schedules of the steamers, rising maintenance costs, and the lack of crews. The lower charter rates offered by schooner owners in the coal trade, for example, usually were not low enough to offset their inability to deliver on a guaranteed date. On the other hand, the schooner rates were computed at so low a margin that a longer than expected passage would wipe out any profit. Few of the younger men would go in sail, where pay was low and working conditions bore little resemblance to those on power-driven vessels. Such was the glamour of sail, however, that by the end of the 1930s the appearance of a weather-worn craft in the harbor of Boston or any other major New England city provided a surefire subject for a newspaper story. Like a magnet, she drew to the waterfront at lunchtime all the frustrated would-be seamen, chafing at their lackluster shore jobs.

In 1929 eight general-cargo steamship lines were operating out of Boston to Atlantic and Gulf Coast ports. Operations through the

Panama Canal between the Atlantic and Pacific coasts grew during the 1920s, and by 1932 five lines were serving Boston. Although there were a few changes during the 1930s, the eight lines were still carrying cargoes out of Boston to Atlantic and Gulf ports at the outbreak of World War II, while the number of lines to Pacific Coast ports had risen to seven.

Conditions in the coastwise trade, however, changed fast. Because of insufficient revenue from the established freight rates, the Mooremack Gulf Lines ended operations in the autumn of 1940. In 1932 the Morgan Line began weekly freight service between Boston and New Orleans and added a run to Galveston, as well as a freight and passenger sailing every three weeks to New Orleans. It canceled these runs in December 1940, also because of insufficient revenues, and the Clyde-Mallory Line followed suit in January 1941. The Lykes Coastwise Line sold its ships to British interests in November 1940. The Merchants' & Miners' and Savannah lines, however, continued their sailings right up to the time when their ships were taken by the government for transport and training use. In 1943 the former Merchants' & Miners' vessel *Dorchester* was torpedoed off Greenland with the loss of eight hundred lives.

The eight steamship lines mentioned above did not include the companies engaged in the coal trade. Between 1920 and 1927 this business amounted to about 68 percent of the entire coastwise trade to Boston; even at the end of the 1930s it still comprised about 45 percent of that city's inbound commerce. As noted earlier, coal arrived at Boston in schooners and steam colliers, but during the 1920s and 1930s tugs and barges were still active, though in steadily declining numbers. Empty American-flag tramps bound for Boston often stopped at Newport News or some other coal port to pick up a cargo.

By the late 1930s coal for Boston was carried primarily in the colliers of three large companies, the Mystic Steamship Company, the Pocahontas Fuel Company, and the Sprague Steamship Company. More than half of the coal carried in Mystic's sixteen colliers was consumed in the manufacture of coke and illuminating gas by the New England Coal & Coke Company in Everett, Massachusetts. The deeply loaded colliers formed almost a steady parade as they slipped into the harbor with cargoes averaging about eight thousand tons. Special shoreside equipment unloaded them in about eight or nine hours, and, riding light, they sailed again to one of the southern coal-loading ports. Round trips averaged between five and nine days.

Coal-unloading gear used to be a prominent feature on the waterfront of every New England port of any size, but since the end of World War II coal has faced a growing challenge as a heating and power-generation source in New England. Several large, steam-powered electric-generating plants were originally constructed to burn coal, and in some instances a plant required the almost exclusive services of one collier. There is, however, a growing tendency, particularly in the large cities, for power plants to shift from coal to oil. A further shift from coal has taken place in the heating of dwellings and commercial buildings. Oil or gas is now employed, but the gas is the natural variety delivered by pipeline and not manufactured from coal. Oil storage tanks have thus replaced the coal-unloading gear in most New England ports and are quite prominent in New Haven, Fall River, Providence, Boston, and Searsport — and above all in Portland.

It was thought that after World War II a few of the coastwise passenger and freight runs in New England, such as the overnight service between Boston and New York, might be reestablished. But many factors — among them, Coast Guard regulations, Interstate Commerce Commission rates, labor costs, the growth of air travel, and, above all, the lack of suitable vessels — worked against any such intentions. Certain war-built, shallow-draft, twin-screw transports were intended for such use, but design features proved unsatisfactory for commercial conversions. Once-busy waterways that had daily steamboat service see now only tankers of varying sizes; some, because of pipeline construction, do not even have these. Aside from pleasure boats and an occasional vessel carrying fish to a processing plant at Bath, the once-busy Kennebec has only the new ships putting to sea from the Bath Iron Works. Most other waterways see only the pleasure boats.

To all this legitimate commerce must be added the rather unusual coastwise traffic from 1920 to 1933, when the Eighteenth Amendment was the law of the land and the country was "dry." Rumrunners, whose wares included many other potables, not only slipped into and out of deserted coves on foggy or moonless nights but brazenly anchored offshore. The apathetic attitude of the public and its sometimes open resentment toward law-enforcing agencies recalled the position of the American colonists toward smuggling before the Revolution.

The rum-runner *Arethusa. Courtesy Mariners Museum, Newport News, Virginia.*

The French islands of St. Pierre and Miquelon in the Gulf of St. Lawrence were the main depot for the smugglers, whose larger vessels, often former fishing schooners, anchored off New England's major ports in well-defined "rum rows" just outside the legal three-mile limit. Sometimes a dozen or more vessels would be anchored in formation. By 1925 the limit of territorial waters had been extended to twelve miles, but it was said that on clear days the rum row between Cape Ann and Cape Cod could be seen from the porch of President Calvin Coolidge's summer White House at Swampscott. Smaller, faster boats transferred the bottled cargoes to the shore.

The Coast Guard was the federal agency charged with the prevention of smuggling, and its operations at times resembled full-fledged naval actions. The Boston-based unit carried out a well-planned attack on the Massachusetts Bay rum row in the autumn of 1924, employing the large cutter *Tampa* and a number of thirty-foot patrol boats. The Coast Guard fleet moved out into the bay on 20 October and for five days was out of contact with the shore. Cruising between Cape Ann and Cape Cod, the squadron found more than a dozen vessels anchored on Stellwagen Bank about twenty miles off the coast. Forming a blockade around them, the Coast Guard closed in at dawn. When the smugglers sighted the *Tampa,* they scattered in all directions. Machine gunners on the patrol boats opened fire, and the three-inch and five-inch guns on the *Tampa* were directed at vessels out of range of the patrol boats. Most of the rumrunners surrendered, but several of the fastest boats escaped. Hundreds of cases of liquor were tossed to Davy Jones, but substantial quantities were confiscated. Among the captured vessels were the British schooner *Marjorie E. Bachman,* with 850 cases of brandy, champagne, and whisky, and seven power boats, each with 100 cases of liquor.

By the mid-1920s speed had become important to the smugglers, and they turned from converted fishing vessels to specially designed craft powered with two or more converted airplane engines that could easily outdistance the best of the Coast Guard vessels. These high-speed craft were designed by some of New England's best naval architects and built in Nova Scotia. Eventually the Coast Guard was forced to employ the same naval architects to design faster patrol boats.

As the running battle between the Coast Guard and the smugglers continued into the late 1920s, the attitude of the public changed from indifference to militant, organized opposition toward enforcement of the law. When three smugglers were killed off the Rhode Island coast in 1929, the episode was denounced at a mass meeting in historic Faneuil Hall as "the Newport Massacre." At the time, government reports indicated that about 150 vessels were engaged in liquor smuggling along the New England coast. The whole "dry" experiment ended in 1933 with the repeal of the Eighteenth Amendment.

The Fisheries

Since the end of World War I New England's fisheries have undergone profound changes. The last whaler to sail from New Bedford was the bark *Wanderer,* which was caught in a summer storm soon after leaving port in August 1924 and was wrecked on Cuttyhunk. The final whaling voyage was settled in 1925 on the return of the schooner *John R. Manta*. The last surviving American whaling vessel, the ship *Charles W. Morgan,* built in 1841, is maintained on exhibit at Mystic Seaport. Many people feel that with foreign fish-factory ships operating as close to New England's shores as Georges Bank and with large quantities of frozen fish caught by them being imported by American firms, other branches of our fisheries eventually may share the fate of whaling.

By the early 1920s big business controlled a large part of New England's fishing industry, owning fleets of trawlers and selling their catches on the floors of fish exchanges. This development brought a change in the fishermen's compensation. As control passed from a fishing boat's master to her owner, some of the expense was also transferred. The men still fished on shares, but as they came to be regarded as employes, they and the master were no longer responsible for an unprofitable voyage, and unpaid bills could be collected only from the owner. With this change came the practice of guaranteeing the men a minimum wage.

In those days the trawlers operated on a fifty-fifty basis. After deductions for docking and weighing expenses, the gross receipts of a trip were divided in half. The owner's share covered company expenses, the fixed charges on the boat, and a bonus to the master. The cost of food, fuel, ice, and certain other items was paid from the crew's half; and the master, mate, cook, engineers, and fishermen shared the remainder. If the crew's half did not cover all the items usually paid by them, the owners met any unpaid bills, and the crew received the guaranteed minimum. The owner-crew percentages and the charges met by each have altered through the years, but the general practice remains essentially unchanged.

In 1921 a new method of processing was introduced, and Boston soon became a leader in the business. This was filleting — the cutting of meaty, boneless chunks from the sides of fish. As a result, fish became much simpler for the housewife to prepare, and the way was opened for the frozen fish industry. Meanwhile, the waste items were used to produce fish meal for livestock and poultry raisers.

The fishing boats too have changed. While the use of mechanically propelled trawlers, first with steam and later with diesel engines, was increasing, schooners driven entirely by sails still set out their dories during the 1920s and early 1930s. But one by one they met mishaps or

The trawler *Boston College,* 116 feet long, built, 1928. *Courtesy Bath Iron Works Corporation.*

had their rigs cut down and power installed. The new schooners were built as auxiliaries, and now all the fishermen, big and little, are power-driven with perhaps only a miniscule riding sail. The last all-sail schooner to fish out of Gloucester was the *Thomas L. Gorton,* designed by Thomas F. McManus of Boston, which was launched from the Tarr & James yard at Essex in 1905. In August of that year the *Gorton* sailed on her maiden voyage for haddock under the command of Captain William H. Thomas; two weeks later she put in to Boston with seventy thousand pounds of fresh fish. During her last years out of Gloucester she was employed in freighting fish from Canada, a task which symbolized both the cause and the effect of the decline in New England's fishing industry. In March 1935 she was sold to Captain Arthur Earle of Carbonear, Newfoundland, who had her rebuilt with a whaleback bow,

The fishing schooner *L. A. Dunton,* built at Essex, Massachusetts, 1921. *Courtesy Mariners Museum, Newport News, Virginia.*

a cut-down rig, and an auxiliary engine. The *Gorton* was lost in 1956 after colliding with an iceberg.

The last all-sail, salt-fish schooner built at Essex was the *Columbia,* launched by Arthur D. Story in April 1923, but she was a racer rather than a regular fisherman, being built to represent the United States in races for the Internationl Fishermen's Trophy. Under the rules, all competitors had to put in a certain period of fishing; so she sailed on a two-month voyage as a dory handliner, returning with 324,000 pounds of salt cod. Later in 1923, after a second trip, she met the Canadian schooner *Bluenose* off Halifax. The latter won the first race but fouled the *Columbia,* whose master, Captain Ben Pine, protested. The *Bluenose* also won the second race, after which her master sailed off in a huff over the protest; there was no third race. The race committee awarded the trophy to the *Columbia,* but Captain Pine refused to accept it. The *Columbia* was lost with all hands off Sable Island in a gale on 24 August 1927.

The last of the great schooners was the *Gertrude L. Thébaud,* which was built with power. Her launching from the Story yard on 17 March

1930 was a gala event for which even the Essex public schools were closed. The *Thébaud* raced the *Bluenose* on three occasions. In October 1930, when the Fishermen's Trophy was not at stake, the *Thébaud* took three straight races, but then off Halifax the following year in a trophy series the *Bluenose* took three straight. The last of the fishermen's races were held off Gloucester in October 1938, and the *Bluenose* won three out of five races.

Two of New England's fishing schooners have been preserved, the *L. A. Dunton* at Mystic Seaport and the second at South Street Seaport in New York City. The *Dunton*, named for a sailmaker of Boothbay Harbor, was designed by McManus and built at Essex by Arthur D. Story, from whose yard she was launched on 23 March 1921. She made the last of many successful trips as a fisherman from Gloucester in 1934. Sold to Newfoundland parties, she continued for a while as a fisherman; but later, with her rig cut down and a diesel engine installed, she served as a freight boat. Mystic Seaport obtained the *Dunton* in 1963.

In 1968 South Street Seaport purchased from Historic Ships Associates of Gloucester what was thought to be the *Caviare*, a clipper-bow schooner that had been designed by Captain G. Melvin McClain of Rockport, Massachusetts, and built in 1891 by Willard A. Burnham at South Essex. After a successful career fishing out of Gloucester, she was sold in 1903 to the E. E. Saunders Company of Pensacola, Florida, for the red snapper fishery. In August 1916 the *Caviare* sank in a hurricane and was stricken from the register, but she was said to have been salvaged, rebuilt, and reregistered as the *Mystic C.* in 1923. Recent investigations have shown, however, that the vessel now at South Street may be the *Lottie S. Haskins,* also designed by McClain, which was built by Moses Adams at Essex in 1890.

At the other end of the seafood scale, the taking of clams, quahogs, and oysters — where the beds have not been polluted by industrial wastes and sewage from the cities and towns — continues to be important in New England. Even the products of polluted beds may be rendered safe, but a large percentage of the fried clams sold in New England in recent years have come from Chesapeake Bay. Scalloping and lobstering are also important businesses with appropriate yearly festivals and popularly elected "Queens." Both shellfish, however, suffer from unexplained cycles and the lobstering in particular from overfishing.

Practically none of the small boats formerly employed in the various fisheries are in service. Perhaps an old oyster sloop might be found near Bridgeport, Connecticut, but the sharpies have disappeared from New Haven waters. From Narragansett Bay east through Buzzards Bay and along the south shore of Cape Cod one can still see old catboats, but their masts are gone and they are pushed along by gasoline engines installed in their ample cockpits. Rebuilt and new Friendship sloops have become popular with many yachtsmen, and yearly regattas are held at Friendship, Maine. Early in 1970 a Camden, Maine, yard started building yacht versions of the Quoddy boat. A few examples of other types — Noank sloops, Block Island boats, Chebacco boats, pinkies, and Hampton boats — occasionally may be seen in New England waters. Fortunately for those interested in the old, working small craft, Mystic Seaport has built up a fine collection and other New England marine museums are acquiring interesting examples.

In the early 1970s the New England fisheries, faced with declining catches, particularly of haddock, are again undergoing changes. The principal developments are in the vessels, although new resources, such as shrimping in Maine waters during the winter season, are being developed, and efforts are being made to interest the fish-eating public in the less popular species. Following the example of the Europeans, whose vessels fish in great numbers off the New England coast, New Englanders are experimenting with factory ships on which the catch is processed at sea to be ready for shipment to inland markets as soon as the vessels dock.

The newer steel trawlers of from 100 to 150 feet in length haul their trawl nets over the stern instead of alongside, and this practice is extending down to the smaller class of draggers, which range from 75 to 100 feet in length. Some of the latter class, both old and new, drag for the large deep-sea scallops. Then there are the smaller-decked vessels of varying sizes, shapes, construction, and equipment which go out for only a day or two at a time. The boats employed for lobstering range from the nondescript outboard-powered skiffs of the part-time fisherman to sleek, high-bowed, low-sterned 45-footers with powerful inboard engines. The average lobster boat is from 25 to 40 feet in length and has a small shelter for the crew, with a large cockpit for stacking the traps. After long resistance, lobstermen are increasingly turning to synthetic materials for construction. While modern fishing boats may not have the glamour of those of yesteryear, perhaps the

The Block Island boat *Roaring Bessie. Courtesy Hart Nautical Museum, M. I. T.*

Setting lobster traps off Monhegan. Photograph by Kosti Ruohomaa. *Courtesy Black Star Publishers.*

latter did not have the glamour for the populace of their day that they do for the romantics of today. Any way of life may be commonplace for those experiencing it.

Although New Englanders had sailed on the sea for several centuries and some had explored beneath the surface, few understood its mysteries and resources. In 1930, with an endowment of $2 million from the Rockefeller Foundation, the Woods Hole Oceanographic Institution was organized to study marine biology, along with the winds, ocean currents, and water temperature changes and their effects on marine life. The institution's first primary research vessel was the Danish-built steel ketch *Atlantis,* designed by Professor George Owen of the Massachusetts Institute of Technology. She was replaced in the mid-1960s by the steam-powered *Atlantis II*. The U.S. Fish and Wildlife Service, formerly the U.S. Bureau of Fisheries, operates a long-established base at Woods Hole, Massachusetts, for studying the conservation and regulation of the fisheries and the utilization of fish by-products. Thus even as New England is losing its old relationship with the sea, some of its scientists are planning ahead.

Safety at Sea and Harbor Improvement

If a deeply laden coal schooner were to sail again around Cape Cod some night in 1970, her master would look in vain for the once-familiar guiding lights. If their absence caused him to go ashore, there would be no red flare from a beach patrolman to tell him that the schooner had been sighted and that help would soon arrive.

The improved Cape Cod Canal, the great reduction in the coastwise trade, and technological advances have led to many changes in aids to navigation and rescue services along the New England coast. Many once-busy ports now see only yachtsmen and an occasional fisherman. A number of minor lighthouses are no longer lighted and serve only as daymarks; others have had automatic equipment installed and are no longer manned. In 1939 the old Lighthouse Service ended its existence as an independent organization, and its functions were taken over by the Coast Guard.

The improvement of the Cape Cod Canal has had a great effect on navigation along the New England coast. The original canal, because of its narrow width, swift currents, and limited depth, did not attract

Cape Cod Canal, with Buzzards Bay in the background. Photograph by Benjamin Harrison, Buzzards Bay, Massachusetts.

the traffic envisioned by its builders. The canal was purchased by the federal government in 1928, but a major program of widening and deepening it was not started by the Army Corps of Engineers until 1933. When completed in 1940, the canal provided a thirty-foot-deep channel between Buzzards and Cape Cod bays; in recent years the controlling depth has been increased to thirty-two feet. Only the largest vessels running between northern New England and ports to the south now sail around Cape Cod.

As the canal was improved, budget-minded authorities gradually removed the chain of light vessels which once led from the eastern end of Long Island Sound through Vineyard and Nantucket Sounds to Pollock Rip off Chatham. Only three lightships are now moored in New England waters — at Portland, Boston, and Nantucket Shoals. The others have been replaced by lighted buoys or fixed platforms, such as the one at the entrance to Buzzards Bay.

The development of electronic equipment for use on shipboard has led to other changes in visual aids to navigation. Government-operated loran stations broadcast signals which enable a mariner equipped with a shipboard receiver to know his exact position at all times. Electronic depth-finders give constant readings of the depth of water under a vessel's keel. Radar gives a ship master "eyes" even in the thickest fogs by showing the positions of other vessels and obstructions. (Too much reliance, however, is often placed on radar, leading to what some courts have labeled "radar-assisted collisions.") With these shipboard aids to navigation and with mechanical propulsion in place of sail for all types of commercial vessels, the elements have not been as much in command as formerly, and shipwrecks are now rare along the New England coast. Because of engine and battery failures, however, vessels still founder in storms, and collisions are not uncommon. In most cases help can be summoned by radio from the Coast Guard, which has also absorbed the functions of the old Life-Saving Service.

Many of the old Life-Saving Service stations have been closed, and patrolmen no longer battle their way along storm-swept beaches looking for wrecks. The Coast Guard's power rescue boats are now stationed at locations where they can be kept in the water or at least on ramps ready for quick launching. The main duties of these rescue boats are aiding yachtsmen and Sunday fishermen who put to sea in small outboard-powered boats with a case of beer, no oars, and little gasoline. Larger Coast Guard vessels based at New Bedford, Boston, and Portland stand ready to help vessels in distress at sea. Amphibious planes and helicopters are available for search missions and often aid foundering vessels by dropping additional pumps.

During this period of change, however, the sea took its toll. On the morning of 5 December 1914 the six-masted schooner *Alice M. Lawrence,* bound from Portland to Norfolk, stranded on Tuckernuck Shoal in Nantucket Sound and brought up on the stone-laden hull of the three-masted schooner *French Van Gilder,* which had been wrecked in 1885. The crew remained on board, and wrecking pumps were employed until it was found that the *Lawrence's* back was broken near her mizzenmast. She was then stripped of all possible material and abandoned. In November of the following year the wrecked *Lawrence* was burned to the water's edge.

In February 1918, Nantucket Sound's light vessel *Cross Rip* and her

The first deep-water off-shore fixed-light tower to replace a lightship—Buzzards Bay Entrance Light Station, commissioned November 1, 1961. *Courtesy United States Coast Guard.*

crew of eight disappeared without a trace. Many bodies of water normally open were frozen over during that severe winter, and heavy pack ice had torn the lightship from her moorings on 1 February. The *Cross Rip* was last sighted on the fifth from Nantucket's Great Point Light as she headed out to sea.

The last of William F. Palmer's fleet of coal schooners, the *Dorothy Palmer*, grounded on the edge of Stone Horse Shoal off the southern end of Cape Cod in a northwest gale in March 1923. The crew of the Monomoy Point Life-Saving Station could not launch a surfboat, but the Coast Guard cutter *Acushnet* stood by. When the gale moderated the next day, the surfboat rescued all eleven of the *Palmer*'s crew, but the schooner eventually went to pieces.

On Monday, 10 March 1924, the greatest of all the six-masted schooners, the Bath-built *Wyoming,* bound from Norfolk to St. John, New Brunswick, with coal, anchored to the northeast of the Pollock Rip light vessel in company with the *Cora F. Cressy,* a Bath-built five-master. In the face of a rising gale the *Cressy* put to sea at dusk, and on the following Thursday, in a blinding snowstorm, she anchored in the shelter of Duck Island, one of the Isles of Shoals. She reached Portland safely on Friday afternoon. On the following Tuesday one of the *Wyoming*'s nameboards came ashore, but this was not held necessarily to be an indication of her loss. Newspaper accounts for the next few days were confusing, and several masters of big sailing colliers were optimistic for her safety, believing she had followed the *Cressy*'s example. As finally more wreckage came ashore, however, it had to be conceded that the *Wyoming* had gone down with her crew of thirteen. Because of her great length (329′6″) she probably struck bottom in the hollows of the seas and pounded to pieces.

On 19 February 1927 the five-masted schooner *Nancy* anchored near Boston Light, expecting to ride out a predicted storm. She had three anchors out the next day when a sleet storm struck, but as the wind increased to fifty-five miles per hour, they dragged. The chains finally parted and the *Nancy* headed for Harding's Ledge. Captain E. M. Baird managed to work her clear by setting a staysail, and she stranded on Nantasket Beach about one hundred yards out. A volunteer crew of eleven launched the Humane Society's lifeboat and brought the entire crew, including the cat, safely to shore. When the storm subsided, the *Nancy* was high on the beach. From time to time efforts were made to haul her off, but all failed, and she there remained a tourist attraction for many years. Eventually she was broken up, her masts going to a Quincy granite quarry, while the inhabitants of Hull got the wood; as late as 1940 her keel was uncovered in a storm.

Not even powerful steamers were able to escape some storms. During a snowstorm on 9 March 1928 the 375-foot *Robert E. Lee,* heading for the Cape Cod Canal from Boston, struck on the Mary Ann Rocks off Manomet Point just south of Plymouth. Shortly after she hit the rocks, her generators failed and she rolled back and forth in darkness. A little later the sea cocks were opened and the *Lee* settled firmly onto the rocks. The next day all passengers were safely ferried by power surf-boats to Coast Guard patrol boats, but three Coast Guardsmen from the Manomet station died when their boat capsized on the way back to shore. Late in the month the *Robert E. Lee* was hauled off the rocks.

For many days in 1930 a pillar of fire and smoke off Scituate marked the site of a collision that claimed forty-seven lives. The Merchants' & Miners' steamer *Fairfax* sailed from Boston at 5:00 P.M. on 10 June 1930, heading for southern ports via the Cape Cod Canal. A heavy fog settled down as she cleared the harbor, and speed was reduced to ten to twelve knots. Just before 7:00 P.M. the Shell Oil tanker *Pinthis* loomed up on her starboard bow. Captain A. H. Brooks of the *Fairfax* ordered full speed astern on the engines and the helm hard aport, but it was too late to avoid collision. The *Pinthis* plowed into the *Fairfax,* oil drenched both ships, and both caught fire. The well-disciplined action of the crew and of some United States Marines and naval personnel traveling as passengers saved the *Fairfax* from serious loss, but the *Pinthis* sank almost immediately.

The Cape Cod Canal provided a safe north-south route for many vessels, but as ships became larger, the old thirty-foot-draft restriction required them to sail around the Cape. On Sunday, 17 February 1952, in a heavy gale and snowstorm, two 503-foot, war-built, all-welded, T2-type tankers, the *Pendleton* and the *Fort Mercer,* were heading north to pass outside Cape Cod. About 6:00 A.M. on Monday the *Pendleton* was struck by several heavy waves near Pollock Rip, where the *Wyoming* and many other vessels had been lost. A crack developed near her mainmast, and she soon broke in two; her radio was out of commission, and there was no way to send an SOS. The stern drifted faster than the bow, but both headed for Monomoy Beach. They were

Watch Hill, Rhode Island, before the 1938 Hurricane. *Courtesy* Westerly Sun *and Lewis R. Greene.*

Watch Hill, Rhode Island, after the 1938 Hurricane. Note the two wooden bulk-heads in both photographs. *Courtesy* Westerly Sun *and Lewis R. Greene.*

soon spotted from the Chatham Coast Guard Station, but neither an amphibious duck nor a surfboat got near enough to take off the crew. In the early evening another attempt by the surfboat rescued thirty-two of thirty-three men from the stern, then aground on Monomoy Beach. None were saved from the bow; in all, nine were lost from the *Pendleton,* and one seaman froze to death on the bow.

At 8:30 A.M. on the same day the *Fort Mercer,* then about thirty miles off Nauset Beach, radioed that she had sprung a leak and required assistance. She too soon broke in halves, and the sections drifted toward the shoals east of Nantucket. Two Coast Guard cutters were dispatched to the scene, and three others were alerted. Four men were rescued from the bow of the *Fort Mercer* after five of her crew had been washed overboard by waves. The bow section was then sunk by gunfire. Nineteen were removed from the stern section, but thirteen men successfully rode out the storm there.

No account of Massachusetts shipwrecks can omit the Italian-owned Liberty ship *Etrusco* that went ashore at Scituate on 16 March 1956. She threatened to become a permanent fixture near the old lighthouse, but on 22 November 1956, Thanksgiving Day, she was successfully refloated and rechristened the *Scituate*. An *Etrusco* Society, founded to aid her crew, still performs charitable services in the town.

For widespread destruction nothing has matched the several hurricanes that have swept through New England in recent decades. The most damaging struck without warning on 21 September 1938 as its center passed up the Connecticut River Valley. Nearly 700 persons lost their lives in the storm, more than 300 of them in Rhode Island, which was hit the hardest, as 121-mile-per-hour winds blew up Narragansett Bay. Lighthouses and summer colonies were washed away, shorelines were altered, and downtown Providence had ten feet of water in its main streets. Thousands of yachts and small commercial craft were reduced to kindling, others were deposited miles from the shore, and a lighthouse tender was set on the railroad tracks at New London.

A second hurricane on 14 September 1944 was well predicted, and only 31 persons lost their lives on shore, although property damage in the New Bedford–Cape Cod region was worse than in 1938. At sea, however, the list of persons killed or missing reached 344 with the sinking of the Vineyard Sound light vessel, the minesweeper *YMS-409,* the Coast Guard cutters *Jackson* and *Bedloe,* and a destroyer, the U.S.S.

Warrington. Two hurricanes in 1954, one in 1955, and another in 1961 also caused extensive marine damage in New England.

At the end of World War I, Boston Harbor had the world's largest drydock, located near the Army Base in South Boston; but because of the limited depth of the Broad Sound North Channel, none of the larger ships could enter the harbor to use it. This situation was remedied in 1925, when the federal government let a contract for dredging the channel to a depth of 40 feet at mean low water. Following the completion of this project, the liner *Leviathan* came to Boston many times for drydocking. Early in 1937 a 40-foot-deep anchorage basin was completed at President Roads just inside of Deer Island, and 1940 saw the finishing of a 40-foot channel from President Roads to Commonwealth Pier No. 1 in East Boston. Work was started in 1938 on a 30-foot-deep, 200-foot-wide channel through Chelsea Creek to the oil terminals.

In 1940 a dragwire survey of Boston Harbor was started to check on unmarked rocks and other obstructions not revealed by normal surveying procedures. Several ships had been damaged by such hazards and one lost. The American freighter *Cold Harbor* had struck a 22-foot ledge in the Broad Sound North Channel where the chart showed 27 feet of water. In the spring of 1938 the British cargo ship *City of Salisbury* had stranded on a previously unknown rock near The Graves and become a total loss. A major improvement since then has been the removal of a pinnacle of rock from Nantasket Gut, through which the largest vessels bound in and out of the Fore River may now pass instead of taking a tortuous channel around the west end of Peddocks Island.

Meanwhile, ironically, Boston's waterfront has contracted steadily since World War I — a decline which typifies that of all of New England's ports. As the many schooners in the coal trade were replaced by a few steamers, the apparent activity in the port dropped considerably. When newer and larger cargo ships came into service, the older wharves in Boston proper no longer were suitable, and steamship companies shifted their operations to the larger wharves in East Boston, South Boston, and Charlestown. By 1940 only six wharves on Boston's waterfront retained any semblance of their former activity. The ships of the Clyde-Mallory Line sailed from Lewis Wharf, which was also the headquarters of the Boston Towboat Company, organized in 1857. The United Fruit Company's "Great White Fleet" unloaded bananas at Long Wharf. The vessels of the Eastern Steamship Lines, operating on the runs to the Maritime Provinces and to New York, berthed at Central and India wharves, while Foster's and Rowes wharves handled the boats carrying summer excursionists to Nantasket Beach and Provincetown.

During the 1920s other Boston wharves and many of those in East Boston and Charlestown became cluttered with old steam and sailing vessels for which there was no more business. They were not cared for and slowly rotted, many sinking with only their superstructures above water. Between 1931 and 1935 a clean-up campaign resulted in the removal of 120 hulks, but 62 remained. A few of the latter were towed to sea and sunk early in 1940. Nothing was done to rehabilitate the old wharves.

More recent spurts of activity have vastly altered the waterfronts of numerous New England ports. In some cases, as in the handling of oil and container cargoes, these changes have brought improvements. In too many instances, however, old waterfront facilities have been torn down without replacement or have been converted into parking lots.

New England Playground

Changing tastes, economics, storms, and the fantastic growth of travel by private automobile have completely altered the character of the old New England seaside resorts and summer colonies. Along the south coast the great hurricanes of 1938 and 1944 wiped out scores of summer cottages and destroyed amusement parks such as Ocean Beach at New London, Rocky Point on Narragansett Bay, and Newport Beach. The parks still open at Nantasket Beach, Revere Beach, and Old Orchard, Maine, are but shadows of their former selves. Summer cottages have been winterized; and seaside towns, while still experiencing an influx of summer visitors, are substantial, year-round communities with such urban problems as schools, sanitation, and rubbish disposal. People in a Connecticut shore town like Old Saybrook think little of a thirty- to forty-minute drive by superhighway to jobs in Hartford, a trip that required more than two hours only fifty years ago.

As the general public became more mobile in their autos and as resorts around the world became more accessible by air, the cottages of Newport and Bar Harbor became less attractive to the wealthy. While many are still in use for family gatherings, others have been demolished or serve other purposes; The Breakers at Newport, for instance, is now a museum of the era. Along with the disappearance of the steamboats came changes in rail service — first reduction, then abandonment. In 1931 the eastern terminus of the famed Bar Harbor Express was shifted from Mount Desert Ferry at the head of Frenchman Bay to Ellsworth, whence the passengers were transferred to Bar Harbor by Maine Central buses. The last Bar Harbor Express pulled out of Ellsworth for New York at the end of the 1960 summer season. Today there are no passenger train services to Boston's South Shore, Cape Cod, or any New England coastal town north of Massachusetts.

Along with the changes in transportation have come changes in accommodations. While some of the great seaside hotels remain, their numbers are dwindling. Many have burned or been torn down, while others have closed their doors for economic reasons; they have been replaced by motels along the highways. Family migrations to a resort hotel for two weeks or more have given way to overnight stops. There has, however, been a trend toward the development of campgrounds in state and national parks suitable for the parking of trailers and the pitching of tents. All these changes have resulted in definite shifts of population. Many who seem to be "natives" are those from other parts of the country who found the New England coast attractive and moved to seaside towns to establish new businesses or simply to rusticate in retirement.

To a large extent, excursion boat services have followed the regular steamboat lines into oblivion. In many cases it was the lack of suitable boats rather than of public interest that closed a line. As with the deep-sea fleet, the boats grew old together, and rising costs of construction and operation precluded the construction of new ones of the same capacity. Many of the lines still operating in the 1960s were forced to employ "motor boats," vessels under sixty-five feet in length which could be operated by small crews. A recent Coast Guard regulation changed the limit for such craft from sixty-five feet to one hundred gross tons; hence New England may again see more suitable excursion craft on its waters.

The longest of the summer excursion runs was that from Boston to Provincetown at the tip of Cape Cod. The Cape Cod Steamship Company's *Dorothy Bradford* operated on that run until the early 1930s, when she was replaced by the *Steel Pier*. The Bay State Steamboat

Company ran various vessels in opposition during the late 1930s, including the *Romance,* which, on a foggy day in September 1936, was cut down and sunk off the Brewsters by the *New York,* fortunately without loss of life. One of the last steamers on the run was the *Provincetown,* formerly the *District of Columbia,* an unsuitable vessel that had been built for night service between Washington, D.C., and Norfolk, Virginia.

The Nantasket Steamboat Company suffered a severe blow in 1930 when fire destroyed four steamers in winter quarters. Subscriptions from the residents of Hull helped the company to purchase three steamers from other waters which, with .the Boston-built *Mayflower,* enabled service to be maintained through the depression years. Following World War II a number of older boats from Chesapeake Bay, the Delaware River, and the Maine coast served on the run from time to time, until a reorganized company had two sixty-five-foot, diesel-propelled craft built in the mid-1960s. For the past several years there has been a year-round commuting service between Pemberton and Boston.

Elsewhere in New England there are still ways of getting afloat in power-driven vessels, if only for relatively short ferry rides. These services have varied from year to year; as of 1970 they included a summer ferry service from Bridgeport, Connecticut, to Port Jefferson, Long Island, and another summer ferry service connecting New London and Orient Point, Long Island. During the harvesting season for Long Island potatoes, motorists crossing from the Connecticut shore to Long Island often must drive their cars into empty potato trucks. New Londoners and others can also take a short boat ride out to Fishers Island. During the summer, motor vessels operate to Block Island from Providence, Newport, Point Judith, and New London. A year-round service connects Woods Hole, Martha's Vineyard, and Nantucket. Besides the little *Sabino* on the Merrimack, the only steamboats in New England waters are on this run. Several Maine coast islands also have year-round services, and two foreign ferry services benefit Maine in particular and New England in general. The automobile and truck ferry *Bluenose,* Canadian-owned and -operated, has run for several years between Bar Harbor and Yarmouth, Nova Scotia. In June 1970 a Swedish company began operating a similar service between Portland and Yarmouth with the *Prince of Fundy.*

Coastal and inland-water cruises are now offered by the American-

Canadian Line based at Warren, Rhode Island, employing the new
(1969) 106-foot motor vessel *Mount Hope,* named for a long-time favorite steamboat on the Providence–Block Island run. Among the
twelve-day cruises offered are one to the Saguenay River via the Hudson
and Lake Champlain, a triangular cruise that includes the New York
Barge Canal and the St. Lawrence Seaway, and an island-hopping trip
along the Maine coast.

People interested in cruising under sail owe a great deal to the
enterprise of Captain Frank Swift of Camden, Maine, who in 1935 organized "Windjammer Cruises" in refurbished, two-masted Maine coasting schooners. These cruises became popular, and many others have
entered the business. Carrying about two dozen dude sailors each, the
schooners sail from Camden and Rockland on weekly cruises around
Penobscot and Blue Hill bays; on special occasions they venture along
the coast as far west as Boothbay Harbor. Itineraries vary as the wind
and weather dictate, but the schooners rendezvous in their home ports
on Saturdays. Power, if needed to meet this schedule, comes from a
yawl boat lashed alongside. The schooners have small professional
crews, but the summer sailors are encouraged to "hand, reef, and steer."

Coming as it did at the end of the era of commercial sail, the dude
cruise business was forced to employ schooners that in most cases were
none too spry. When with advancing age it became impossible for some
to meet Coast Guard inspections, replacements were sought far and
wide; the fleet at various times has included a Long Island Sound brick
schooner, a freight schooner from Chesapeake Bay, and an oyster
schooner from the Delaware. Recently yachts and fishermen built in
the 1920s have entered the business. In 1962 Captain H. S. Hawkins,
who had owned the well-known *Alice S. Wentworth* and the *Stephen
Taber,* put the new 83-foot *Mary Day* in service; designed by Captain
Hawkins, she was built by Harvey Gamage at South Bristol, Maine.

Dude cruising is not confined to the coast of Maine. The 100-ton
steel *Mystic Whaler,* sporting painted ports, carries forty-four passengers on trips out of Mystic, Connecticut, while the 108-foot topsail
schooner *Shenandoah* sails out of Vineyard Haven. The latter, another
product of the Gamage yard at South Bristol, is a close reproduction of
the Coast Guard cutter *Joe Lane* of 1849. Three sail training vessels are
also based on New England's south coast — the Coast Guard's bark

The dude schooner *Mercantile*, off Camden, Maine. *Courtesy Maine Department of Economic Development.*

Eagle at New London, the schooner *Brilliant* at Mystic Seaport, and Tabor Academy's *Tabor Boy* at Marion, Massachusetts. Cruises in these vessels may be vacations for some but hard work for others. Not to be overlooked is the reproduction of Captain Joshua Slocum's *Spray,* which offers short cruises around Boston Harbor.

The bright spot in New England's current maritime activities is the pleasure-boating field, with numerous craft ranging from *America*'s Cup yachts and deep-sea ocean racers to noisy outboards, the latter hardly pleasurable to those alongshore on a quiet evening. In summer, mooring space in most of New England's yachting centers is at a premium, and the construction of marinas is increasing. The simplest of these provide only mooring slips, while the more elaborate offer showers, laundry facilities, restaurants, and even motel accommodations. These developments have made it possible for some boats to become little more than floating summer cottages.

Major yacht-racing activities, suspended during World War I, resumed in 1920 with Sir Thomas Lipton's postponed fourth challenge for the *America*'s Cup. Herreshoff's 1914 candidate, the *Resolute,* won the honor of defending the Cup. In the July match off Sandy Hook, after losing the first two races to the *Shamrock IV,* the *Resolute* took the last three to retain the Cup. Sir Thomas challenged for the fifth and last time in 1929 for a match to be sailed in 1930, naming a cutter with a seventy-seven-foot waterline. The New York Yacht Club suggested that the boats be built to the universal rule of measurement and raced boat for boat, rather than employing time allowances as in previous matches. Sir Thomas agreed and chose the seventy-six-foot rating class, which carried the distinguishing letter *J*; hence the popular but erroneous designation *J-boat.* Four defense candidates were built — the *Enterprise,* designed by W. Starling Burgess; the *Yankee,* Boston's favorite, designed by Frank C. Paine; the *Weetamoe,* designed by Clinton H. Crane; and the *Whirlwind,* designed by L. Francis Herreshoff, a son of Nathanael G., the "Wizard of Bristol." These boats and the challenging *Shamrock V* were all jib-headed or Bermuda-rigged cutters carrying about 7,500 square feet of sail and varying in waterline length from eighty to eighty-six feet. The *Enterprise* was selected to defend the *America's* Cup and did so handily on new courses off Newport, Rhode Island.

In 1934 and again in 1937, T. O. M. Sopwith of England's Royal

The seventy-six rater *Ranger,* built at the Bath Iron Works, 1937. Photograph by Stanley Rosenfeld. *Courtesy Morris Rosenfeld & Sons, New York City.*

Yacht Squadron unsuccessfully challenged for the Cup with the *Endeavour* and the *Endeavour II*. In 1934 Harold S. Vanderbilt, in the new Burgess-designed *Rainbow,* lost the first two races but took the next four in succession. The defender in 1937 was the *Ranger,* designed by Burgess and young Olin J. Stephens, which won four races in a row and, in the fourth race, set a record for the thirty-mile equilateral triangular course of three hours, seven minutes, forty-nine seconds.

In all probability we shall never see the likes of the seventy-six-raters again. Recognizing the economic changes brought about by World War II, the New York Yacht Club was permitted by the court to allow racing by yachts of forty-four-foot waterline and to remove the restriction that challenging yachts must sail to the scene on their own bottoms. This resulted in a challenge in 1958 from a Royal Yacht Squadron syndicate on behalf of the *Sceptre* of the International Rule twelve-meter class. She was defeated in four straight races by the Stephens-designed *Columbia,* the third of the name to defend the Cup. During the 1960s the American yachts *Weatherly, Constellation,* and *Intrepid* have succeeded in defending the Cup from both British and Australian challenges.

In the smaller racing classes, Universal Rule boats predominated during the 1920s both north and south of Cape Cod, but an interest in international competition led to the introduction on Long Island Sound of the International Rule six-meter class early in the decade. These were followed by eight-, ten-, and twelve-meter boats, which gradually displaced the equivalent Universal Rule twenty-raters (R), twenty-five-raters (Q), and forty-six-raters (M). In the opinion of many yachtsmen, the International Rule boats were poorer all around than the Universal Rule boats. Again economics played its part, and the 1930s saw the end of these open classes and a widespread trend toward one-design racing classes.

The 1920s also saw the beginning of long-distance racing on a yearly or biennial basis. The biggest such event now originating in New England is the biennial race to Bermuda. The first such race started at Gravesend Bay, Long Island, in 1906, when 3 participants crossed the starting line; four more races were held between then and 1910. The race was revived in 1923, when 22 boats racing in one class crossed the line at New London; in 1924 a total of 14 boats started in three classes. From 1926 on, except during World War II, the Bermuda Race has

The twelve-meter *Intrepid*. Photograph by Stanley Rosenfeld. *Courtesy Morris Rosenfeld & Sons, New York City.*

been a biennial event under the auspices of the Cruising Club of America. Through 1934 all starts were at New London, except in 1932, when the race started off Montauk Point. Difficulties in sailing through The Race at the eastern end of Long Island Sound led to the selection of Newport as the starting point in 1936. The contest became so popular that the number of entries taxed facilities at the "Onion Patch," as yachtsmen have called Bermuda. The number of boats is now limited to about 150, and entry is by invitation only.

At the other end of the yachting fleet are the little open boats for juniors — and for those of their elders who are still young in heart — which dot the waters of all harbors in the summer. The hardy indulge in the well-named "frostbite" racing all winter. While many classes of little boats may be found, New England's own Turnabout class, a nine-foot, eight-inch catboat that even carries a miniscule spinnaker, numbers in the thousands.

A New Era

We have followed the rise and fall of the New England merchant marine through two worldwide conflicts, which demonstrated that its poor peacetime condition was the result of economics, not of technical incompetence. Unlike the period before World War I, the years since have seen several efforts by the federal government to bolster the country's deep-sea merchant marine, the varied success of the programs depending on the determination of the federal agencies involved and on the Congress's mood as it controls the purse strings. In view of recently announced measures, there is hope that American merchant ships may again carry a substantial portion of the country's foreign commerce; but present shipping patterns suggest that only Boston, of all New England's ports, would benefit.

Since the close of World War I we have seen the end of commercial sail and of the coastwise steamboat lines. Except for oil tankers, a few colliers, and fewer special chemical carriers, there is at present no New England coastwise trade and little possibility of improvement. Once-important rivers are now only obstacles to be bridged by the expanding net of highways for motor transport. Even yachting no longer preserves the maritime traditions as carefully as it once did. The ubiquitous outboard motorboat is too often a means of escape from the congested highways on shore, and sailing is frequently just a sport indulged in at the expense of prudent seamanship. Yet many new enthusiasts are discovering each year the challenge and pleasure of sailing in New England's waters.

The preservation of New England's maritime past is now the province of museums, which are gaining public interest and support. Their number is growing and their quality improving as they are transformed from local historical societies into nationally recognized institutions. Among those outstanding in the field is Mystic Seaport, operated by The Marine Historical Association, Inc., at Mystic, Connecticut. Its most popular attraction (and perhaps its biggest headache) is the whaleship *Charles W. Morgan*. Not only does this museum preserve many of the smaller types of commercial vessels and yachts; it has also reconstructed the shops and offices that built them, manufactured their equipment, and handled their business. These practical exhibits are backed by a growing research library and publications program, and summer courses are offered in American maritime history.

Since whaling out of New Bedford ended in the 1920s, it has fallen to the Whaling Museum of the Old Dartmouth Historical Society to preserve the memories and records of that business. In recent years this museum has been complemented by the Kendall Whaling Museum in Sharon, Massachusetts, and there is a small whaling museum on Nantucket. Also in southern Massachusetts is the Marine Museum at Fall River, specializing in the history of steam vessels. The Peabody Museum in Salem, Massachusetts, continues to be of prime importance to researchers, with numerous models, large collections of paintings, prints, photographs, and documents, and a fine library. The small, technically oriented Hart Nautical Museum at the Massachusetts Institute of Technology has a fine collection of ship models and plans of merchant ships, naval vessels, and yachts. In Maine there are two important institutions in the field, the Bath Marine Museum — which in five years grew from exhibits in a downtown store to fill a twenty-six-room, shipbuilder's mansion with an air-conditioned archives room — and the older Penobscot Marine Museum in Searsport. Smaller collections of marine materials may be found at the Wadsworth Atheneum in Hartford; the Old State House and the Museum of Fine Arts in Boston; the Salem Maritime National Historic Sites; the Cape Ann Historical Association in Gloucester; Phillips Academy in Andover,

The whaleship *Charles W. Morgan,* one of the main attractions at Mystic Seaport. *Courtesy Connecticut Development Commission.*

Massachusetts; the Athenaeum in Portsmouth, New Hampshire; and the headquarters of numerous local historical societies.

Apart from those at Mystic, there are few actual historic vessels to be seen in New England. Top billing, of course, goes to the United States Navy, which maintains the U.S.S. *Constitution* at Boston. Also at Boston are the Hudson River steamboat *Peter Stuyvesant* and the schooner *Alice S. Wentworth*. A three-quarter-size version of Donald McKay's *Flying Cloud* is at Salem, and in Hull the old Nantasket steamer *Mayflower,* hauled out about two decades ago, serves as a nightclub. Plimoth Plantation maintains at Plymouth, Massachusetts, the *Mayflower II,* a reproduction of a vessel of the size and type of the Pilgrims' ship of 1620, which sailed the Atlantic in 1957. The Bath Marine Museum owns the tug *Seguin* of 1884 and is building up a collection of small craft, as is the museum at Searsport. A reproduction of H.M.S. *Rose,* a ship-sloop of 1756, is based at Newport, Rhode Island, and in nearby Fall River the battleship *Massachusetts* of 1942 is open to visitors. While not an actual vessel, the half-size model of the whaling bark *Lagoda* in the museum at New Bedford is an impressive display. With these museums and vessels and many dedicated workers in the field, the role of New England in America's maritime past will not be forgotten.

Epilogue

In the foregoing chapters we have seen the many ways in which ten generations of New Englanders have used the sea. They have relied on its fish as foodstuff and as cargo in coastal and foreign trade. The ocean itself has been an avenue of commerce that took them all over the world. Most recently the sea has become a summertime playground. But there is one other purpose to which New Englanders have put the sea. They have used it as a dump.

The rivers of New England drain many square miles of forest and farm into the sounds and bays along the coast. The advent of agricultural spraying, particularly the use of DDT and other chemicals of persistent life, has brought tons of pesticides down the streams and rivers to the sea. As a result, marine life from the tiniest phytoplankton to the largest game fish has become contaminated. Birds and larger fish eat the smaller species, and the poisons become ever more concentrated within them. Osprey counts have dropped steadily since World War II, while scavengers like the bald eagle, which feed on dead fish, are even more seriously endangered. The only hope for survival among these species, claim officials of the Audubon Society, is the effective prohibition of DDT and similar chemicals throughout the world.

But agriculture is not the primary source of the pollutants that contaminate New England's waters. With the coming of the industrial revolution to New England in the early nineteenth century, most millowners placed their plants along the riverbanks. In so doing, they naturally assumed the right to use the river for whatever purposes their business required. Many mills operated at first by waterpower, and the steam mills required water for their boilers. Some rivers served as important transportation lines for the mill operators, and in almost every case the river was used to carry off whatever waste products the plant produced. Until late in the nineteenth century, these industrial wastes were not extremely dangerous. With the increasing use of chemical dyes in the textile mills, however, and with the rise of paper mills, tanneries, and other industries that use chemicals, wastes were no longer easily broken down. Today we are just beginning to realize the deadly effects of substances like lead, mercury, and polychlorobiphenyl (PCB).

New Englanders, like people everywhere, have also used their waterways as sewers to carry off human wastes. Until recent decades, sewage treatment plants were not considered necessary, and one might argue that the amount of sewage from the small population centers of pre-twentieth-century America was literally but a drop in the bucket of the broad Atlantic. Furthermore, human wastes are organic and are therefore more readily absorbable by the ocean waters. In fact, when cleansed of their disease-bearing bacteria, these effluents are a benefit to the aquatic life cycle. The problem today is to assure proper treatment and to prevent such heavy concentrations of effluent that marine life is overstimulated.

Along with industrial chemicals come two other modern substances that cause dangerous pollution — oil and heat. Oil pollution comes from a number of sources. Transferring crude oil from tanker to refinery often produces minor spillages. Most of this oil is easily trapped in the immediate area of the refinery, but as the supertankers make increasing use of offshore facilities, the difficulty of containing spillages is multiplying. The proposed facilities along the coast of Maine have generated considerable opposition from conservationists and others because of these dangers. The process of cleansing tanks, although prohibited in coastal waters, pumps still more oil into the sea. Worst, of course, is the kind of marine disaster that spilled 36 million gallons of oil from the tanker *Torrey Canyon* off the coast of England in 1967. New Englanders shudder at the thought of such a tanker striking one of the many ledges off the coast of Maine or foundering in Long Island Sound. The fact that tankers of the future will be three or four times as large as the *Torrey Canyon* is not encouraging.

As Jacques Cousteau has pointed out, however, private yachts are responsible each year for thirty times as much oil as was spilled from the *Torrey Canyon*. One study, disputed by industry authorities, has estimated that the high-horsepower, two-cycle outboard engine pumps up to 50 percent of its fuel directly through the exhaust system into the water. The ability of coastal waters like Long Island Sound to absorb oil pollution at this rate is limited. Offshore oil drilling is still another source of danger, as the Santa Barbara case in 1969 dramatically illustrated.

Optimists are confident that pesticides can be curbed, industrial chemicals can be neutralized at the plant, sewage can be treated. Some might argue that a combination of more careful piloting, tighter international regulations, and more effective clean-up procedures can check the dangers from oil spills. Prohibiting the two-cycle engine and preventing leakage from offshore oil wells may not be so easily accomplished. To some conservationists, however, the most dangerous threat to coastal waters is from an altogether different source — heat.

Thermal pollution results from the steam-generating plants located along many of New England's major rivers. Whether powered by fossil fuels or atomic energy, these plants require millions of gallons of water each hour to cool their condensers. The water is returned at temperatures ranging from 10 to 30 degrees above that of the river or bay. Temperature is a critical factor in the reproductive cycle of marine organisms, most of which cannot tolerate water much above 90 degrees. One need not dwell long on the effect that increased ocean temperatures will eventually have on the polar ice cap. Yet our civilization must have power, and most conservationists look to electricity as a hopeful alternative to the internal combustion engine. The use of atomic energy eliminates the smoke pollution now associated with fossil fuel generators, but such plants, because of their thermal inefficiency, require even greater amounts of water for cooling purposes. And then there is the problem of disposing of the used-up fuel cells. Will they too be consigned ("out of sight, out of mind") to the Atlantic, as was the army's deadly nerve gas?

Marine interests themselves are responsible for considerable damage to the coastal environment, as when they demand the dredging of a local harbor without concern for the place where the silt will be dumped. Dredging of the harbor at Belfast, Maine, by the Army Corps of Engineers has deposited tons of mud, polluted by the town's chicken processors, onto some of the best shellfish beds in Penobscot Bay. Yet the maritime future of Belfast harbor seems dependent on the project. Still more harmful is the use of dredged silt to fill in salt marshes, for the marshes are the nurseries in which much of the coastal marine life is spawned.

Until recently New Englanders have used the sea as they saw fit, without much thought for the consequences. In this respect they are little different from people everywhere. But as the 1960s ended, many New Englanders living along the coast had become aware that an environmental crisis was at hand. Only by the narrowest of margins did the inhabitants of the economically depressed area around Machias approve the idea of a major oil depot there. At Portland, already the terminal for oil lines into Canada, plans for new facilities in Casco Bay have met with determined opposition. Maine has adopted the nation's first water-pollution act, and vigorous enforcement has begun. A leading conservation group, the Nature Conservancy, has accepted for perpetual preservation numerous parcels of coastal shoreline, and residents of other New England states are working toward similar goals.

As in so many areas of American life, the decade of the 1970s is one in which New Englanders will be reexamining the priorities involved in their uses of the sea. If they wish still to depend on the ocean for its fish, lobsters, and clams and to attract tourists to its coasts, they will have to protect man's greatest natural resource from destruction by man. Whether New Englanders can show the way in human self-restraint remains to be seen.

Index

Abnaki Indians, 13
Acadia, S.S., 241
Acushnet, cutter, 262
Acushnet, whaler, 114
Adams, Charles F., 156
Adams, Capt. Isaac, 62
Adams, John, 52–53, 69
Adams, John Quincy, 52–53
Adams, Moses, 255
Adams family, 193
Adventure, ketch, 22
Africa, trade with, 107, 109, 111, 168.
    See also Slave trade
Aids to navigation, 198–201, 258, 260, 261
A. J. Fuller, Down-Easter, 169
Akerman, John, 63
Alabama, C.S.S., 153, 155, 156–159
Alabama Claims, 156
Alaska, 124
Albany, N.Y., 21, 127
Alert, ship, 113
Aletes, yacht, 232
Alewives, 26
Algonquin Indians, 12–13
Alicante, Spain, 83
Alice M. Lawrence, schooner, 260
Alice S. Wentworth, schooner, frontispiece,
    270
Allyn's Point, Conn., 130
Amanda, bark, 158
America, yacht, 218
American-Canadian Line, 270
American Coast Pilot, 92
American Export Lines, 238
American Steamship Co., 164

America's Cup races, 218–223, 272–276
Ames, Fisher, 52, 63
Ames, Nathaniel, 52
Amsterdam, 62, 107
Andrew Jackson, clipper, 146
Andrews, Israel D., 123
Anglo-French War (1793–1815), 60–66
Ann & Hope, ship, 107
Anna F. Schmitt, ship, 157
Annapolis, Md., 39–40, 42
Annie & Rueben, 184
Antarctica, 112
Antigua, 35, 36, 122
Antigua, S.S., 234
Archangel, 81, 83
Archer, C.S.S., 158, 159
Architecture, 46–53
Arctic Ocean, 197
Arethusa, schooner, 250
Argentina, 113–114
Arnold, Benedict, 69
Arrow, steamer, 241
Arrow, yacht, 225
Asia, trade with, 56–60. See also
    individual countries
Asia, ship, 62
Atlantic Corporation, 228
Atlantic Works, 149, 170, 234
Atlantis, ketch, 258
Augusta, Me., 141–142, 179, 243
Augustus P. Loring, S.S., 235
Australia, trade with, 58, 98, 146, 166, 168
Axes, 40
Azores, trade with, 27, 33, 40, 115, 156

Bahia, Brazil, 158
Bainbridge, U.S.S., 238
Baird, Capt. E. M., 262
Baltic Sea, 81, 121
Baltick, schooner, 34
Baltimore, Md., 127, 131, 181
Baltimore clipper, 93, 142
Bananas, 166
Bangor, Me., 78–79, 102, 122, 130, 133,
    155, 158, 164, 179, 181, 182, 212, 244
Banks, Gen. Nathaniel P., 153
Bar Harbor, Me., 179, 211, 212, 214, 215,
    223, 244, 262, 268, 269
Barbados, 34, 35, 36, 122
Barbary pirates, 73–75
Barnard, Rev. John, 29
Barnes, James, 146
Barnstable, Mass., 26, 49–50, 102, 136, 191
Barrel staves. See Wood products
Bartlet, William, 62
Batavia, Java, 107
Bath, Me., 30, 78–79, 101, 102, 103, 122,
    130, 150, 152, 161–162, 168, 169, 170,
    171, 172, 174, 176, 179, 185, 186, 189,
    198, 228, 232, 238, 242, 243, 249, 262
Bath Iron Works, 172, 174, 175, 176, 179,
    223, 229, 236, 237, 238, 249, 253, 273
Bath Marine Museum, 279
Bay State Steamboat Co., 268–269
Beans, 40, 62
Beavertail Light, R.I., 87
Bêche-de-mer, 58, 112, 113
Bedloe, cutter, 265
Beer, 36
Beets, 33, 62
Belfast, Me., 102, 130, 179, 237, 244,
    282–283
Belfast, steamer, 175, 179, 241, 242
Bering Sea, 115, 159, 197
Bermuda race, 276
Bertram, John, 109
Berwick, Me., 74
Bethel, ship, 65
Bethlehem Fore River (Quincy) Yard,
    228–231, 233, 234, 237, 238, 239. See
    also Fore River Ship & Engine Co.
Betsey, schooner, 40
Beverly, Mass., 102, 210
Biddeford Pool, Me., 211
Bills of exchange, 25, 36, 40, 60
Black Ball Line, 98, 118, 127, 146
Black Joke, sloop, 68
Blankets, 68

Block, Adriaen, 17
Block Island, R.I., 6, 16, 199, 200, 269, 297
Blockade (War of 1812), 85; (Civil War),
    150. See Revolution & War of 1812
Blue Hill, Me., 185, 214
Bluenose, motor vessel, 269
Bluenose, schooner, 254–255
Blunt, Edmund March, 92
Bombay, India, 59
Boon Island Light, Me., 89, 199
Boothbay Harbor, Me., 193, 242, 243, 255
Boston, Mass., 6, 19, 29, 37, 45, 50, 52, 57,
    66, 69, 85, 87, 90, 102, 103, 104, 105,
    113, 119, 120, 124, 127, 129, 131, 143,
    145, 149, 150, 151, 154, 156, 157, 160,
    164, 167, 175, 176, 179, 181, 186, 188,
    189, 192, 193, 201, 204, 208, 229, 238,
    240, 241, 244, 245, 247–248, 249, 252,
    260, 266, 268, 272, 279. See also East
    Boston, Mass.
Boston, ship, 59
Boston, steamer, 239, 241
Boston & Bangor S.S. Co., 175, 179
Boston and Gloucester Steamboat Co., 242
Boston & Hingham Steamboat Co., 208
Boston College, trawler, 253
Boston Light, 87
Boston Marine Society, 198, 201
Boston Navy Yard at Charlestown, 152,
    153, 231
Boston Port Act, 67
Boston Tea Party, 66
Bowditch, Nathaniel, 92
Bowdoin College, 110, 151
Bradford C. French, schooner, 185
Braintree, Mass., 173
Brandon, steamer, 242
Brazil, 81
Brazil Banks, 31
Bread, 33, 38
Breakwaters, 205
Bremer, Germany, 61
Brereton, John, 3
Bricks, 33
Bridgeport, Conn., 175, 195, 269
Bridges, Horatio, USN, 151
Briggs, Enos, 94
Brilliant, schooner, 272
Bristol, R.I., 49, 69, 102, 107, 176, 217
Britannia, S.S., 119, 120, 131
"Broken voyage", 61, 75
Brooklin, Me., 244
Brooks, Capt. A. H., 263

Brooks, Van Wyck, 97
Brown, John Bundy, 123
Brown, Moses, 49, 63
Brown, Nicholas, 60, 62
Brown family (Providence), 48–49, 59–60
Brown and Ives, 107
Brown University, 49
Browne, Samuel, 35–36
Brownstone. See Stone.
Bryant, William C., 212
Bryant & Sturgis, 113
Buenos Aires, Argentina, 113–114
Bucksport, Me., 244
Bulfinch, Charles, 53
Bulloch, Capt. James D., C.S.N., 156
Bunker, Capt. Elihu, 129
Bunker Hill, steamer, 241–242
Buoys, 89, 198
Burgess, Edward, 193, 219–220
Burgess, W. Starling, 272, 274
Burke, Edmund, 55
Burnham, Willard A., 255
Burnham family, 193
Butler, Gen. Benjamin F., 153
Butler's Hole, Mass., 205
Butter, 62
Buzzards Bay, 3, 7, 16, 19, 215, 261

Cabot, John and Sebastian, 15
Cabot family, 56, 63
Cadet, brig, 60
Cadiz, Spain, 40
Calais, Me., 159
Calcutta, India, 62, 109, 110, 156
Caleb Cushing, cutter, 158
California, 97, 98, 113, 142
Cambria, yacht, 218
Camden, Me., 101, 130, 185, 187, 237, 244, 270, 271
Camden, steamer, 174, 175, 179, 241, 242
Campobello Island, N.B., 79
Canada, 164, 253–254, 277. See also Maritime Provinces
Canary Islands, 40
Candles, spermaceti, 31, 33, 40
Cannibalism, 112, 114
Canton, China, 58, 59, 105–108, 112, 143
Cap François, 35
Cape Ann, Mass., 7, 26, 87, 89, 139, 141, 205, 210, 215
Cape Breton Island, 13, 123
Cape Cod, Mass., 6, 7, 16, 19, 30, 85, 89, 100, 122, 125, 126, 128, 136, 138–139,

175, 179, 181, 185, 196, 202–203, 215, 216, 241, 262, 265
Cape Cod Canal, 204, 205–206, 258–260, 263
Cape Elizabeth, Me., 7
Cape Horn, 98, 112, 124, 143, 156, 157
Cape Town, So. Africa, 158
Cape Verde Islands, 115
Caribbean. See West Indies
Carnes, Capt. Jonathan, 60
Casco Bay, Me., 6, 135, 185, 283
Casco Bay Lines, 244
Cashes Ledge, 26
Castine, Me., 79, 85
Cattle, 33
Caviare, schooner, 255
Celia, brig, 75
Champlain, Samuel de, 4, 17
Champlin family, 48–49
Charles D. Stanford, schooner, 245
Charles Hunt Co., 168
Charles W. Morgan, whaler, 116, 118, 257, 277, 278
Charles River, Mass., 19
Charleston, S.C., 119, 127, 153
Charlestown, Mass., 23, 164
Charlotte, ship, 62
Chebacco boats, 23, 93–94, 138
Chebeague Island, Me., 135, 185
Cheese, 62
Cheeseman, James L., 135
Cherbourg, France, 158
Chesapeake, U.S.S., 76, 79
Chesapeake-Leopard affair, 76, 78
Chesapeake Bay, 39–40, 85
Child, Josiah, 27–28
Chile, 57, 114, 149
China, trade with, 56–60, 97, 98, 104–105, 112–113, 143, 146, 157
Chinaware, 57
Cigarette, yacht, 225
City of Bangor, steamer, 179, 242
City of Lowell, steamer, 173
City of Rockland, steamer, 242
City of Salisbury, S.S., 266
Civil War, 150–160
Clams. See Shellfish
Clark, Capt. Arthur H., 142
Clark, David, 185
Clippers, 97, 98, 107, 142–149, 160
Cloves, 109
Clyde-Mallory Line, 248, 266–267
Coal, 123, 126, 132, 135, 151, 182, 186,

188, 191–192, 245, 247, 248–249, 262,
Coastal Trade, 23, 25, 33, 37, 38–41, 78–
79, 110, 118, 124–135, 175–191, 247–
249, 277
Coastal navigation, 200
Coastwise Transportation Co., 188
Cocoa, 38
Coconuts, 35
Cod, 15, 26, 27, 29, 78, 126, 135, 136, 193,
254. See also Fish, Fisheries
Coffee, 38, 59, 61, 62, 68, 81, 83, 107
Cold Harbor, S.S., 266
Cole, Thomas, 212
Collins, Capt. Joseph W., 193
Columbia, schooner, 254
Columbia, ship, 57, 59
Columbia, yacht (1871), 219, 220; (1890),
220; (1957), 274
Comet, steamer, 241
Commission merchants, 100
Commonwealth, steamer, 176
Congregational church, 48, 52
Connecticut, 4–12, 38, 39, 47–48, 53, 57,
67, 68, 69, 79, 85, 99–100, 101, 102,
129, 131, 135, 139, 150, 151, 164, 175,
206–207, 228, 231, 237–238
Connecticut, steamer, 129
Connecticut River, 6, 17, 19, 21, 89, 185,
195, 206, 265
Connolly, James B., 192
Constellation, yacht, 274
Constitution, U.S.S., 279
Constitution, S.S., 238
Continental Association, 67
Continuous voyage, 75
Cook, John, 57
Cook, Zebedee, 63
Coolie trade, 149
Coombs, John and Philip, 81
Cooperage, 35
Copenhagen, 60, 62
Cora F. Cressy, schooner, 262
Corbin, James, 244
Cordage, 83
Corn, 38, 40
Corn Laws, 97–98
Corsair IV, yacht, 232, 233
Cottage City (Oak Bluffs), Mass., 207
Cottage City, steamer, 173
Cotton goods. See Textile Manufactures
Cotton trade, 35, 38, 59, 98, 118, 132, 141,
166
Council for New England, 17, 18

Cousteau, Jacques, 281–282
Crane, Clinton H., 272
Crescent, frigate, 74
Cressy, Capt. J. P., 153
Crowell & Thurlow, 245
Crowley, Capt. John G., 188
Crowninshield, B. B., 193
Crowninshield family, 56, 63
Crowninshield Shipbuilding Co., 247
Cruising Club of America, 276
Cuba, trade with, 122, 123
Cudworth & Flint, 146
Cunard Line, 119, 164
Currents, 7–8, 26
Currier & Townshend, 146
Curtis, J. O., Yard, 146
Cushing, Caleb, 97
Cushing, John P., 105
Customs districts, statistics, 101
Cutler, Carl C., 127, 142–143, 160

Damariscotta, Me., 12, 243
Damariscove, Me., 17
Dana, Richard H., 113
Dane, Ernest B., 232
Darby, schooner, 40
Dartmouth, Mass. See New Bedford
Dashing Wave, ship, 143
Davis, Charles H., USN, 151
Davis Strait, 31
Deane, Silas, 67–68
Deer Isle, Me., 133, 135
Defiance, yacht, 223
Deford, Benjamin, 131
Delano, Warren, 106
Delaware Bay, 126–127
Denmark, trade with, 81
Depth finders, 260
Derby, Elias Hasket, 59
Derby, Elias Hasket, Jr., 59, 73
Derby family, 56, 63
Desmoines, U.S.S., 173
Devereux, Capt. James, 57
Dewey, U.S.S., 232
Diamond Shoals, lightship, 173
Dickens, Charles, 119
Dighton, Mass., 102
Dilemma, yacht, 220
Diligence, mast ship, 42
Dirigo, bark, 170, 171, 172
Disasters, marine. See Shipwrecks.
Disunion, 80, 84
Dodge, William E., 100

Dorchester, S.S., 248
Dorothy Bradford, steamer, 268–269
Dow, Neal, 122
Down-Easters, 149, 168–170
Downer, Samuel, 208–210
"Drawbacks", 61
Dreadnought, clipper, 146
Dredging, 204–205
Dwight, Timothy, 48

Eagle, bark, 270–272
East Boothbay, Me., 243, 244
East Boston, Mass., 145, 146, 164, 168, 170, 180, 185
East Haddam, Conn., 206
East India Marine Society (Salem), 91
East River, N.Y., 145
Eastern Steamship Co. (later Eastern Steamship Lines), 179, 181, 239, 241, 266–267
Eastport, Me., 7, 179, 244, 245
Eben Dodge, whaler, 157
Ecology, 280–283
Ecuador, 114
Eggemoggin Reach, 8
Eleanor A. Percy, schooner, 185–186
Electric Boat Co., 231, 236
Elizabeth, schooner, 39–40
Elizabeth Islands, Mass., 6
Embargo Act, 76–80
Emergency Fleet Corporation, 228
Emery, John S., 168
Endeavour, sloop, 35
Endeavour, yacht, 274; *II,* 274
English Pilot, 91
Enterprise, yacht, 272
Enumerated articles, 32
Ericsson, John, 151
Erie, S.S., 163
Erikson, Lief, 14
Essex, Mass., 94, 141, 192, 193, 194, 196, 198, 253, 254–255
Essex decision, 75
Essex, whaleship, 114
Etrusco, S.S., 265
Eunice, brig, 91
European trade, 38, 40, 60, 61–62, 81
Evangeline, S.S., 241
Everett, Mass., 249
Everett, steamer, 186
Excursion boats, 207
Exploration, 13–18

Fair Haven, Conn., 195
Fairfield, Conn., 102
Fall River, Mass., 122, 130, 176, 211, 249, 279
Fall River Line, 130, 176, 177, 211, 241
Fall River Marine Museum, 277
Fanning, Edmund, 112
Farragut, David G., USN, 152
Farragut, U.S.S., 234
Farrell Lines, 240
Federalists, 48, 50–53, 75, 76, 80, 83–84
Fertilizer, 245. See also Guano
Figs, 121
Fiji Islands, 112
Firewood, 124, 134
Fish, preserved, 100
Fish, 15, 19, 33, 37–40, 42, 55, 59–62, 83, 121, 124, 132, 135–139. See also Cod and other species
Fish oil, 42
Fisheries and fishing, 13, 15–17, 23, 25–31, 50, 54, 67, 78, 79, 93–94, 103–104, 137–139, 158, 191–198, 251–258. See also Shellfish
Fishers Island, N.Y., 48, 269
Flax, 83
Fleeting, yacht, 216
"Flight from the flag", 160
Flint, Charles R., 225
Flint & Chapman, 170
Florida, C.S.S., 153, 156–159
Florida, S.S., 201
Flour, 33, 38, 39, 40, 42, 59, 79, 124, 126, 135
Flying Cloud, clipper, 142, 145, 146, 147, 153, 160, 270
Fog, 200
Foote, Andrew, USN., 151
Forbes, John M., 106
Forbes, Capt. Robert B., 106–107
Fore River Ship & Engine Co., 173, 186, 193. See also Bethlehem Fore River (Quincy) Yard
Fort Mercer, tanker, 263, 265
Forests, 19, 21
Fox, Gustavus V., 150
Fox Island Thoroughfare, 8
France, trade with, 55, 60, 61, 67–68, 83, 121
Franco-American Alliance, 1778, 69
Frank A. Palmer, schooner, 185
Franklin, ship, 57
French, in America, 17–18, 27, 28–29

Frenchman's Bay, Me., 102, 136
Fredonia, schooner, 193
"Free ships", 163
Friendship, ship, 109
Fruits, 121
Fulton, Robert, 129
Fulton, steamer, 129
Furlong, Capt. Lawrence, 92
Furniture, 33, 40, 62
Furs, 19, 57, 110–112

Gardiner, Me., 130, 179, 237, 242, 243
Gardner, William, 222–223
Galatea, yacht, 219
Galena, U.S.S., 153
Gamage, Harvey, 270
Galveston, Tex., 248
General Dynamics Corp., 238. See also Electric Boat Co.
General Lincoln, steamer, 209
General Washington, ship, 59
Genesta, yacht, 219, 220
George, ship, 109
George W. Wells, schooner, 185–186, 187
Georges Bank, 6, 15, 26, 29, 138, 191, 252
Gertrude L. Thébaud, schooner, 254–255
Gin, 62
Ginger, 35
Ginseng, 57
Glasgow, Scotland, 172
Glaciers, 4–7
Glassware, 83
Globe, whaler, 114
Gloriana, yacht, 220, 221
Gloucester, Mass., 19, 30, 69, 85, 102, 103–104, 127, 136, 138, 158, 191–193, 210, 242, 253
Gold dust, 109
Gold rush, 98, 142, 143, 144
Golden Rocket, ship, 155
Gómez, Estev*á*n, 16
Goodhue, Jonathan, 100
Gosnold, Bartholomew, 3, 16–17
Goss & Sawyer (Goss Marine Iron Works), 168, 173, 185. See also New England Shipbuilding Co.
Governor, steamer, 131, 151
Governor Ames, schooner, 184, 185, 191
Governor Prence, steamer, 242
Grain, 55
Grand Banks, 11, 15, 27, 31, 138, 191–192
Grand Manan Island, N.B., 79
Grand Trunk Railroad, 120

Granite. See Stone
Gray, Capt. Robert, 57
Gray, William, 75
Great Britain, trade with, 38, 42–43, 54, 60, 66–67, 97–98, 107, 117–124, 166
Great Republic, clipper, 146, 148
Grindstones, 123
Grinnell, Moses H., 145
Grinnell family, 100, 106
Griswold, N. L. & G., 100
Griswold family, 105–106
Groton, Conn., 175, 228, 231, 237, 238
Groton Iron Works, 228. See also Electric Boat Co.
Guadeloupe, 35, 62
Guano, 149
Gulf Coast, 181, 247–248
Gulf Stream, 31
Gum arabic, 59
Gum copal, 109
Gunpowder, 67, 68, 109
Gypsum, 123

Haddock, 15, 26, 138, 253
Hadlock, Samuel, 78
Hakluyt, Richard, 16
Halibut, 138, 192, 193
Halifax, N.S., 78, 119, 120, 179
Hallowell, Me., 130, 141–142, 179, 182
Hamburg, Germany, 61
Hampton Beach, N.H., 210
Hannah, schooner, 137
Hannah, sloop, 40, 41
Hanseatic ports, 61
Happy Return, brigantine, 68
Hart Nautical Museum, M.I.T., 277, 279
Hartford, Conn., 19, 21, 48, 129, 164, 166, 175, 241, 279
Harvard College, 113
Harvard, steamer, 180, 187
Haskell, Capt. David, 83
Hats, 62
Havana, 75, 110, 122
Hawaii, 58, 115, 116, 124
Hawkins, Capt. H.S., 270
Hawthorne, Nathaniel, 109–110
Hay, 127
Hedges, James B., 107
Helen B. Thomas, schooner, 194
Hemp, 83
Henrietta, yacht, 216
Henry B. Hyde, Down-Easter, 169, 170

Herald, brig, 111
Herjolfsson, Bjarni, 14
Herreshoff, John B., 217
Herreshoff, L. Francis, 272
Herreshoff, Nathanael G., 217, 219, 220, 221–223, 272
Herreshoff Manufacturing Co., 224–225
Hero, sloop, 112
Herring, 15, 26, 29, 138, 193, 197
Hesper, schooner, 246, 247
Hides, 112–113, 166
Hingham, Mass., 208–210, 237
Holmes Hole, Mass. See Vineyard Haven
Hope, ship, 60
Horses, 33
Houghton family, 142
Hound, H.M.S., 73
Houqua, 105
Housatonic, U.S.S., 153
House frames, 33
Howe, Octavius T., 142–143
Howland family, 100, 105–106
Hull, Mass., 7, 198, 204, 208, 263, 269
Humane Society of Mass., 14, 89–90, 201, 212
Hurricanes. See Storms
Hyannis, Mass., 208
Hyde, Gen. Thomas W., 173

Ice, as cargo, 110, 127, 134, 135, 179, 182–183
Ice, as hazard, 10, 179, 198, 262
Ice King, ship, 167
Ile de France. See Mauritius
Immigration, 97, 98, 119–120, 124, 163, 166
Impressment, 75–76, 83
Independence, S.S., 238
India, trade with, 56, 59–60, 62, 110, 116
Indian Ocean, 58–59
"Indian-headers", 193
Indians (American), 12–13, 18, 21, 28, 36–37
Indigo, 32, 35, 55, 60
Insurance, marine, 74, 91
Insurance, war-risk, 73, 159–160, 162
Internal combustion engine, 193, 225
International Fisherman's Trophy, 254, 255
International Steamship Co., 179
Intrepid, yacht, 274, 275
Ipswich, Mass., 7, 12, 19, 26, 101, 102
Ireland, 97, 121

Irish, 124
Iron, 39, 83
Iron ships, 162, 170
"Iron works", 149
Isherwood, Benjamin F., USN, 153–154
Islander II, steamer, 243
Isles of Shoals, N.H., 26
Islesboro, Me., 244
Italy, trade with, 61, 121
Ivory, 109

Jackson, cutter, 265
Jackson, Jonathan, 53
Jackman, George W., Jr., 164
Jamaica, 27, 34, 35, 36, 73, 122
James, John, & Son, 198
James, Capt. Joshua, 204
James family, 193
Jane Palmer, schooner, 185
Japan, 115
Java, trade with, 59, 62, 107
Jay's Treaty, 73
"J-boats", 272–274
Jefferson, Thomas, 48, 52, 76–77
Jeffries Ledge, 26
Joe Lane, cutter, 270
John R. Manta, whaler, 252
Jones, John Paul, USN, 70
Jones-White Act, 234
Jordan, Eben, 130
Joseph, schooner, 137
Joseph Whitney, S.S., 131
Juan Fernandez Island, 112

Kaiulani, bark, 172
Karlsefni, Thorfin, 14
Katahdin, U.S.S., 152, 173
Katahdin, steamer, 179
Kearsarge, U.S.S., 153, 155, 158
Kendall Whaling Museum, 277
Kennebec River, 6, 8, 12, 22, 89, 110, 130, 135, 141, 168, 179, 182, 238, 242, 244, 249
Kennebec, steamer, 178, 179, 189–190
Kennebec, motor vessel, 245
Kennebec Steamboat Co., 179, 242
Kennebunk, Me., 102, 132
Kennebunkport, Me., 157, 185
Kineo, U.S.S., 152
Kineo, schooner, 186
King Philip's War, 28
King William's War, 28
Kipling, Rudyard, 138

Kittery, Me., 25, 153. See also Portsmouth, N.H.
Kittery, brig, 40
Knight, Thomas, 146

L. A. Dunton, schooner, 254, 255
Labor, 162, 168, 241, 245
Labrador Current, 10
Lagoda (whaler replica), 279
Langdon, Tobias, 25
L'Anse aux Meadows, Newfoundland, 14
Lawley, George, & Sons, 223, 225
Lawlor, Dennison J., 193
Lawton, Capt. Samuel, 73
Lead, 68
Leander, H.M.S., 75
Leander, ship, 109
Leather, 40, 112, 124, 166. See also Hides
Ledyard, John, 57
Lee, Jeremiah, 42
Leopard, H.M.S., 76
Letters of marque, 64–65, 73
Levart, ship, 108
Leviathan, S.S., 266
Lewis, William, 198
Lewiston, steamer, 179
Lexington, U.S.S., 230, 231, 233–234
Libbey, John, 63
Liberty ships, 234–237
Lifeboats, 90, 203
Lifesaving, 89–90, 201–202, 258, 260
Lighthouses, 87–89, 198–201, 258
Lightships, 87–89, 200, 260, 262, 265
Lime, 133, 182
Limes, 36
Lincolnville Beach, Me., 244
Lipton, Sir Thomas, 222–223, 272
Little Brewster Island, Mass., 87
Little Cranberry Island, Me., 78
Liverpool, 110, 118, 119, 121, 127, 146, 156, 172
Liverpool Packet, Canadian privateer, 84
Livestock, 55
Livingston, Robert, 129
Livonia, yacht, 218–219
Lobsters. See Shellfish
Long Beach, U.S.S., 238
Loran, 260
Loring Works, 149
Long Island Sound, 48, 128, 129, 175, 176, 181, 189, 195, 196, 197, 206–207, 216, 223–224, 260
Lopez, Aaron, 42–43

Lord, William, 132
Lottie S. Haskins, schooner, 255
Low family, 100, 105–106
Lowell, John, 53
Loyalists, 54, 68–69
Lubec, Me., 244
Lumber. See Timber
Lurline, S.S., 234
Luther Little, schooner, 246, 247
Lydia, schooner, 81, 82, 83
Lykes Coastwise Line, 248
Lynch, John, 162

MacDonald, Joseph A., 232
Machias, Me., 102, 179, 283
Mackerel, 15, 29, 126, 136, 192, 193
MacKibbon, Capt. John, 68
Macon Act, 81
Madeira, trade with, 27, 33
Madge, yacht, 219
Madison, James, 81
Madras, India, 59–60
Maffitt, Capt. John, C.S.N., 156
Magic, yacht, 218
Main, Archibald M., 232
Maine, 4–12, 42, 69, 85, 89, 102, 103–105, 110, 122, 123, 125, 127, 128, 130, 132–135, 136, 139, 141, 142, 152, 153, 154, 155, 159, 162, 164, 168–175, 176, 179, 182, 185, 186, 192, 195, 202, 211–215, 227, 228–229, 232, 235–237, 242, 243–245, 247, 249, 258, 270, 283
Maine, U.S.S., 173
Maine, pinky, 139
Maine, steamer, 241
Malays, 109
Malden, steamer, 186
Manhattan, S.S., 237, 239
Manila, 112
Manomet Point, Mass., 263
Marblehead, Mass., 7, 19, 26, 29, 40, 54, 85, 102, 104, 136, 137, 139, 145, 153
Marconi, Guglielmo, 200
Marine Historical Association, 277–279
Marine societies, 90–91
Mariner ships, 238
Mariners, 99, 163
Marion, Mass., 272
Mariposa, S.S., 234
Maritime Provinces, trade with, 33, 39, 40, 107, 121, 122, 123, 124, 166, 175, 179, 241

Marjorie E. Bachman, schooner, 251
Marseilles, France, 83
Marshfield, Mass., 67, 201, 208
Martha's Vineyard, Mass., 6, 207–208, 269
Martinique, 35, 62
Mary and Helen, whaler, 198
Mary Day, schooner, 270
Massachusetts, 3–12, 38, 62, 66, 67, 80, 81, 83, 87, 89, 100, 101, 113, 122, 126, 136, 150–151, 164, 172–173, 176–179, 186, 188, 192, 195, 202, 229–231, 232–238, 240, 242
Massachusetts, U.S.S., 279
Massachusetts, steamer, 241–242
Massachusetts Bay Company, 19
Massachusetts Bay Steamship Corp., 242
Masts, 15, 19, 42
Matanzas, Cuba, 122, 123
Matinicus Island, Me., 26
Matson Line, 234
Matthews, Frederic C., 142–143
Mauritius, 58–59
Mayflower, ship, 19, 205; *II* (replica), 20, 279
McClain, Capt. G. Melvin, 255
McDonald, John, 170
McIntire, Samuel, 53
McKay, Donald, 119, 145–148
McManus, Thomas F., 193, 253, 255
Meat, 124, 166
Medford, Mass., 122, 168
Mediterranean, trade with, 83, 121
Melrose, steamer, 186
Melville, Herman, 114
Menhaden (porgies), 193
Mercantile, schooner, 271
Merchant Marine Act of 1936, 234
Merchants, 51, 54, 55–56
Merchants' & Miners' Line, 131, 181, 190, 241, 248, 263
Merrill, Orlando, 94
Merrimack River, 6, 19, 23, 50, 54, 89, 164, 244, 269
Middletown, Conn., 47–48, 79, 84, 102, 105
Milo, schooner, 128
Moby-Dick, 114
Mobile, Ala., 127, 132
Mocha, 59
Mohawk, yacht, 216
Molasses, 35, 36, 38–40, 42, 62, 68, 103, 122–123, 170

Molasses Act, 36
Monhegan Island, Me., 17, 26, 244
Monhegan, steamer, 242
Monitor, U.S.S., 151
Monomoy Point, Mass., 205, 262
Montauk Point, N.Y., 4
Montecristi, 35
Monterey, S.S., 234
Monts, Sieur de, 17
Mooremack Gulf Line, 248
Morgan, Edwin D., 220
Morgan, J. P., 232
Morison, Samuel Eliot, 105, 109, 110, 145
Morning Light, clipper, 147
Morrill, Capt. Benjamin, 112
Morse, Charles W., 179, 181, 182
Mosher, Charles D., 225
Mt. Desert Island, Me., 4, 7, 212–215
Mount Hope, motor vessel, 270
Mount Vernon, ship, 73, 74
Mugford, Capt. James, 72
Muscat, 59
Museums, maritime, 277
Muskets, 68
Mutiny, 114
Mystic, Conn., 116, 146, 153, 270
Mystic River (Mass.), 23, 168
Mystic Seaport, Conn., 117, 252, 272, 277–279

Nahant, Mass., 7
Nails, 62
Nancy, schooner, 262–263
Nantasket Beach, Mass., 26, 30, 31, 201, 208, 209, 262–263, 267
Nantasket Steamboat Co., 208, 269
Nantes, France, 55, 68
Nantucket, Mass., 6, 7, 16, 42, 49–50, 67, 87, 89, 90, 102, 103, 114, 116, 200, 207–208, 269, 277
Nantucket Sound, 6, 7, 89, 181, 200, 205, 215, 260
Napoleon, 81
Narragansett Bay, 6, 16, 17, 21, 48, 195, 207, 215, 265, 267
Narragansett Indians, 13
Nature conservancy, 283
Naumkeag Steam Cotton Factory, 109
Naushon, steamer, 243
Naval construction, 229–231, 232, 234, 237, 238
Naval forces, American, 64, 66, 73–75, 84, 150, 241, 242

Naval forces, British, 69, 75–76, 84–85
Naval stores, 19, 32, 38, 42, 121
Navarch, yacht, 224
Navigation, 91–92, 93, 95, 99
Navigation Act, U.S. (1817), 124
Navigation Acts, British, 23, 32, 67, 97, 146
Netherlands, trade with, 31, 60, 61, 62
Neutral trade, 60–63, 64–85, 81, 83
New American Practical Navigator, 92
New Bedford, 31, 42, 49–50, 69, 85, 117, 151, 154, 157, 159, 160, 197–198, 208, 241, 251, 252, 260, 265, 277, 279
New Brunswick, 79, 123, 179
New England coast, description, 3–12, 13
New England Coasting Pilot, 91
New England Gas & Coke Co., 186
New England Shipbuilding Co., 168, 235, 236. See also Goss & Sawyer
New England Steamship Co., 176
New Hampshire, 38, 42, 102, 195, 202, 228, 231, 238
New Haven, Conn., 21, 47–48, 57, 100, 102, 129, 175, 195, 200, 241, 249
New Jersey, U.S.S., 173
New Ledge, 26
New London, Conn., 47–48, 68–69, 87, 92, 102, 116, 129, 151, 198, 207, 237, 241, 265, 267, 269, 272
New London Ship & Engine Co., 231
New Orleans, 119, 127, 132, 152, 248
New York, 16, 36, 45, 60, 85, 101, 104, 105–106, 118, 121, 122, 126, 127, 145, 146, 159, 160, 164, 175, 181, 216, 223, 241
New York, steamer, 241, 269
New York, New Haven & Hartford Railroad Co., 176, 181
New York Yacht Club, 210, 211, 219, 272, 274
New Zealand, 112, 115, 116
Newbury, Mass., 19, 23, 26
Newburyport, Mass., 50–52, 55–56, 62, 63, 66, 73, 80, 82, 83, 89, 92, 94, 102, 104, 114, 122
Newcastle, steamer, 243
Newell, William S., 232
Newfoundland, 13, 14, 15, 27, 40, 179, 191
Newington, N.H., 230
Newport, R.I., 34, 42–43, 45, 48, 49, 69, 73, 79, 81, 102, 107, 176, 207, 210, 211, 215–216, 233, 267–268, 269, 272, 274–275, 279

Newport News, Va., 186
Niantic Bay, Conn., 197, 207
Nickerson & Co., F.W., 181
"Night boats", 128–132, 175–181, 189–191
Nightingale, clipper, 104
Noank, Conn., 195
Non-Intercourse Act, 80–81
Norfolk, Va., 127, 245
Norsemen, 13–15
North Haven, Me., 244
North Haven, steamer, 244
North River, Mass., 141, 204
Northampton, U.S.S., 234
Northern Virginia Company, 17, 18
Northwest Passage, 237
Norwich, Conn., 47–48, 100, 129, 207
Nova Scotia, 13, 15, 28, 29, 123, 124, 126, 127, 145, 179, 269
Novelty, brig, 170
Nutmeg Mariner, S.S., 238

Occupations, 51
Oceanic Steamship Co. (Matson Line), 234
Oceanography, 258
Oil, 118, 197, 227, 249, 281. See also Whale oil
Old Colony Mariner, S.S., 238
Old Dartmouth Historical Society, 277
Old Lyme, Conn., 100, 145
Old Orchard Beach, Me., 210, 267
Old Saybrook, Conn., 267
Olive oil, 121
Oneida, ship, 157
Ontario, S.S., 164
Opium, 106–107
Opium War, 97, 106–107
Oporto, Portugal, 78
Oranges, 36
Orders in Council (1807), 76
Oregon, S.S., 165
Orient Point, N.Y., 6
Outlook, yacht, 221
Owen, George, 223, 258
Oxner family, 193
Oysters. See Shellfish

Pacific coast, 181, 247–248
Pacific Ocean, 31, 57, 110–112, 159
Packets, 47, 98, 118, 120–121, 127–129
Paine, Frank C., 272
Paine, Capt. Robert T., 41
Paint, 62

Palm oil, 109
Palmer, Capt. Nathaniel B., 112
Palmer, William F., 188, 262
Panama, 98, 124
Panama Canal, 247–248
Parsons Steam Turbines, 175
Passamaquoddy Bay (Quoddy), 8, 79, 85, 102, 121, 123, 124, 130, 164
Patent, steamer, 130
Patten family, 142
Paving stones, 127, 135
Pawtucket, R.I., 49
Peabody, Joseph, 107, 109
Peabody Museum, Salem, 277
Peanuts, 109
Pearls, 166
Peas, 33
Peck, Elisha, 100
Pemaquid, Me., 17, 19, 26
Pemberton Point, Mass., 198
Pendleton, tanker, 263, 265
Penobscot Bay, 6, 50, 89, 130, 136, 199
Penobscot (customs district), Me., 102
Penobscot Indians, 13
Penobscot Marine Museum, 279
Penobscot, motor vessel, 244
Penobscot River, 179, 244
Pepper, 62, 100, 107–109
Pepperrell, William, 40
Pepys, Samuel, 42
Pequot Indians, 13, 21
Percy & Small, 186
Perit, Pelatiah, 100
Perkins, Thomas H., 105, 106
Perseverance, ship, 88
Peru, 57, 114
Peter, Rev. Hugh, 26
Peter Stuyvesant, steamer, 279
Petit Manan Island, Me., 8
Petroleum. See Oil
Phelps, Anson G., 100
Philadelphia, Pa., 40, 68, 85, 118, 126, 127, 131, 151, 181
Philadelphia, U.S.S., 75
Phippsburg, Me., 141–142
Phoenix, clipper, 146
Phosphates, 245
Pickering, John, 75
Pickering, Timothy, 80
Pigeon Cove, Mass., 139
Pilgrim, brig, 113
Pilgrim, steamer, 176
Pilgrims, 19

Ping, Capt. Ben, 254
Pine Tree Mariner, 238
Pinky, 138, 139
Pinthis, tanker, 263
Pioneer, whaler, 198
Pirates, 64, 73–75
Piscataqua River, 23
Pitt, William, the Younger, 55
Plaster of paris, 123
Ploughboy, coaster, 78–79
Plum Island, Mass., 203
Plymouth, Mass., 19, 30, 49–50, 87, 90, 166, 210
Point Judith, R.I., 129–130, 269
Politics, 51–53, 101. See also Federalists, Republicans
Pollock, 26
Pollock Rip, Mass., 10–11, 205, 260
Pollution, 280–283
Pomona, ship, 62
Pook, Samuel Hartt, 146
Poor, John A., 120
Popham, George, 17
Pork, 33, 38, 40
Port Clyde, Me., 244
Port Royal, S.C., 151
Portland, Conn., 185
Portland Gale, 204, 210
Portland Head Light, 177
Portland Locomotive Works (Portland Co.), 149, 176
Portland, Me., 50, 69, 102, 103, 105, 118–121, 122, 123, 124, 127, 130–131, 132, 133, 136, 150, 152, 155, 158, 164, 165, 175, 176, 179, 181, 183, 212, 227, 242, 244, 247, 249, 260, 269
Portland, steamer, 176, 177, 179
Portland Steam Packet Co., 176, 179. See also Eastern Steamship Co.
Portland Sugar House, 123
Ports, 45–53, 104
Portsmouth Navy Yard, Kittery, Me., 151, 231, 288
Portsmouth, N.H., 25, 40, 42, 50, 66, 68, 75, 84, 102, 104, 153, 238
Portugal, trade with, 27, 29, 42, 60, 78, 247
Potato famine, 97, 121
Potatoes, 124
Potomac, U.S.S., 109
Poultry, 33
Pray, Samuel, 25
Presbyterian Church, 52
Prince, Hezekiah, 127–128

Prince Edward Island, 123
Prince of Fundy, motor vessel, 269
Priscilla, yacht, 219–220
Privateering, 64–65, 69, 71, 184
Privateers, French, 73; Danish, 81; Canadian, 84
Prohibition, 249–251
Prohibitory Act of 1775, 68
Providence, R.I., 48–49, 58, 59, 60, 62, 107, 122, 129, 130, 164, 166, 175, 181, 207, 231, 237, 241, 249, 265, 269
Providence, steamer, 177
Provincetown, Mass., 19, 85, 116, 210, 242, 268–269
Provincetown, steamer, 269
Provisions, 33, 36, 39, 55, 58, 59
Puerto Rico, 122, 124
Puritan, yacht, 219–220
Puritans, 19–20, 21

Quallah Battoo, 109
Quasi-War (1798–1800), 73
Quebec, 21
Queen Anne's War, 28
Quincy, Mass., 168, 172–173, 177, 185, 187, 228, 237, 238
Quincy, U.S.S., 234
Quirigua, S.S., 234
Quisset, Mass., 3
Quoddy. See Passamaquoddy

Race, the (Long Island Sound), 7
Radar, 260
Radio, 200–201
Raiders, Confederate, 154–160, 162
Railroads, 120, 128, 164, 175, 182, 186
Rainbow, clipper, 143
Rainbow, yacht, 274
Raisins, 121
Rajah, schooner, 60
Raleigh, U.S.S., 66
Ranger, U.S.S., 70
Ranger, yacht, 273–274
Reading Railroad Co., 186
Red Jacket, clipper, 146
Red-paint people, 12
Reed Brothers, 247
Re-export Trade, 60–61, 80, 81
Reid, U.S.S., 231
Reliance, yacht, 220, 221–222
Republic, S.S., 201
Republicans (Jeffersonian), 52, 80, 83
Research, 258

Resolute, ketch, 192
Resolute, yacht, 222–223, 272
Resorts, 206–215, 267–270
Restraining Act, 67
Revere Beach, Mass., 208, 210, 267
Revolution, American, 64–71
Rhode Island, 4–12, 30, 38, 48–49, 53, 58, 59, 60, 62, 68, 100, 102, 107, 126, 164, 175, 176, 195, 202, 211, 265
Rhode Island, U.S.S., 123
Rice, 32, 36, 37
Richard Peck, steamer, 190, 241
Richmond Island, Me., 26
Richmond, Me., 2, 141–142, 178, 182
Rob Roy, schooner, 193
Robert E. Lee, S.S., 263
Robinson, Capt. John, 128
Rockland, Me., 101, 130, 133, 146, 179, 182, 212, 244, 247, 270
Rockport, Me., 101, 133, 134, 182
Rockport, Mass., 185, 205, 255
Rogers & Webb, 247
Roosevelt, Franklin D., 106
Roosevelt, Theodore, 181
Rose, H.M.S. (replica), 279
Rotch family, 31
Roulette, schooner, 193
Rowe, William H., 142
Rowley, Mass., 26
Royal Yacht Squadron, 274
Rule of 1756, 61
Rum, 35, 36, 38, 39, 40, 48, 53, 59–60, 109, 121, 122, 123
Rumrunners, 249–251. See also Prohibition
Russell & Co., 105–106
Russell, Samuel, 105
Russia, trade with, 60, 81, 83
Rye Beach, N.H., 210

Sabino, steamer, 244, 269
Sable Island, N.S., 27
Saco, Me., 101, 102
Safety at sea, 198–206, 258–266
Sag Harbor, N.Y., 116
Sagadahoc, steamer, 179
Sailcloth, 83
Sailing directions, 91–92
St. Bartholomew, 81
St. Christopher, 35
St. Croix River, 17
St. Eustatius, 35
St. John, N.B., 120, 130, 159, 242

St. John, S.S., 241
St. John's, Newfoundland, 179
St. Mary's River, 79
St. Petersburg, Russia, 60
Salem Marine Society, 89
Salem Maritime National Historic Sites, 279
Salem, Mass., 19, 26, 28, 29, 30, 35, 40, 50, 53, 56, 59, 60, 66, 69, 73, 75, 80, 86, 91, 92, 94, 100, 102, 107–109, 111, 112, 116, 210, 277, 279
Salmon, 16, 26
Salt, 35, 40, 83, 245
Saltpeter, 156
Salvage, 202–203
Samuel Knight, ship, 140
Samuels, Capt. Samuel, 146
San Francisco, 98, 143–144, 146, 157, 172, 198
Sandalwood, 58
Sandwich Islands. See Hawaii
Santo Domingo, 62
Sappho, yacht, 219
Sarah Sands, S.S., 120
Saratoga, U.S.S., 231
Sardines, 245. See also Herring
Sardinia, 83
Savannah, Ga., 119, 127, 181
Savannah Line, 181, 241, 248
Saybrook, Conn., 48, 175
Scallops. See Shellfish
Sceptre, yacht, 274
Schooners, 183, 184, 185–186, 187, 188, 192–193, 196
Scituate, Mass., 26, 67, 208, 265
Scott, Gen. Winfield, 150
Sea Bride, bark, 158
Sea otters, 57, 110–112
Sea smoke, 10
Sea Witch, clipper, 143
Sealing, 57, 101
Searsport, Me., 249, 279
Seawanhaka Corinthian Yacht Club, 220
Sebenoa, steamer, 212
Seekonk River, 49
Seguin, tug, 279
Seguin Island, Me., 8, 89
Semmes, Raphael, CSN, 155–158
Seven Years' War, 29
Seventy-six raters, yachts, 272–274
Sewall family, 142, 168, 170, 172, 186
Shad, 195
Shadow, yacht, 217, 218, 219, 220

Shamrock III, yacht, 221; *IV,* 223, 272; *V,* 272
Shanghai, China, 97, 107, 143
Shattuck, L. H., Inc., 230
Shaw, Nathaniel, 68
Shelburne, Earl of, 55
Shellfish (clams, lobsters, oysters, scallops), 139, 193, 195, 196–197, 255–256, 257, 282–283
Shenandoah, C.S.S., 156, 159
Shenandoah, schooner, 270
Shingles, 33
Ship design, 93–94
Ship ownership, 102
Ship Registry Act (1914), 163
Shipbuilding, 21–25, 54–55, 63, 93–94, 99, 103, 139–149, 152–153, 161–162, 163–175, 185–186, 188–191, 192–193, 228–240
Shipmasters, 33–34, 51, 59, 61, 99, 150
Shipowners, 186
Shipping Act of 1916, 228
Shipwrecks, 86–92, 133, 137, 138–139, 151, 198–206, 251, 260–266. See also Lifesaving
Shipwrights, 21
Shoes, 40, 42, 62, 66
Silk, 57, 166
Simpson Dry Dock Co., 234
Sinclair Navigation Co., 234
Singapore, 159–160
Slater, Samuel, 49
Slave trade, 37, 48, 53, 109, 122
Slavery, 37, 53, 122
Slocum, Capt. Joshua, 272
Smith, Adam, 55
Smith, Capt. John, 4, 18–19
Smith, Joseph, USN, 150–151
Smuggling, 79, 249–251
Smyrna, Turkey, 121
Soap, 62
Social structure, 51, 56
Somerset, Mass., 247
Sopwith, T.O.M., 274
South America, trade with, 62, 100, 107, 110, 113–114, 166, 168, 181, 245
South Bristol, Me., 270
South Portland, Me., 146, 235, 236
South Portland Shipbuilding Corp., 235
South Shetland Islands, 112
South Street Seaport Museum, 255
Southack, Cyprian, 91
Southern trade, 40, 53

Sovereign of the Seas, clipper, 146
Spain, trade with, 27, 40, 60, 61, 68, 81, 83
Specie, 58
Sperm oil, 68
Spermaceti, 31
Sprague, Phineas, 131, 181
Spray, sloop, 272
Spray, trawler, 193
Springfield, Mass., 21
Stamford, Conn., 145
Star of Peace, ship, 156
Star of the East, steamer, 179
State of Maine, steamer, 180
Statistics, 38, 102
Steam navigation, 98, 118, 128–132, 149,
    151, 163–164, 173, 174, 177, 178, 180,
    188–191, 193, 209, 223, 228–229, 231–
    240, 241–252
Steel, 62
Steel vessels, 170–172, 186
Stellwagen Bank, 26, 251
Stephen Taber, schooner, 270
Stephens, Olin T., 274
Stiletto, U.S.S., 224–225
Stockton Springs, Me., 182
Stone, 133–135, 184
"Stone fleet", 151, 152
Stones, precious, 166
Stonington, Conn., 47–48, 69, 100, 101,
    102, 112, 116, 129, 175
Stonington, Me., 135, 184
Storms and hurricanes, 8–10, 40, 41, 86–
    87, 139, 140, 204, 210, 262–265, 267
Story family, 193, 254–255
Straits of Sunda, 158
Stratford, steamer, 245
Sturgeon, 26
Sturgis, Capt. William, 105
Submarines, 153
Subsidies, 98, 162
Sugar, 21, 32, 35, 36, 37, 38, 40, 47, 59,
    61, 62, 68, 81, 83, 122–123
Sumatra, trade with, 56, 60, 107–109, 158
Sumter, C.S.S., 155–156, 157
Surinam, trade with, 35
Swampscott, Mass., 250
Swasey, Raymond, & Page, 225
Sweden, trade with, 81
Swift, Capt. Frank, 270

Tacony, C.S.S., 157–158, 159
Tallahassee, C.S.S., 159
Tampa, cutter, 251

Tarr & James, 253
Taunton, Mass., 188
Taunton Locomotive Works, 149
Tea, 57, 62, 100, 104, 107, 124, 143, 157
Texas Co., 228, 237
Textile manufactures, American, 33, 47,
    49, 63, 96, 101, 107, 109, 110, 113,
    114, 121, 124, 126
Textile manufactures, British, 19, 33, 40,
    42, 55, 56, 78, 85, 117, 126
Textile manufactures, other, 59
Thaddeus, brig, 116
Thames River, Conn., 48, 175
Thatcher Island Light, 89
Thermal pollution, 282
Thomas, George, 146
Thomas, Capt. William H., 253
Thomas, schooner, 84
Thomas L. Gorton, schooner, 253–254
Thomas W. Lawson, schooner, 173, 181,
    186, 187
Thomaston, Me., 101, 127, 136, 182
Thompson, Jeremiah, 119
Thoreau, Henry David, 110
Thunder Hole (Mt. Desert, Me.), 7
Tides, 7–8
Timber and lumber, 14, 15, 21–22, 23, 25,
    32, 36, 37, 39, 40, 42, 55, 60, 61, 62,
    94, 101, 103, 108, 121, 126, 132–133,
    141, 166, 182, 245, 249. See also
    Wood products, Masts
Tobacco, 21, 32, 36, 37, 55, 59, 60, 67, 109
Todd-Bath Iron Shipbuilding Corp., 235–
    237
Tonnage, 102–103, 125, 150, 160, 161, 162,
    164, 227, 231, 238–240
Torrey Canyon, tanker, 281
Tortuga, 35
Tourist, steamer, 244
Touzell, Capt. John, 35
Tracy, John, 55–56
Tracy, Nathaniel, 55
Train, Enoch, 119, 146
Trumbull, John, 48
Tudor, Frederic, 110, 135
Turks Island, 35
Tuscany, ship, 110
Twilight, steamer, 165

United Fruit Co., 166, 234, 266–267
U.S. Army, Corps of Engineers, 205, 282
U.S. Coast Guard, 87, 90, 250, 258, 260,
    263, 270, 272. See also U.S. Life-

saving Service, U.S. Lighthouse Service, U.S. Revenue Cutter Service
U.S. Fish Commission, 193
U.S. Fish & Wildlife Service, 258
U.S. Lifesaving Service, 90, 201–202
U.S. Lighthouse Service, 87, 201
U.S. Maritime Administration, 238
U.S. Maritime Commission, 234, 240
U.S. Revenue Cutter Service (Revenue Marine), 90, 202. See also U.S. Coast Guard
U.S. Shipping Board, 228, 229
United States Lines, 238
Universal Rule (yachting), 222–223
Uruguay, 113
Utrecht, Treaty of, 28

Valparaiso, Chile, 115, 116
Vanda, yacht, 232
Vanderbilt, Harold S., 274
Vanitie, yacht, 222–223
Varnish, 109
Veragua, S.S., 234
Vermont, U.S.S., 173
Verrazano, Giovanni da, 16
Vessel types, 23, 29, 39, 93–95, 98, 127, 132, 135, 138, 141–149, 152–153, 162, 168, 170, 172–173, 185–186, 188–191, 192–193, 195, 216–225, 228–240, 240–251, 252–258, 272–276
Vesta, yacht, 216
Vinalhaven, Me., 135, 197, 244
Vinalhaven II, motor vessel, 244
Vineyard Haven, Mass., 181, 270
Vineyard Sound, Mass., 200, 260
Viola, whaler, 198
Virginia, 17, 21, 126
Virginia Company, 17
Virginia, pinnace, 17, 18, 22
Virginia, steamer, 243
Vulture, ship, 42

W. S. White, steamer, 244
Wachussett, U.S.S., 153, 158
Waddell, Capt. James I., CSN., 159
Waldoboro, Me., 50, 102, 103, 121, 141–142, 184, 185
Walrus skins, 16
Walsh-Kaiser Co., 237
Wampanoag Indians, 13
Wanderer, whaler, 251–252
Wanton family, 48–49
War, effects of, 60–85, 91, 150–160, 223, 228–240, 241, 274, 276

War material, 67–68
War of 1812, 71, 81, 91
Wardwell, John J., 185
Warren, R.I., 49, 270
Warrington, U.S.S., 265–266
Washington, George, 69
Watch Hill, R.I., 201, 264
Waterfronts, 46
Watson, Thomas A., 173
Weather, 8–11
Weatherly, yacht, 274
Webb, Isaac, 145
Webb, William H., 145
Weetamoe, yacht, 272
Weld, William F., & Co., 166, 168
Welles, Gideon, 150
Wellfleet, Mass., 196
Wellington, Frank O., 173
Westerly, R.I., 48
Western Way, the, 8
West Indies, British and general, 22–23, 25, 29, 33–37, 38, 40, 48–49, 53, 55, 60, 61, 81, 107, 122–123, 168, 245
West Indies, Danish, 81
West Indies, Dutch, 35–36, 48, 61, 68, 81
West Indies, French, 35–36, 48, 61, 62, 68, 81
West Indies, Spansh, 35–36, 61, 75, 81
West Indies, Swedish, 81
West Quoddy Head Light, 10–11
Weybosset, schooner, 185
Weymouth Fore River, Mass., 173
Whale oil, 16, 31, 42, 55, 101, 118, 197
Whaling, 30–31, 48, 50, 67, 100, 101, 104–118, 135, 151, 152, 157, 159, 197–198, 207–208, 251–252, 278
Wheat, 38, 39, 40, 42, 126
Wheelwright, William, 114
Whitby, Henry, RN, 75
Whitney, Eli, 47
Whitney, Joseph, 131
Wm. Boyce Thompson, S.S., 234
William L. Douglas, schooner, 186
William L. White, schooner, 185
Williams, Roger, 21
Wilson, Capt. Andrew, 62
"Windjammer Cruises", 270
Wine, 83, 121
Winsor, Henry, 131
Winter Harbor, steamer, 243
Winthrop, John, Jr., 21
Wiscasset, Me., 102, 243, 246, 247
Wood products, 33, 39, 62, 123. See also Timber and Lumber

Woods Hole, Mass., 7, 17, 208, 269
Woods Hole Oceanographic Institution, 258
Wool, 114, 166
Woolen goods. See Textile manufactures
World War I, 223, 228–240, 241
World War II, 234–239, 241, 242, 274, 276
"Wreckers", 202–203
Wyoming, schooner, 186, 262

Yacht design and building, 173, 175, 215–225

Yachting, 195, 211, 215–225, 272–276, 277
Yale College, 47, 116
Yale, steamer, 181
Yankee, yacht, 272
Yarmouth, N.S., 179
Yarmouth, S.S., 241
YMS-409, U.S.S., 265
York, Me., 101, 122, 210

Zaine, brig, 111
Zanzibar, 109

ABBREVIATIONS OF BOTTOMS

Materials in Capitals	Colors or Shades two small letters	Other qualities three small letters
M. for Mud	bk. for black	hrd. for hard
S. „ Sand	wh. „ white	sft. „ soft
G. „ Gravel	rd. „ red	fne. „ fine
Sh. „ Shells	yl. „ yellow	crs. „ coarse
P. „ Pebbles	gy. „ grey	brk. „ broken
Sp. „ Specks	bu. „ blue	sml. „ small
C. „ Clay	dk. „ dark	rky. „ rocky
St. „ Stones	lt. „ light	
R. „ Rock	gn. „ green	
	bn. „ brown	

Note. *The principal materials and their qualities are represented by larger letters than the subsidiary.*
+ *Signifies Sunk Rock,* * *Rock awash at Low-water.*

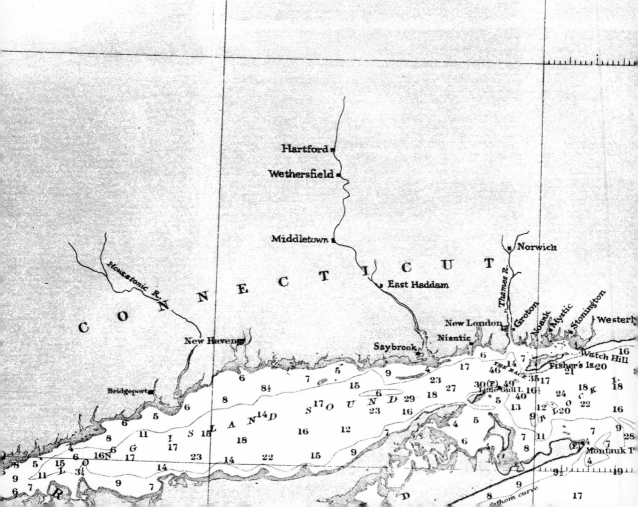

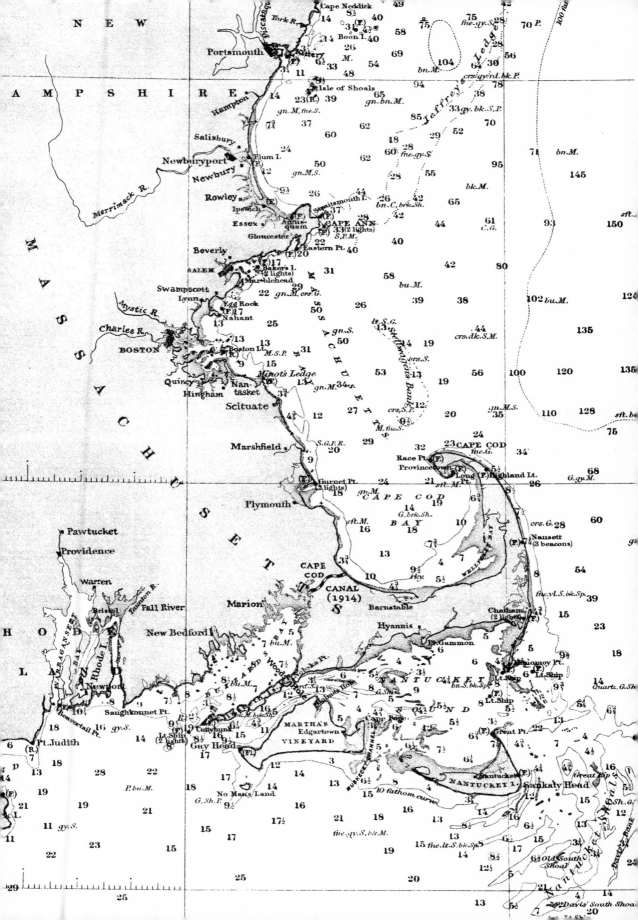

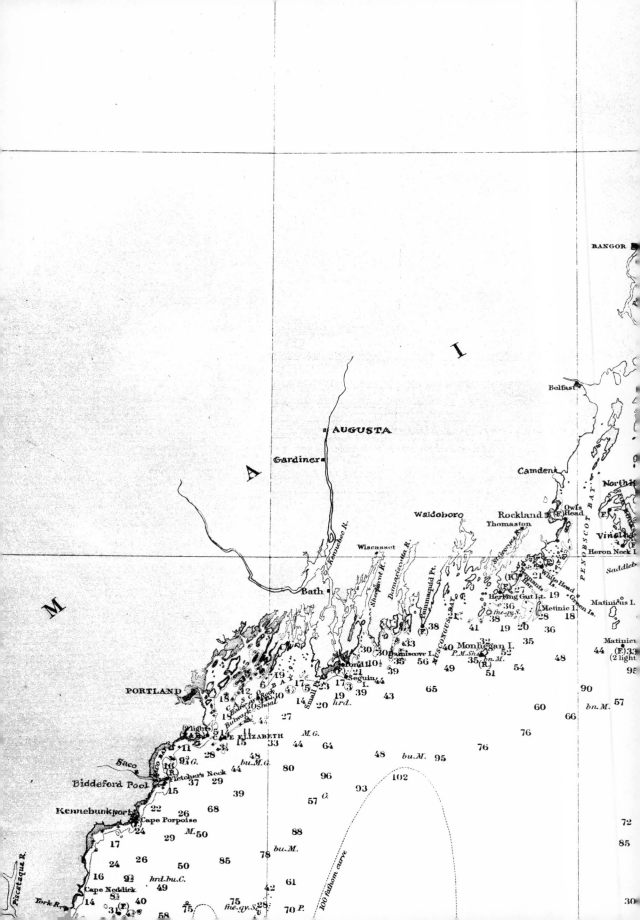

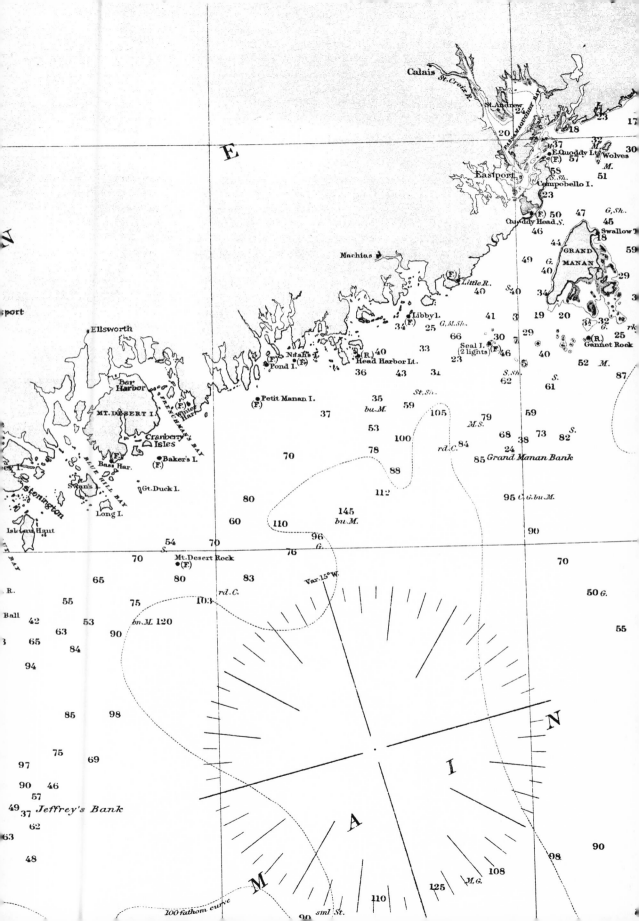